The Art of Intelligence

SECURITY AND PROFESSIONAL INTELLIGENCE EDUCATION SERIES (SPIES)

Editor: Jan Goldman

In this post–September 11, 2001, era, there has been rapid growth in the number of professional intelligence training and educational programs across the United States and abroad. Colleges and universities, as well as high schools, are developing programs and courses in homeland security, intelligence analysis, and law enforcement, in support of national security. The Security and Professional Intelligence Education Series (SPIES) was first designed for individuals studying for careers in intelligence and to help improve the skills of those already in the profession; however, it was also developed to educate the public in how intelligence work is conducted and should be conducted in this important and vital profession.

Books in the series include:

Communicating with Intelligence: Writing and Briefing in the Intelligence and National Security Communities, by James S. Major. 2008.

A Spy's Résumé: Confessions of a Maverick Intelligence Professional and Misadventure Capitalist, by Marc Anthony Viola. 2008.

An Introduction to Intelligence Research and Analysis, by Jerome Clauser, revised and edited by Jan Goldman. 2008.

Writing Classified and Unclassified Papers for National Security, by James S. Major. 2009.

Strategic Intelligence: A Handbook for Practitioners, Managers, and Users, revised edition by Don McDowell. 2009.

Partly Cloudy: Ethics in War, Espionage, Covert Action, and Interrogation, by David L. Perry. 2009.

Ethics of Spying: A Reader for the Intelligence Professional, edited by Jan Goldman. 2006.

Ethics of Spying: A Reader for the Intelligence Professional, edited by Jan Goldman. Volume 1. 2006. Volume 2, 2010.

Handbook of Warning Intelligence: Assessing the Threat to National Security, by Cynthia Grabo. 2010.

Handbook of Scientific Methods of Inquiry for Intelligence Analysis, by Hank Prunckun. 2010.

Keeping U.S. Intelligence Effective: The Need for a Revolution in Intelligence Affairs, by William J. Lahneman. 2011.

Words of Intelligence: An Intelligence Professional's Lexicon for Domestic and Foreign Threats, Second Edition, by Jan Goldman. 2011.

Balancing Liberty and Security: An Ethical Study of U.S. Foreign Intelligence Surveillance, 2001–2009, by Michelle Louise Atkin. 2013.

The Art of Intelligence: Simulations, Exercises, and Games, edited by William J. Lahneman and Rubén Arcos. 2014.

Scientific Methods of Inquiry for Intelligence Analysis, Second Edition, by Hank Prunckun. 2014.

Communicating with Intelligence: Writing and Briefing in National Security, Second Edition, by James S. Major. 2015.

International Journal of Intelligence Ethics, edited by Jan Goldman. https://rowman.com/page/IJIE.

The Art of Intelligence

Simulations, Exercises, and Games

Edited by William J. Lahneman and Rubén Arcos

ROWMAN & LITTLEFIELD
Lanham • Boulder • New York • Toronto • Plymouth, UK

Published by Rowman & Littlefield
4501 Forbes Boulevard, Suite 200, Lanham, Maryland 20706
www.rowman.com

10 Thornbury Road, Plymouth PL6 7PP, United Kingdom

Copyright © 2014 by Rowman & Littlefield

British Library Cataloguing in Publication Information Available

Library of Congress Cataloging-in-Publication Data
The art of intelligence : simulations, exercises, and games / edited by William J. Lahneman and
Rubén Arcos.
    pages cm
Includes bibliographical references and index.
 ISBN 978-1-4422-2896-2 (cloth : alk. paper)—ISBN 978-1-4422-2897-9 (pbk. : alk.
paper)—ISBN 978-1-4422-2898-6 (electronic)
 1. Intelligence service—Study and teaching. 2. Simulation games. I. Lahneman, William J.,
1952–, editor of compilation. II. Arcos, Rubén, 1977–, editor of compilation.
 JK468.I6A87 2014
 327.12—dc23   2013045391

Printed in the United States of America

Contents

Foreword

Series Introduction

When I established this series, back in 2006, my goal was to offer professional educational books that went beyond the current issues facing the intelligence profession. Up to that year, intelligence agencies were hiring new analysts and operators at unprecedented levels. Unfortunately, there were few books available to the general public that seemed to focus on the education or training of intelligence analysts or intelligence operators. From learning to communicate intelligence reports, to the discussion of moral and ethical dilemmas, this intelligence series has since sought to go beyond the descriptive landscape of the intelligence business. It is more about "doing" intelligence rather than "speaking" about intelligence, and this volume takes the series to its natural progression.

The Art of Intelligence will challenge anyone interested in knowing what an intelligence professional does. It will also allow readers to challenge their own assumptions of correctly digesting and producing intelligence reports. For the trainer or educator, this book should be the beginning of hours of discussion. Each chapter will test the reader's critical thinking skills, no matter his or her level of experience.

Additionally, I have known the coeditors for many years, and I am extremely pleased and honored to have them develop and publish this book for the series. Each of the coeditors is knowledgeable about the intelligence profession, as both scholars and educators anchored in the international intelligence community. The coauthors are professors in the United States and Spain, which has allowed them to assemble the best educators teaching intelligence from several countries. This international dimension greatly enhances the real-world experience of this publication.

This book is everything this series was meant to be: a textbook for educating and training the next generation of intelligence professionals from an international perspective of experts. A book about "doing" rather than "speaking," about intelligence—a perfect addition to the series.

Jan Goldman
Editor, Security and Professional Intelligence Education Series (SPIES)
Washington, DC

Acknowledgments

Our acknowledgments must begin with our most sincere thanks to the talented scholars and practitioners who have made this volume possible by contributing their original simulations, exercises, and games. When we decided to pursue this kind of volume, we could only hope that we would end up with such an interesting and diverse set of offerings from a distinguished international group of contributors. We are pleased that our hope has become a reality.

We wish to thank Jan Goldman, editor of the Security and Professional Intelligence Education Series (SPIES); Marie-Claire Antoine, our acquisitions editor; and Stephanie Scuiletti, our production editor at Rowman & Littlefield; for their outstanding work in guiding us through the publication process.

The views contained in this volume are those of the respective authors alone. Any other persons thanked above are not responsible for its content and should not be blamed for any defects that might be present. The views expressed in this volume do not represent the views, attitudes, or policies of the authors' parent institutions, or any agency or component of their respective national governments.

Introduction

William J. Lahneman and Rubén Arcos

Education and training in intelligence have evolved considerably and have been consolidated at campuses since the mid-1980s. Students have the possibility to attend both undergraduate and graduate courses dealing with the historical, political, and legal aspects of intelligence. These educational offerings continue to grow each year across the world. Some institutions offer major programs of study in intelligence and intelligence analysis. Also, there is a growing demand for distance learning courses on intelligence. Former intelligence officials, university professors, and practitioners from businesses converge in academic programs on intelligence analysis, primarily in the United States, Canada, and Europe.

Because these programs aim to produce graduates who are prepared to commence careers as intelligence analysts in both government (e.g., in intelligence agencies and policy-making departments at all levels of government) and the business sector (e.g., in competitive intelligence organizations), developing proper methodologies to optimize teaching and learning in intelligence programs and courses is an important issue. A good program should not only *educate* students by enabling them to learn how to think about and perform analyses, but it should also *train* them by teaching them the ethics, terminology, structures, processes, and pitfalls associated with the intelligence profession. It is common for instructors to emphasize the former over the latter—to educate more than they train. This is understandable because the most common vehicle for conveying information is the lecture. Lectures are certainly a necessary tool for both training and educating students in intelligence matters. And, in many instances, lectures are both necessary *and* sufficient to the task. After all, even though many educators do not like to admit it because it sounds old fashioned, future intelligence professionals must become familiar with (okay, *memorize!*) a huge amount of information if they are to become effective intelligence practitioners. Lectures by highly qualified teachers who explain concepts, processes, and techniques of intelligence tradecraft form an essential element of any program. However, we have noted that students sooner or later find a strict diet of lectures monotonous. Also, too often former practitioners provide just a catalog of interesting but barely useful anecdotes for training students in analytic tradecraft techniques. Lastly, we believe that some, if not most, of the concepts and practices central to achieving high-quality analytic tradecraft will not sink in unless students can *practice* the application of these concepts and tools in some way.

There is a need for reflection in the field of intelligence education to address two basic questions: What kind of intelligence courses should institutions offer, and how should the students be educated and trained? The former question has to do with the objectives of intelligence education and training. And it depends on the education requirements for government or business applicants, the level of intelligence literacy that a society possesses, and policymakers' knowledge of intelligence affairs. In other words, what should intelligence education be for? Is intelligence an institution whose origin, history, functions, or basic processes should be known by citizens of democratic societies? Why? Also is it desirable that institutions of higher education provide education and training on intelligence? Should this education and training be considered important qualifying criteria in potential selection processes?

It seems clear that as intelligence enterprises become increasingly professionalized, entry-level knowledge and skills will be more and more important, and the standard for what constitutes an acceptable level of competence and qualification will rise. In this sense, and as in other professions, higher education should play a role in providing such knowledge and skills to intelligence professionals. The International Association for Intelligence Education (IAFIE) has established standards for the initial training of intelligence analysts. These standards deal with critical and creative thinking, structured analytic techniques, analytic writing and briefing, ethics, and collector or analyst integration, among others. These standards can only be met through both education and training; accordingly, both institutions of higher learning and in-house intelligence schools have an important role to play. Also, many of these capabilities are essential for industry analysts, business managers, and for policymakers and analysts in virtually all government agencies, not just those that deal directly with the production of intelligence.

Regarding the latter question, the response is clear, and it is the underlying reason for the birth of this volume: students of intelligence courses can learn analytic tradecraft best through experiential learning methodologies such as simulations and games. These learning vehicles allow students to experience intelligence analysis and issues related to its practice by performing analyses and then derive other meanings from their experiences through reflection. It often happens that, after we have run a simulation in class, a student will say (in the American vernacular), "I didn't *get it* before. Now I *get it*!" Usually he or she is referring to things such as the difficulty associated with working with information gaps, or with trying to convey uncertainty in words that a policymaker will understand, or with the need to respond to a requirement even though there is little raw intelligence on the topic, or with the effect that denial or deception had on the outcome of the student's analysis. The student had heard about these kinds of challenges in lectures, but participation in the simulation raised the student's understanding to a new level.

We need to highlight that we are not speaking about opposite approaches to intelligence education or training or advocating for a single approach. Rather, it is a matter of balancing the use of lectures, reading assignments, and discussion on concrete case studies, on the one hand, with experiential activities such as simulations, exercises, and games, on the other.

According to David A. Kolb (1984, p. 38), "learning is the process whereby knowledge is created through the transformation of the experience." Experiential learning is rooted in Dewey's, Lewin's, and Piaget's learning models and can be described as a cyclical process involving four learning modes: "concrete experience, reflective observation, abstract conceptualization and active experimentation" (Kolb, 1984, p. 40). As explained by Kolb and Kolb:

> Immediate or concrete experiences are the basis for observations and reflections. These reflections are assimilated and distilled into abstract concepts in which new implications for action can be drawn. These implications can be actively tested and serve as guides in creating new experiences. (2009, pp. 298–299)

And, as stated by Mel Silberman (2007, p. 8), "experiential learning can be based on both real work/life experiences (e.g., working on a current project) and structured experiences that simulate or approximate real work/life."

The idea behind this book was born in June 2011 when we initiated this "inclusive" approach to intelligence analysis education or training within the intelligence analysis master's program at Rey Juan Carlos University in Madrid, Spain. At that time, both "Estimating Iraqi Weapons of Mass Destruction" (reprinted as Chapter 1 of this volume) and "Multimedia Intelligence Products" (Chapter 15 of this volume) were incorporated into the program and conducted. The former had been published in 2009 in the journal *Simulation & Gaming*, and the degree of structure of the simulation and its ready-to-run format gave us the initial inspiration for the production of this volume. After an initial discussion on the idea of preparing a practical casebook of intelligence simulations and exercises, including national security intelligence and competitive intelligence experiential learning activities, the volume began to take shape. By late July 2011 the nature of the volume was clear for us: the book should contain interactive teaching devices that place students in active roles rather than emphasizing reading cases or other materials and then discussing them. It should contain activities that require students of intelligence analysis courses to perform some activity and then discuss what they learned. An inclusive approach to interactive and experience-based learning methodologies would be adopted. In addition to simulations, in which students assume roles, the volume should also include other interactive learning tools such as exercises (e.g., ACH Exercise from Chapter 2) and games (e.g., Kim's Game from Chapter 6). As noted by Abt (1987, p. 9), "while all games simulate something from the real world, not all simulations are games." Additionally, not all games involve a contest among adversaries;

rather, sometimes cooperation is required to achieve common desired goals. The origin of the term *serious game* has been attributed to Abt's book of the same title. "Games may be played seriously or casually. We are concerned with serious games in the sense that these games have an explicit and carefully though-out educational purpose and are not intended to be played primarily for amusement" (Abt, 1987, p. 9).

Based on this approach, and assuming that many instructors of intelligence courses were already using experiential learning techniques but kept these activities unpublished, we began to invite potential contributors for a volume aimed at enhancing the learning experience through simulations, games, and other interactive or experiential methodologies. We were extremely pleased when our suspicions proved accurate, and we were able to fill this volume with many excellent original simulations, exercises, and games by a distinguished, international group of scholars and practitioners. Their contributions to this volume not only provide superb, ready-to-use experiential learning tools for classrooms but also provide valuable windows into the issues, challenges, and methodologies being experienced by a diverse set of national intelligence agencies and business entities.

As far as we know, this book is the first volume of this kind in the field of intelligence studies, although the use of simulations, exercises, games, or debriefing in the field of intelligence services for training purposes is anything but new. The use of simulations for teaching and research aims in the field of international relations is also not new and includes the work of remarkable figures such as Harold Guetzkow (1963).

As noted by David Crookall (2010), the so-called field of simulation/gaming comprises a wide set of methods, theories, and practices. These include simulations, serious games, computerized simulations, virtual worlds, role playing, and debriefing, among many others (Crookall, 2010, p. 899). And it is a field that is growing exponentially in both size and scope. Accordingly, we look forward to publishing successive volumes of additional simulations, exercises, and games to continue to improve experiential learning and the quality of intelligence education in the future.

It is our hope that this volume successfully meets its primary objective of providing a tool for enhancing the learning experience of participants in intelligence analysis courses. We have emphasized providing the simulations, exercises, and games contained in this book in the most usable and ready-to-run formats possible to facilitate instructors' ease of incorporating them into their courses.

As editors of this book, we wish to express our sincere gratitude to the contributors of the volume for their generosity and willingness to share their know-how in this enterprise, and we hope this book will fill a significant gap in the literature on intelligence education and training.

REFERENCES

Abt, Clark C. 1987. *Serious games.* Lanham, MD: University Press of America.
Crookall, David. 2010. Serious games, debriefing, and simulation/gaming as a discipline. *Simulation & Gaming, 41*(6), 898–920.

Guetzkow, Harold. 1963. *Simulations in international relations: Developments for research and teaching.* Englewood Cliffs, NJ: Prentice-Hall.

Kolb, Alice Y., and Kolb, David A. 2009. The learning way: Meta-cognitive aspects of experiential learning. *Simulation & Gaming, 40*(3), 297–327.

Kolb, David A. 1984. *Experiential learning: Experience as the source of learning and development.* Englewood Cliffs, NJ: Prentice-Hall.

Silberman, Mel (Ed.). 2007. *The handbook of experiential learning.* San Francisco: Pfeiffer.

Part I

ONE- OR TWO-CLASS SESSION SIMULATIONS

1

Simulating Iraqi WMD: A Ready-to-Use Simulation

William J. Lahneman and Hugo A. Keesing

ABSTRACT

This simulation offers a way to improve student understanding of the analytic process used by intelligence analysts as well as analysts in other fields such as business and public policy. The simulation places participants in the role of intelligence analysts in the months leading up to the Iraq War. Participants prepare an outline of a National Intelligence Estimate (NIE) that assesses the status of Iraq's weapons of mass destruction (WMD) programs. This simulation has several stages that mimic the actual process that the U.S. intelligence Community (IC) uses to produce NIEs. This simulation gives participants a better understanding of the ambiguity that IC analysts face in their jobs, the difficult assessments they must make based on limited information, the complexities of collaboration between different agencies in the IC to produce unified judgments, and the different perspectives of analysts and policymakers. The simulation takes about 2.5 hours to conduct and requires very little preparation by instructors and participants. It is a valuable addition to courses in intelligence, national security, foreign policy, and international relations.

KEYWORDS

Analysis and production; analytic tradecraft; intelligence analysis; intelligence cycle; intelligence process; intelligence simulation; Iraq; National Intelligence Estimate (NIE); teaching intelligence analysis; U.S. intelligence community; U.S. national security; weapons of mass destruction (WMD)

The September 11, 2001, attacks on the World Trade Center and the Pentagon by members of the al Qaeda transnational terrorist group placed the performance of the U.S. intelligence community (IC) and the topic of intelligence in general under the spotlight of public scrutiny. This attention intensified even further when, less than a year and a half later, the IC failed to estimate correctly Iraq's weapons of mass destruction (WMD) programs. Although the intensity of this spotlight has now dimmed, the U.S. IC will never be the same, for this scrutiny ignited a wave of ongoing intelligence reforms that has encompassed all aspects of the intelligence enterprise.

Why did the IC fail to detect al Qaeda's plans for the 9/11 attacks? Anyone who has studied the matter will tell you that the IC's failure to share information—to "connect the dots"—among its many parts was a principal contributor to the intelligence failure. Analysis is the part of the intelligence process that connects the dots. As the 9/11 Commission stated in its report investigating the causes of the attack, "The importance of integrated, all-source analysis cannot be overstated. Without it, it is not possible to 'connect the dots'" (*9/11 Commission Report*, 2004, p. 408). Analytic problems also played a significant role in the Iraqi WMD intelligence failure. However, in this case it was poor analytic tradecraft rather than a failure to connect the dots that was largely to blame. Given these facts, a large share of intelligence reforms have directly targeted analysts and the analytic process.

One of the post-9/11 intelligence reforms that has been of particular significance for universities and colleges is the decision to increase dramatically the size of the IC's analytic workforce. Universities have responded to the increased demand for intelligence analysts by designing a wide array of new courses and programs at both the undergraduate and graduate levels to help prepare students for employment as analysts.

At its core, intelligence analysis involves trying to make sense of incomplete information. Intelligence analysts try to solve complex puzzles that are missing a number of pieces. The resulting intelligence products must state several things in addition to offering analysts' best estimate of the "picture" the incomplete puzzle represents. Analysts must:

1. Assess what the puzzle represents based on the pieces they have collected through various secret and open sources (allowing for the possibility of denial and deception).
2. Estimate the things that they do not know (i.e., what pieces are they missing).
3. Judge the importance of the missing pieces (i.e., to what degree might missing pieces contain information that would invalidate their analysis).

A good analytic product thus clearly states the IC's best estimate of the status of an issue (step 1) *and* quantifies in some way the "substantive uncertainty" of the analysis (steps 2 and 3).

Although this description is straightforward, teaching the basic principles of intelligence analysis is challenging. John Gannon, former deputy director of intelligence at the CIA and former chairman of the National Intelligence Council, stated "most intelligence community (IC) analysts do not learn their trade primarily from books, training manuals, or courses but rather 'in the heat of the shop floor,' under the supervision of experienced managers and mentors" (cited in George & Bruce, 2008, p. 213). Gannon, like many other intelligence professionals, does not oppose formal education for analysts. In fact he is a leading advocate of formal programs. Rather, he recognizes the difficulty of teaching the analytic process through lectures alone.

This ready-to-use simulation offers a way to improve students' understanding of the analytic process used by intelligence analysts by giving them the opportunity to construct an intelligence product on their own. I have run this simulation many times for groups composed of students, university professors, and intelligence analysts. Every group felt that the simulation provided valuable insights they could not obtain from lectures, discussions, and their readings.

In this simulation, participants play the role of intelligence analysts in the months leading up to the Iraq War. Their task is to produce an NIE that assesses the status of Iraq's WMD programs.

> NIEs are the IC's most authoritative written judgments concerning national security issues. NIEs contain the coordinated judgments of the Intelligence Community regarding the likely course of future events. The National Intelligence Council (NIC) in the Office of the Director of National Intelligence leads the IC's effort to produce NIEs. The goal is to provide policymakers with the best, unvarnished, and unbiased information—regardless of whether analytic judgments conform to US policy. (National Intelligence Council, 2008)

Iraq's WMD programs were a vital U.S. national security concern in late 2002. The prospect of war literally hung in the balance depending on the status of these programs. In September 2002, at the instigation of several members of the Senate Select Committee on Intelligence, the IC produced an NIE on Iraq's WMD programs (*Report of the Select Committee*, 2004). The NIE painted a fairly strong assessment that Iraq was pursuing WMD programs. Members of Congress also prompted the IC to produce an unclassified version of the NIE—a "White Paper." The White Paper's purpose was to distribute information about Iraq's WMD programs to as wide an audience as possible to stimulate informed public debate about this important issue.

After the U.S. invasion of Iraq, it became apparent that both the NIE and White Paper were wrong. Both documents had considerably overstated Iraq's WMD programs. In particular, many criticized the White Paper for making a stronger case than the classified NIE that Iraq possessed WMD. The inaccuracies in the NIE and White Paper resulted in a number of investigations into this intelligence failure. In particular, a congressional investigation included a list of actual declassified excerpts from the classified NIE as well as the corresponding excerpts from the White Paper (*Report of the Select Committee*, 2004). These excerpts of finished intelligence constitute the pieces of "raw" intelligence used in the simulation.

The simulation's subject matter adds to its pedagogic value in three principal ways. First, the NIE was one of the main justifications for the U.S. invasion of Iraq in March 2003. Thus, the simulation underscores the critical contribution that good intelligence analysis makes to effective policy making.

Second, the simulation gives participants the opportunity to gain insights into the kinds of uncertainties and ambiguities inherent in intelligence analysis. The fact that they are using the same intelligence available in 2002 heightens participants' interest. Can participants produce more accurate results than the IC? The vast majority of participants have found this opportunity very interesting and challenging.

Third, the simulation is designed so that half of the participants work with raw intelligence consisting of statements extracted from the NIE while the other half uses corresponding items of raw intelligence extracted from the White Paper. This approach provides many superb examples of how small changes in the wording of statements can produce significant changes in perceived meaning. It also allows participants to test the validity of claims that the White Paper made a stronger case for war than the classified NIE. Did the teams that used excerpts from the White Paper become more convinced that Iraq possessed WMD than the teams that used excerpts from the classified NIE?

Although the simulation deals with intelligence analysis, many other fields in government, business, and the nonprofit sector require large numbers of competent analysts. This simulation can be a useful addition to any course that emphasizes students' critical thinking, writing, and briefing abilities.

BASIC DATA

Instructional Objectives

The instructional objectives of this simulation are: to impart appreciation for the ambiguity that U.S. IC analysts face in their jobs; to experience the difficult assessments analysts must make based on limited information; to demonstrate the complexities involved in constructing unified judgments through collaboration among different IC agencies; to show the difficulty in estimating and conveying uncertainty to intelligence consumers; to reveal the different perspectives of analysts and policymakers; to emphasize the challenges policymakers face when they feel the need to act on incomplete information.

Simulation Objectives

Participants prepare an outline of an NIE that assesses the status of Iraq's WMD programs. The simulation has several stages that mimic the actual process used to produce NIEs. Participants first prepare individual assessments, then work as part of a team to prepare their agency's formal assessment, and finally participate in the NIE process with analysts from other IC agencies to produce a single, IC-wide assessment. The simulation uses "raw intelligence" excerpted from the classified NIE and the subsequent unclassified White Paper. It has several stages that mimic the actual process used to produce NIEs (e.g., assessments by individual analysts, team analyses within single IC agencies, and the final step in which participants representing different agencies must produce a final analysis representing the IC's consensus on Iraqi WMD).

Debriefing Format

The instructor facilitates a group discussion among all participants at the end of the simulation. Several key questions guide the discussion to ensure that the class discusses the various learning objectives.

Target Audience

Undergraduate and graduate students in an introductory or advanced course about intelligence. The simulation is also suitable for courses in national security, U.S. foreign policy, and international relations. I also have conducted the simulation for groups of university professors and intelligence analysts. All groups have found the simulation to be a very effective tool for cementing a number of important concepts central to successful intelligence analysis.

Playing Time

2 hours (NOTE: Instructors can conduct the simulation and debriefing in one 2.5-hour class session, two 75-minute class sessions, or three 50-minute class sessions.)

Debriefing Time

30–45 minutes

Number of Players Required

12+. The simulation requires a minimum of four groups/teams, each of which should contain a minimum of three persons. I have conducted the simulation successfully with 24 persons (four teams of six participants each). Above approximately 25 participants, I recommend raising the number of teams to six or eight to keep each team below about six persons.

Participation Materials Included

Appendices A and B (raw intelligence)

Debriefing Materials Included

Appendix C (Primary Differences in Key Judgments of the Classified National Intelligence Estimate [NIE] and Unclassified White Paper)

Computer/Internet

Not required

Other Materials/Equipment Required

The classroom should be large enough to allow each group to have its own area to conduct discussions without disturbing the other groups. Each group should have markers and large sheets of paper for recording their probabilities and lists (classrooms with adequate blackboard/erasable board space can use them instead).

FACILITATOR'S GUIDE: MATERIALS

Appendix A: Raw Intelligence

Appendix A contains a list of nine statements concerning Iraq's WMD programs from Table B of the U.S. Intelligence Community's Prewar Intelligence Assessments on Iraq (National Intelligence Estimate) (*Report of the Select Committee*, 2004, p. 294). Six of the nine Classified NIE conclusions were altered slightly either to accentuate differences between the NIE and the corresponding statements in the White Paper or to sharpen details to provide participants with meaningful information. None of these changes is inconsistent with the findings. These changes are highlighted in Table 1.1.

Appendix B: Raw Intelligence

Appendix B contains a list of nine statements from Table B of the U.S. Intelligence Community's Prewar Intelligence Assessments on Iraq (White Paper). This list parallels the list in Appendix A. However, the White Paper utilizes different phraseology in many instances.

Appendix C: Copy of Table B, Primary Differences in the Key Judgments of the Classified National Intelligence Estimate (NIE) and Unclassified White Paper

This appendix facilitates comparison of how the two documents conveyed raw intelligence.

Presimulation Briefing

The facilitator informs the participants that they will be learning about intelligence analysis by serving as analysts. In this simulation, it is September 2002 and their task is to summarize the U.S. intelligence community's position on whether Iraq has some form of WMD or WMD program. This is an extremely important matter since a finding that Iraq possesses WMD could be cause for the United States to go to war! In a moment, the facilitator will give each participant a list containing nine pieces of raw intelligence. To increase interest, tell participants that the nine items on this list are actual pieces of raw intelligence used by the IC in developing its 2002 NIE on Iraq's WMD programs.

Table 1.1. Revisions to NIE Phraseology for Use in the Simulation (revisions are in italics)

Item Number	National Intelligence Estimate	Appendix A (Used in simulation)
1	We judge that Iraq has continued its weapons of mass destruction (WMD) programs in defiance of United Nations (UN) resolutions and restrictions. Baghdad has chemical and biological weapons as well as missiles with ranges in excess of UN restrictions; if left unchecked, it probably will have a nuclear weapon during this decade. (See INR alternative view at the end of these key judgments.)	We judge that Iraq has continued its weapons of mass destruction (WMD) programs in defiance of United Nations (UN) resolutions and restrictions. Baghdad has chemical weapons *(CW)* and biological weapons *(BW)* as well as missiles with ranges in excess of *600 km; it may have a nuclear weapon during this decade. (INR, the State Department's intelligence office, does not concur with this assessment).*
3	In the view of most agencies, Baghdad is reconstituting its nuclear weapons program.	In the view of most agencies, Baghdad is reconstituting its nuclear weapons program. *(INR does not concur with this assessment.)*
4	Most analysts believe that Saddam's personal interest in and Iraq's aggressive attempts to obtain high-strength aluminum tubes for centrifuge rotors . . . provide compelling evidence that Saddam is reconstituting a uranium enrichment effort for Baghdad's nuclear weapons program. (DOE agrees that reconstitution of the nuclear program is under way but assess that the tubes probably are not part of the program.)	Most analysts believe that Saddam's personal interest in and Iraq's aggressive attempts to obtain high-strength aluminum tubes for centrifuge rotors . . . provide compelling evidence that Saddam is reconstituting a uranium enrichment effort for Baghdad's nuclear weapons program. *(The Department of Energy's intelligence office assesses that the tubes are not part of the program.)*
6	Although we have little specific information on Iraq's CW stockpile, Saddam probably has stocked at least 100 metric tons (MT) and possibly as much as 500 MT of CW agents—much of it added in the last year.	We have little specific information on Iraq's CW stockpile. Saddam *possibly* has stocked at least 100 metric tons (MT) and possibly as much as 500 MT of CW agents—much of it added in the last year.
7	We judge that all key aspects—R&D, production, and weaponization—of Iraq's offensive BW program are active and that most elements are larger and more advanced than they were before the Gulf War.	We judge that all key aspects—*research & development* (R&D), production, and weaponization—of Iraq's offensive BW program are active and that most elements are larger and more advanced than they were *a decade ago.*
9	Iraq maintains a small missile force and several developmental programs, including for a UAV probably intended to deliver biological warfare agents.	Iraq maintains a small missile force and several developmental programs, including for an *unmanned aerial vehicle* (UAV) *possibly* intended to deliver biological warfare agents.

Participants will analyze this intelligence in a series of steps involving both independent and team analyses to construct an NIE. The facilitator cautions participants to be as objective as possible regarding the raw intelligence despite the fact that it is now known that Iraq did not possess WMD. Participants should place themselves in the position of the analysts working this issue in late 2002 and base their judgments only on the raw intelligence available to them rather than hindsight.

Step 1: Getting Organized

Divide participants into at least four groups. Each group should sit in a different part of the classroom so that members of each group cannot readily overhear the discussions of the other groups. Next, hand out copies of Appendix A to members of half of the groups (e.g., to the members of groups A and B) and copies of Appendix B to members of the other groups (e.g., to members of groups C and D). This means that, for the duration of the simulation, half of the groups will work with the (modified) Classified NIE intelligence contained in Appendix A and the other half will work with the White Paper intelligence contained in Appendix B. *Do not tell the groups that they are using different summaries. All participants should believe that they are using the same raw intelligence.*

Step 2: Developing Individual Assessments (15 minutes)

Participants work *individually* during this step. Tell participants that this phase of the simulation mimics the fact that analysts initially develop their own individual analyses of an issue. Participants will assign a numerical probability to each of the nine statements on their lists of raw intelligence. Each probability will indicate a participant's confidence, based only on the single statement under consideration, that Iraq has some form of WMD or WMD program. For instance, if statement 1 on the list makes a participant believe with absolute certainty that Iraq has some form of WMD (nuclear, biological, chemical, or radiological weapon), then that participant should assign a probability of 100 percent to that statement. Tell the participants to pay particular attention to words/phrases that they feel are ambiguous or create uncertainty ("we judge . . ." and "probably") and keep a list of these terms for use later in the simulation.

Once participants have assigned a probability to each of the nine statements, tell them to use all nine statements to determine a single probability that summarizes their personal assessment whether Iraq has some form of WMD or WMD program. Tell participants that this part of the simulation mimics the process of intelligence fusion. Participants should not simply average their nine probabilities to determine their single overall probability. Rather, they should consider the relative weights they attach to each of the nine pieces of raw intelligence. For example, a participant might assign low probabilities to seven of the nine pieces of intelligence and very high probabilities to the remaining two pieces. If the participant feels that the two items with high probabilities are particularly important indicators that Iraq has WMD, then it is appropriate to assign an overall probability that is quite high.

When everyone has finished, participants will list their probabilities in a location where all members of their team can view them. It is preferable but not essential that each group cannot see the other groups' results at this point. *Do not discuss these results at this time.*

Step 3: Preparing Agency Positions (25 minutes)

Participants now work as team members within their groups. This phase mimics the work of analytic teams within individual intelligence agencies. The facilitator should assign a name to each group (for example, one could be the Central Intelligence Agency [CIA], one could be the Defense Intelligence Agency [DIA], another could be the State Department's Office of Intelligence and Research [INR]). This measure encourages the members of each group to identify themselves as team members.

Instruct the members of each group to reach agreement (consensus) among themselves on a single probability for each of the nine pieces of raw intelligence, as well as on a single overall probability that Iraq has WMD/programs (i.e., repeat the steps of step 2 as a group). Caution groups to base their consensus on analytical reasoning rather than averaging or a similar compromise approach.

When every team has finished, each team (A, B, C, D, etc.) should list the group's conclusions. Do not disclose these results to the members of other groups.

Step 4: Addressing Intelligence Gaps (20 minutes)

Direct each group to draw on its previous work and generate from three to five additional collection requirements. These requirements should address what participants perceive as critical intelligence gaps. Do not disclose these results to the members of other groups. Participants will discuss these lists during the debrief.

Step 5: Producing NIEs (25 minutes)

The facilitator now combines groups that have been working with the same list of raw intelligence (i.e., all participants using Appendix A [classified NIE] should work as one group and all participants using Appendix B [White Paper] should work as another, separate group). This phase mimics the fact that all agencies of the IC work together during the final stages of the NIE process. The facilitator should emphasize that each group's analysis represents the position of one of the IC's all-source agencies (i.e., the CIA, DIA, and INR).

Tell each of the two "multiagency" groups to repeat step 3 as a single team (reach a single probability for each of the nine items as well as an overall probability). This result represents the consensus of the entire IC. Do not disclose these results to the members of the other group.

Step 6: Briefing NIEs to Policymakers (25 minutes)

Direct each of the two combined groups to prepare an intelligence briefing for policymakers. Participants should pay particular attention to the language they use to convey their overall probability (i.e., the substantive uncertainty) that Iraq possesses WMD or WMD programs. This briefing summarizes each group's NIE.

Have each group brief its conclusions to the entire class. This concludes the active phase of the simulation.

DEBRIEFING THE SIMULATION (30–45 MINUTES)

Objectives

An effective debriefing session can help participants reach a better understanding of a number of factors that makes intelligence analysis so challenging.

Gaps in Information

Participants experienced that the raw intelligence available for producing their NIEs lacked many important elements. (They identified specific gaps in step 4.) Participants usually find it difficult to produce a set of collection requirements that the IC can collect in a reasonable amount of time, if at all. This is an important realization. It helps students appreciate that intelligence analysts routinely must produce analyses about issues for which they feel important if not vital parts of the puzzle are missing.

The IC often obtains raw intelligence through "sensitive sources and methods" (spies, wiretaps, various forms of covert observation). The agencies using these sensitive sources and methods try hard to keep them secret so that the groups they target do not learn of them and take actions to neutralize their effectiveness. This secrecy applies within the IC: collection agencies will not disclose their sources and methods to other parts of the IC that do not have a "need to know." The result is that IC analysts might be given a piece of raw intelligence but not told how the intelligence was obtained. Analysts can perceive this practice as a type of information gap. Analysts want to know how the IC obtained the intelligence so they can personally assess its validity. This is not always possible.

Assessing Substantive Uncertainty

Gaps in information are one source of uncertainty in an analysis, but they are not the only one. Analysts are likely to disagree among themselves about the degree of uncertainty associated with a particular piece of raw intelligence. This tendency also manifests itself as analysts combine the pieces of raw intelligence into a finished analysis. This process is called *intelligence fusion*. Participants perform intelligence fusion throughout the simulation, first as individuals and then as members of groups. Group analyses are particularly important because they are where knowledge creation is more likely to occur. Knowledge creation refers to the generation of insights based on the knowledge that individual analysts possess but do not tap until stimulated by other analysts' comments.

Analysts can reach different conclusions from the same raw intelligence for several reasons, including differences in their education and experience. These differences cause them to assign greater weight to pieces of raw intelligence that resonate with their own experience. An analyst's organizational affiliation can also be important. Different parts of the IC are responsible for collecting intelligence by specific methods (e.g., human sources, communications intercepts, or imagery). Members of these organizations often assign greater importance to intelligence collected by their methods.

Interpretation problems are another source of disagreement. Analysts must produce written summaries of their analyses at some point. The nine pieces of raw intelligence in the simulation are examples. Other analysts, managers, and, ultimately, policymakers—from a number of government agencies—subsequently read these summaries. Each reviewer might attach different levels of substantive uncertainty to the same statement. One reason for this phenomenon is that the IC lacks a standard lexicon to express uncertainty. As a result, one person interprets the expression "We judge . . ." to indicate a high level of certainty while another assigns a lower degree of certainty to the same phrase.

Cognitive Biases

Intelligence analysts learn to avoid a number of common cognitive biases that degrade the critical thinking that is so important to effective intelligence analysis. Two such biases that might occur among participants are "mirror imaging" (supposing that Iraqis act as Americans would act in the same circumstances) and "preexisting attitudes" (unwillingness to challenge the preexisting knowledge that Iraq did not have WMD).

Layering is another natural tendency that is particularly relevant to this simulation. *Layering* occurs when analysts assume that previous analyses on the same subject are valid. They analyze the issue by updating the old assessment based on any new intelligence that has become available since the last assessment instead of taking an entirely fresh look at all aspects of the issue. Layering predisposes analysts to produce a new assessment that agrees with previous ones (Lowenthal, 2009).

Organizational Dynamics

The simulation provides an excellent setting to discuss phenomena associated with the dynamics of small groups. These phenomena detract from the quality of group decision making. Typical pitfalls for groups of analysts include "groupthink" (a group ignores a team member who disagrees with the majority view) (Janis, 1972),[1] "satisficing" (lowest common denominator thinking—accepting the least objectionable position) (Simon, 1972),[2] and the emergence of a leader who dominates the discussion.

The Tyranny of Deadlines

Participants had limited time to conduct the simulation. Although the IC takes much longer to compile an NIE, deadlines are an unpleasant fact for the IC and participants alike. Insufficient time can degrade the quality of an analysis.

Briefing Skills

Drafting briefs that estimate effectively the status of an issue is difficult. Capturing substantive uncertainty is particularly difficult. Moreover, policymakers are extremely busy. This means that even briefings on complex issues must be very concise. (This partially explains the brevity of the pieces of raw intelligence that the participants used.)

The Role of Intelligence

The participants' NIE outlines (the briefings) are important. Policymakers must make decisions under conditions of uncertainty and incomplete information. In this case, the NIEs summarized by the briefings would form a vitally important component of the knowledge that policymakers would use in deciding to go to war!

DEBRIEFING

Step 1. Comparing Results

NOTE: This outline is a guide. It is more important to cover all of the topics than to adhere rigorously to the order of events described below.

Participants should display all results (all probabilities and lists of collection gaps) so everyone can see them.

Give each participant a copy of Appendix C. Tell the participants that half of the groups had used statements from the NIE and the other half the corresponding statements from the White Paper. The facilitator should explain that the IC produced the classified NIE first, then the White Paper when it became clear that the issue of Iraqi WMD would be an important element in the decision to go to war. The purpose of the White Paper was to make as much as possible of the intelligence about Iraq's WMD programs available to the public in order to expand meaningful debate beyond persons—mostly government officials—who possessed the necessary security clearances to view the classified NIE. (Many later alleged that the White Paper had presented a stronger case than the classified NIE that Iraq possessed WMD.)

Use this background as a starting point for assessing the various probabilities developed during the simulation.

Key questions to stimulate discussion:

- Do the simulation's results support the contention that the White Paper overstated the classified NIE's findings?
- Did the overall probability that Iraq possessed WMD vary significantly between the groups that used the NIE and those that used the White Paper?

Step 2. Issues in Conveying Uncertainty

Step 1 leads into a detailed examination of the probabilities that individual analysts assigned to the nine pieces of raw intelligence (questions 1 and 2). Discuss issues of terminology when they inevitably arise at some point in this discussion (questions 3–6). This leads to a discussion about the difficulty in determining the substantive uncertainty contained in written statements.

Key questions:

- What were the principal factors that led participants to arrive at their estimates?
- Why did individual participants assign significantly different values to the same piece of raw intelligence?
- Did particular phrases convey (or fail to convey) important meaning, such as substantive uncertainty?
- Would participants have liked to see different language used in their raw intelligence?
- What terms are more useful as descriptors?
- To what degree do participants agree on a set of standards?

Step 3. Intelligence Fusion, Cognitive Biases, and Group Dynamics

Cover intelligence fusion issues next. Start with individual analyses (question 1) and then discuss group analyses (questions 2–7). Participants should raise issues associated with group dynamics, cognitive biases, and deadlines during these discussions. Terminology will remain an issue; participants will discuss instances in which they disagreed on the meaning of a term or phrase.

Key questions:

- Why did one participant assign a given overall probability while another, who had similar individual probabilities, arrive at a different overall value?
- What were the major factors involved in obtaining agreement during group sessions?
- Was the initial view adopted by the group the one that made it into the group's briefing?
- How did participants persuade analysts who disagreed with their position?
- Did anyone feel pressure to conform to another analyst's views? How was this issue resolved? Was there evidence of groupthink, satisficing, dominant leader, or layering? Were any group members excluded from discussions because they held unpopular views?
- During the final group session, did analysts in each "agency" prove reluctant to change their group's views?
- Did teams feel pressure because of time constraints? How did these constraints affect individual and group performance?

Step 4. Intelligence Collection Issues

Discuss collection issues using the lists that participants constructed in step 4 of the simulation. Tell participants that analysts can task the IC's collection agencies to focus their efforts on filling important gaps in the analytic picture. Have each group brief the contents of its list to the entire class. If the class has already discussed intelligence collection techniques, participants should identify the parts of the IC that might be capable of obtaining the required information and discuss the collection sources and methods involved.

Key questions:

- What things could the IC have done to improve the quality of its raw intelligence on this issue?
- How long would it take the IC to accomplish these tasks?

Step 5. Conveying Meaning to Policymakers

Discuss the written and oral briefings. Discuss the problems participants encountered in trying to write such concise briefs about such a complex issue. Emphasize the importance of these kinds of briefings and the NIEs upon which they are based, particularly their direct impact on important policy decisions.

Key questions:

- Ask participants to place themselves in the role of policymakers and assess how they would interpret the intelligence about Iraq's WMD programs contained in the briefings/NIEs. Did the briefings/NIEs help policymakers who were considering whether to go to war with Iraq?
- To what degree might policymakers' preexisting attitudes about this issue affect their interpretation of the contents of the briefing/NIE?

Step 6. Self-assessment of Performance

Conclude the debrief by asking participants to assess how they would rate their group's use of critical thinking. This should lead to a discussion of whether individual participants or groups would do anything differently if given another chance.

CONCLUSION

This simulation exposes participants to a number of important issues associated with producing high-quality intelligence products for policymakers. Many of these issues are difficult for students to grasp through lectures alone. The simulation gives students firsthand experience with making difficult choices based on incomplete information.

The simulation also gives participants important insight into how intelligence products affect the quality of national security and foreign policies. This simulation is thus not only a way to enhance student learning in an intelligence policy course but also an appropriate addition to any course dealing with foreign policy, national security policy, or homeland security policy.

The need to act based on incomplete information is in no way limited to the intelligence and policymaking communities. Rather, high-quality analysis is an essential ingredient for success in virtually all fields. Accordingly, the simulation's lessons in critical thinking, writing, and briefing skills are equally applicable for analysts in business and other fields.

The simulation's structure and scope allow instructors to emphasize aspects that pertain to their fields. Although the simulation translates readily to business intelligence courses, professors teaching psychology courses might want to emphasize the aspects of the simulation dealing with cognitive biases and group dynamics. Instructors of courses in foreign policy might choose to stress the connection between good (or bad) intelligence, resulting policies, and the downstream effects on U.S. security and influence. Courses in many fields can profit from the simulation's requirement to translate analytic discussions into thoughtful written and oral briefings.

The simulation requires 2.5 hours to conduct. It can be run in a single 2.5-hour class session or conducted over two 75-minute sessions, or three 50-minute sessions. It requires no preparation on the part of participants and only minimal preparation by the instructor. All of the materials necessary for conducting the simulation are contained in Appendices A through C. Students and others who have participated in the simulation have found it both educational and enjoyable.

APPENDIX A: RAW INTELLIGENCE

1. We judge that Iraq has continued its weapons of mass destruction (WMD) programs in defiance of United Nations (UN) resolutions and restrictions. Baghdad has chemical weapons (CW) and biological weapons (BW) as well as missiles with ranges in excess of 600 km; it may have a nuclear weapon during this decade. (INR, the State Department's intelligence office, does not concur with this assessment.)

2. We judge that we are seeing only a portion of Iraq's WMD efforts, owing to Baghdad's vigorous denial and deception efforts.

3. In the view of most agencies, Baghdad is reconstituting its nuclear weapons program (INR does not concur with this assessment).

4. Most analysts believe that Saddam's personal interest in and Iraq's aggressive attempts to obtain high-strength aluminum tubes for centrifuge rotors . . . provide compelling evidence that Saddam is reconstituting a uranium enrichment effort for Baghdad's nuclear weapons program. (The Department of Energy's intelligence office assesses that the tubes are not part of the program.)

5. We assess that Baghdad has begun renewed production of mustard, sarin, GF (cyclosarin), and VX (types of CW).

6. We have little specific information on Iraq's CW stockpile. Saddam possibly has stocked at least 100 metric tons (MT) and possibly as much as 500 MT of CW agents—much of it added in the last year.

7. We judge that all key aspects—research & development (R&D), production, and weaponization—of Iraq's offensive BW program are active and that most elements are larger and more advanced than they were a decade ago.

8. We judge that Iraq has some lethal and incapacitating BW agents and is capable of quickly producing and weaponizing a variety of such agents, including anthrax, for delivery by bombs, missiles, aerial sprayers, and covert operatives.

9. Iraq maintains a small missile force and several developmental programs, including for an unmanned aerial vehicle (UAV) possibly intended to deliver biological warfare agents. USAF Intelligence believes UAV's primary role is reconnaissance.

APPENDIX B: RAW INTELLIGENCE

1. Iraq has continued its weapons of mass destruction (WMD) programs in defiance of UN Resolutions and restrictions. Baghdad has chemical weapons (CW) and biological weapons (BW) as well as missiles with ranges in excess of UN restrictions; if left unchecked, it probably will have a nuclear weapon during this decade.

2. Baghdad hides large portions of Iraq's WMD efforts.

3. Most analysts assess Iraq is reconstituting its nuclear weapons program.

4. Iraq's aggressive attempts to obtain proscribed high-strength aluminum tubes are of significant concern. All intelligence experts agree that Iraq is seeking nuclear weapons and that these tubes could be used in a centrifuge enrichment program. Most intelligence specialists assess this to be the intended use, but some believe that these tubes are probably intended for conventional weapons programs.

5. Baghdad has begun renewed production of chemical warfare agents, probably including mustard, sarin, cyclosarin, and VX (types of CW).

6. Saddam probably has stocked a few hundred metric tons of CW agent.

7. All key aspects—research & development (R&D), production, and weaponization—of Iraq's offensive BW program are active and most elements are larger and more advanced than they were before the Gulf War.

8. Iraq has some lethal and incapacitating BW agents and is capable of quickly producing and weaponizing a variety of such agents, including anthrax, for delivery by bombs, missiles, aerial sprayers, and covert operatives, including potentially against the U.S. Homeland.

9. Iraq maintains a small missile force and several developmental programs, including for an unmanned aerial vehicle (UAV) that most analysts assess probably is intended to deliver biological warfare agents.

APPENDIX C: PRIMARY DIFFERENCES IN THE KEY JUDGMENTS OF THE CLASSIFIED NATIONAL INTELLIGENCE ESTIMATE (NIE) AND UNCLASSIFIED WHITE PAPER

Classified NIE

We judge that Iraq has continued its weapons of mass destruction (WMD) programs in defiance of United Nations (UN) resolutions and restrictions. Baghdad has chemical and biological weapons as well as missiles with ranges in excess of UN restrictions; if left unchecked, it probably will have a nuclear weapon during this decade. (See INR alternative view at the end of these key judgments.)

We judge that we are seeing only a portion of Iraq's WMD efforts, owing to Baghdad's vigorous denial and deception efforts.

In the view of most agencies, Baghdad is reconstituting its nuclear weapons program.

Most analysts believe that Saddam's personal interest in and Iraq's aggressive attempts to obtain high-strength aluminum tubes for centrifuge rotors . . . provide compelling evidence that Saddam is reconstituting a uranium enrichment effort for Baghdad's nuclear weapons program. (DOE agrees that reconstitution of the nuclear program is under way but assess that the tubes probably are not part of the program.)

We assess that Baghdad has begun renewed production of mustard, sarin, GF (cyclosarin), and VX.

White Paper

Iraq has continued its weapons of mass destruction (WMD) programs in defiance of UN resolutions and restrictions. Baghdad has chemical and biological weapons as well as missiles with ranges in excess of UN restrictions; if left unchecked, it probably will have a nuclear weapon during this decade.

Baghdad hides large portions of Iraq's WMD efforts.

Most analysts assess Iraq is reconstituting its nuclear weapons program.

Iraq's aggressive attempts to obtain proscribed high-strength aluminum tubes are of significant concern. All intelligence experts agree that Iraq is seeking nuclear weapons and that these tubes could be used in a centrifuge enrichment program. Most intelligence specialists assess this to be the intended use, but some believe that these tubes are probably intended for conventional weapons programs.

Baghdad has begun renewed production of chemical warfare agents, probably including mustard, sarin, cyclosarin, and VX.

Although we have little specific information on Iraq's CW stockpile, Saddam probably has stocked at least 100 metric tons (MT) and possibly as much as 500 MT of CW agents—much of it added in the last year.

Saddam probably has stocked a few hundred metric tons of CW agent.

We judge that all key aspects—R&D, production, and weaponization—of Iraq's offensive BW program are active and that most elements are larger and more advanced than they were before the Gulf War.

All key aspects—R&D, production, and weaponization—of Iraq's offensive BW program are active and most elements are larger and more advanced than they were before the Gulf War.

We judge that Iraq has some lethal and incapacitating BW agents and is capable of quickly producing and weaponizing a variety of such agents, including anthrax, for delivery by bombs, missiles, aerial sprayers, and covert operatives.

Iraq has some lethal and incapacitating BW agents and is capable of quickly producing and weaponizing a variety of such agents, including anthrax, for delivery by bombs, missiles, aerial sprayers, and covert operatives, including potentially against the U.S. Homeland.

Iraq maintains a small missile force and several developmental programs, including for a UAV probably intended to deliver biological warfare agents.

Iraq maintains a small missile force and several developmental programs, including for a UAV that most analysts assess probably is intended to deliver biological warfare agents.

Source: *Report of the Select Committee on Intelligence on the US Intelligence Community's Prewar Intelligence Assessments on Iraq*, July 7, 2004, p. 294. (www.gpoaccess.gov/serialset/creports/iraq.html)

ACKNOWLEDGMENTS

William J. Lahneman and Hugo A. Keesing. 2011. Estimating Iraqi weapons of mass destruction. *Simulation & Gaming, 42*(6), 803–821, copyright © 2011 by SAGE Publications. Reprinted with Permission of SAGE Publications.

The authors wish to thank Dr. Lenora Peters Gant, director of the Intelligence Community Centers of Academic Excellence Program, for commissioning us to devise a simulation for the IC CAE's 2006 summer seminar and for her advice and encouragement as we developed and refined this simulation.

NOTES

1. For an introduction to Groupthink, see the Wikipedia site http://en.wikipedia.org/wiki/Groupthink.

2. For an outline of satisficing and bounded rationality, see the Wikipedia site http://en.wikipedia.org/wiki/Satisficing.

REFERENCES

George, R. Z., & Bruce, J. B. (Eds.). 2008. *Analyzing intelligence: Origins, obstacles, and innovations.* Washington, DC: Georgetown University Press.

Janis, I. 1972. *Victims of groupthink: A psychological study of foreign-policy decisions and fiascoes.* Boston, MA: Houghton Mifflin.

Lowenthal, M. M. 2009. *Intelligence: From Secrets to Policy* (2nd ed.). Washington, DC: CQ Press.

National Intelligence Council. www.dni.gov/nic/NIC_home.html.

Report of the Select Committee on Intelligence on the US Intelligence Community's Prewar Intelligence Assessments on Iraq. July 7, 2004. Washington, DC: U.S. Government Printing Office. Available at: www.gpoaccess.gov/serialset/creports/iraq.html.

Simon, H. A. 1972. Theories of bounded rationality. In C. B. McGuire & R. Radner (Eds.), *Decision and organization* (pp. 161–176). New York: North Holland.

The 9/11 Commission Report: Final Report of the National Commission on Terrorist Attacks Upon the United States. 2004. New York: Norton. Available at: www.gpoaccess.gov/911/.

These ee

2

Competing Hypotheses in Contemporary Intelligence Analysis

Julian Richards

There are two persistent and very resilient debates in the academic discipline of intelligence studies. The first is the question of how, precisely, we define "intelligence" and related factors such as the nature of the intelligence analysis activity and the nature and shape of the intelligence analyst. The second frequently heard debate is that of whether intelligence analysis is an art or a science. In both cases, the general outcome of discussion is that it is impossible to define such issues exactly, and that they will encompass a wide range of activities and factors depending on the specific context.

At one level, the debate as to whether intelligence analysis is an art or a science is a largely academic one in the worst sense of the word. For intelligence practitioners it is almost certainly the case that such debates would be considered a wasteful luxury. No intelligence practitioners whom I have met have spent time sitting around pondering whether what they do is an art or a science. Particularly in the fiercely operational culture that seems to have accelerated since the turn of the twenty-first century, there is scarcely time for analysts to define what they are doing, as all of their time must be taken up with getting on and doing it.

Sherman Kent's injunction, delivered in the 1960s, that there "can never be a time when the thoughtful man can be supplanted as the intelligence device supreme" (Kent, 1965, p. xviii) remains as important and pertinent today as it did then, and most intelligence practitioners would probably agree. However, with the passing of time, the belief among technologists that machines could start to think and make judgments for us, in certain cases, will be gathering pace. This critical boundary, between machines and techniques that help us do intelligence analysis and the human processes of thought and judgment that still drive the process, is essentially the boundary between the art and science of intelligence analysis. Both are critical elements of the intelligence process and both define it (Richards, 2010, p. 172),

23

although the boundary between both activities and the question of which drives the other will become increasingly blurry, with dangerous consequences.

For the time being, intelligence analysts and students of their craft can usefully consider these different elements of the process and consider how to employ them to the best effect. At this stage, it is useful to go slightly further in defining what we mean by "art" and "science" in this context. Leaving aside complex questions of whether creative and critical thinking processes are innate or can be learned, the "art" of intelligence analysis is situated in processes of human analysts making best-guess judgments, predictions, and recommendations based on the information before them. This is not a precise business, and different analysts at different times may make different judgments on the basis of exactly the same information. There are also a host of human factors that can sometimes pervert or warp the judgment process, such as bias, mistakes in perception, political factors within and between organizations, or, indeed, deception. Such factors are the curse of any situation in which humans come together. At the point of judgment, the individual analyst may not be able to say how or why he or she arrived at a particular conclusion; he or she will just "feel" it to be right (this is the "Blink" phenomenon that Gladwell [2006] so aptly described). At one level, it is akin to the difficulty of a Mozart or a Picasso explaining where his ideas came from (both were notoriously unable and, in some cases, unwilling to do so!).

The "science" part of the equation, if deployed appropriately, offers a set of opportunities for improving these judgments and mitigating the pitfalls that arise from the human factors described. (At the same time, they should never be seen as panaceas or be relied upon to always deliver the right answers.) In practice, I suggest this breaks down into three dimensions of activity. First, there is the business of academic inquiry within intelligence studies. This is very much an interdisciplinary activity; not just formal intelligence studies, but the host of other scientific disciplines that look at human behavior in its various manifestations, from biology to psychology and sociology. All of these activities have value to offer in considering how humans make analytical judgments and how they can improve their performance. And academics will have more time to consider such issues than the analysts themselves.

The second point at which science interacts with intelligence analysis is in the technological realm, and particularly the application of advanced information technology to the collection, codification, databasing, mining, and presentation of large amounts of complex data. Essentially, the task here is to reduce the amount of time an analyst spends on preparing the data and maximize the time he or she can spend on analyzing it.

The third and final scientific approach is the development and use of tradecraft techniques and procedures, which, while not replacing the essential thinking processes of the analyst, help to make their task more efficient and more accurate. Pherson and Heuer (2011) described these techniques as "Structured Analytic Techniques." One of the earliest and most well known of these is Richards Heuer's (1999) "Analysis of Competing Hypotheses" (ACH), which we consider in this exercise.

Heuer was one of a group of Central Intelligence Agency (CIA) analysts with a background in social sciences, who, during the height of the Cold War, developed a notion of analytic tradecraft and the need to train and professionalize the intelligence analyst, with a particular emphasis on the role played by human factors such as cognitive psychology. One of the first and most influential of this group was the aforementioned Sherman Kent, a former historian from Yale University who ended up working for the CIA after World War II and eventually became the namesake for the CIA's Sherman Kent School for Intelligence Analysis. Kent, Heuer, and others, such as Jack Davis, collectively established a number of studies and techniques that have largely set the standards for intelligence analysis training up to the present day, not only in the Anglo-Saxon world but also beyond it to a certain extent. Heuer's "Psychology of Intelligence Analysis," developed over several decades through his direct experience of analysis within the CIA during the Cold War but eventually published as a single and openly available document in 1999, has become something of a core text for analysts and trainers alike across the global intelligence community.

There is an argument to say that, given that this school of thinking was developed during the Cold War and within the specific intelligence environment of the CIA, there is a need to evolve the thinking about intelligence analysis and tradecraft to better account for the post–Cold War world, and, perhaps, of a wider set of cultural and political environments than that of the Anglo-Saxon setting. Heuer's ACH technique is certainly one that is best suited to the large, set-piece strategic intelligence challenges that the Cold War typified, but that seem to occur less frequently in the faster-moving and more operational contemporary period. For this reason, many contemporary analysts will express suspicion about techniques such as ACH, seeing them as heavy and burdensome procedures for which much time and resources are needed. In a rapidly moving tactical situation, neither is in good supply.

There is some validity in this argument, and it probably is the case that studies of intelligence analysis techniques and tradecraft do indeed need to evolve further and to move beyond the CIA, Cold War legacy. That is work at hand. At the same time, I would argue that there is still a great deal to be learned by contemporary analysts from these techniques, and they should still remain the bedrock of thinking on intelligence analysis techniques and tradecraft. Similarly, although many contemporary challenges are fast-moving and tactical, not all of them are, and a great deal of strategic intelligence analysis is still necessary. There is not one type of intelligence analysis nor one species of intelligence analyst. Additionally, some of the principles of strategic analysis can be applied to all types of intelligence analysis, even if the specific techniques and procedures of the ACH model are not present in every case. This is the key to the use of these techniques, namely, to see them in flexible ways as pointers toward some key principles of analysis, which can and should be adapted and developed to suit a range of different environments. It is a mistake, in my view, to slavishly follow these techniques in the fashion of proscribed processes, but much better to understand the underlying principles and messages of these techniques and to think about how to employ those most effectively to the particular intelligence challenge at hand.

Such principles apply to ACH as much as they do to a range of other structured analytic techniques developed by Heuer and by more contemporary analysts such as Randy Pherson. With these thoughts in mind, it is worth considering the particular analytic challenges and pitfalls that ACH aims to tackle.

THE IMPORTANCE OF COMPETING HYPOTHESES
AND EVALUATION OF EVIDENCE

Most discussions of intelligence analysis success and failure in the post–Cold War world tend to focus fairly quickly on the intelligence case for invading Iraq in 2003 and the fact that the bedrock of this case—the belief that Saddam Hussein was stockpiling weapons of mass destruction (WMD)—turned out to be erroneous. Numerous studies and inquiries followed this revelation. In the United Kingdom, Lord Butler was tasked with an inquiry into the wider question of how intelligence on weapons of mass destruction and their proliferation was collected and analyzed. The report he published in 2004 came to be known as the Butler Report. Since accusations were mounting at the time that the intelligence process around Iraq had been politicized, in the sense that the intelligence case was being made to fit around the policy objectives of removing Saddam from power, Butler's report looked at the two dimensions of intelligence failure: the process of intelligence collection and analysis; and the process of moving that intelligence through the bureaucratic machinery. On the latter, to the dismay of critics, the report gave the British government a largely clean bill of health and suggested that there had not been willful attempts to politicize the intelligence case. Butler focused instead on institutional problems with intelligence analysis, which, he felt, were more to blame for the failure.

The list of analytic failures that Butler identified provide a useful starting point for thinking about how and why to apply ACH as a technique. The five key problems that Butler identified were:

- "Groupthink" (or prevailing wisdom)
- A lack of experts on key issues, which tended to mean that idiosyncratic expert assessments on technical matters went unchallenged
- "Mirror-imaging" when looking at how adversaries might react
- A general failure to understand how the threat picture had changed after the Cold War
- A general lack of imagination across the analytic community, particularly in the area of thinking of alternative scenarios and hypotheses to the norms.

The last of these points in particular provides a good case for deploying a technique such as ACH. In the case of Iraq, it appears that the prevailing wisdom across the Western intelligence community that Saddam Hussein had hidden stocks of WMD tended to become the single most dominant hypothesis about the situation. Once this was the case, it was very difficult for individual analysts to challenge the situation or suggest that alternative scenarios might apply. It was also the case that all incoming information was filtered against this single hypothesis and either made to fit or rejected out of hand (a process that typifies "confirmation bias"). Thus, the lack of cooperation with UN weapons inspectors and continual obfuscation of details surrounding weapons stocks, for example, were interpreted as the Saddam regime attempting to hide the reality of covert stockpiles of WMD. An absence of evidence was not taken as evidence of absence, but quite the opposite. During this process, and with the benefit of hindsight, the correct application of a process such as ACH, which forces consideration of alternative scenarios, may have been beneficial. The salience of this point is still strong, as, at the time of writing, very similar situations are being experienced by UN weapons inspectors who are attempting to find the truth surrounding Iran's purported nuclear capability.

Noel Hendrickson (2008) provides another very useful critique for thinking about how and why a technique such as ACH can be useful. Hendrickson looks at problems analysts may unwittingly encounter when tackling data connected with an investigation. He places these data problems within a heuristic centered around four I's, namely:

- Insufficiency
- Irrelevance
- Indeterminacy
- Instrumentality.

This causes the analyst to think not only about the hypotheses that may be applicable in a given situation but also about the nature and validity of the evidence that he or she is collecting and using to build a case for any particular hypothesis. It is very often the case that collected intelligence is neither relevant nor useful to the particular case in hand, but analysts will tend to overlook this fact, particularly if that intelligence has been difficult and costly to collect. It is also the case that we tend to simplify the world and think in terms of one thing naturally leading to another. Unfortunately, humans are notoriously nondeterministic and will often make seemingly irrational or illogical decisions. The psychologist Daniel Kahneman (2011, p. 76) describes this phenomenon as a bias toward finding "causality," which manifests itself as the tendency of the human brain to infer logical explanations for everything it sees. Such a cognitive phenomenon can lead to conspiracy theories and more general erroneous theories about situations, when often the available data do not actually add up to any sort of coherent story at all. One of the things that ACH allows the analyst to do is to think of each incoming piece of evidence in an objective and isolated way, without being tempted to fit it into an evolving pattern or story.

This is essentially all about the *diagnosticity* of evidence. Use of this word causes us to think of the medical environment, because doctors have to deliver a diagnosis of a patient's condition when they visit the surgery. What the doctor does is to ask for a description of symptoms and then develops a hypothesis around the diagnostic value of the various symptoms in relation to specific conditions. Some symptoms have very low diagnostic value: a raised temperature, for example, might be present in a very wide range of conditions and would not in itself give much of a clue as to the problem with the patient. Coupled with a very specific type of rash on the skin, however, the window of possible conditions might narrow considerably; this symptom might therefore carry much greater diagnostic value in helping to establish a solid hypothesis.

Specific pieces of evidence can be diagnostic both in their presence *and* their absence. The case of Sherlock Holmes's "dog that didn't bark in the night" is a fine example. Indeed, the classic scenario that helps to explain this particular part of the analytical process is that of the detective investigating a murder. In a scene replicated in countless detective stories, the investigating officer will ask suspects where they were at the time of the murder and whether their location can be corroborated by someone else. If a suspect was not in a particular location within a significant time frame and indeed was too far away to have been able to travel to and from the relevant location within the time frame in question, then he or she can be ruled out of the investigation. A corroborated piece of evidence on location and time in this scenario is highly diagnostic in establishing whether a particular suspect was the possible murderer.

Thus, as Pherson and Heuer describe (2011, p. 161), the power of ACH is in refuting rather than supporting hypotheses. This can be slightly counterintuitive for new analysts. It means that the ACH exercise usefully starts with some discussion around diagnosticity of evidence against hypotheses. In the ACH model, individual pieces of evidence are assessed as being either "consistent," "inconsistent," or "ambiguous" when placed against each hypothesis. This determines the diagnosticity of each piece of evidence, and it is the inconsistent pieces of evidence that carry more weight, since they help to refute hypotheses.

For example, a particular piece of evidence or argumentation might be consistent with a particular hypothesis. However, in a natural analytical tendency called "satisficing" that Alexander George (1980, p. 19) identified in strategic foreign policy analysis, we tend to find an explanation for something that seems "good enough" and then stop looking for alternative hypotheses. This is a manifestation of confirmation bias, whereby we tend to seek evidence that supports a theory we already favor for a given situation and give more credence to such evidence. In our Iraq case, for example, the fact that officials at potential weapons sites in Iraq were obstructive when receiving visits from UN weapons inspectors was consistent with the hypothesis that the Iraqi regime had something to hide. As this was the preferred hypothesis around which Western foreign policy was coalescing, it was taken as a "good enough" explanation and one that confirmed institutional suspicions. Unfortunately, the obstructive behavior of the Iraqi officials would also have been consistent with any number of other hypotheses: they could have been bluffing; they could have been feeling that their sovereignty was being questioned and thus wanted to be awkward to make a point; or they could have been just deliberately making life difficult for the UN inspectors because they could. Suddenly, this piece of evidence becomes less diagnostic because it is consistent with a range of different scenarios, like the raised temperature of the patient in the doctor's surgery.

Conversely, evidence that is strongly inconsistent with a particular hypothesis can sometimes be more useful in narrowing down the range of possible hypotheses. If a murder suspect was not in a particular location at a particular time, it does not tell us where he or she was. But it does tell us that the hypothesis in which that person is the murderer can be contested, if not completely refuted, since this particular piece of evidence makes it fundamentally flawed. We can then narrow down the range of potential hypotheses.

Pherson and Heuer (2011, pp. 160–161) suggest that ACH can be used "for almost any analysis where there are alternative explanations for what has happened." Given the weight and complexity of the ACH process when applied to a large problem, however, I find that it is particularly useful when applied to a big, strategic question that is not necessarily time sensitive. There are really two scenarios in which ACH can usefully be applied, one of which looks backward in time, while the other looks forward. The first case is a situation in which an intelligence mystery needs unraveling. This concerns a situation that has already happened, such as a murder, to which deductive analysis needs to be applied to work out what happened. The second scenario in which ACH can be useful concerns looking forward, in a predictive manner, to consider possible future scenarios and outcomes. A foreign policy outlook on a long-running and complex issue that is still developing is a good scenario, such as the question of what will happen if a state develops a nuclear weapon capability in the future. These questions allow more time to be taken on detailed analysis of the evidence and for longer consideration of such issues as diagnosticity of the evidence.

At the time of designing and delivering this exercise, the Arab Spring was unfolding in the Middle East. This provided a number of particularly useful and compelling test cases for an exercise such as ACH. First, the questions of where the Arab Spring was going, what was underpinning it, and what the implications of it for regional and global affairs are all pressing and difficult intelligence questions with which every observer country would grapple in their strategic intelligence function. At the same time, the lack of predictability of the phenomenon makes it a good case for developing and evaluating alternative hypotheses and scenarios.

Contemporary and unpredictable test cases for exercises of this nature can be very stimulating, since they can be of more immediate interest and relevance to the participants and can avoid the pitfalls of hindsight bias or guilty knowledge. The other benefit of basing the exercise on a contemporaneous situation is that there is often a great deal of open source information available, which acts as the intelligence information on which analysts can make their judgments.

THE EXERCISE

For this exercise, I focused on the unfolding uprising in Syria and posed the question: What are the prospects for Syria? As discussed, such a question was likely being asked within a number of governments around the world at the beginning of 2011, and intelligence agencies were undoubtedly being asked to contribute intelligence assessments of the situation. While the analysts in our exercise obviously did not have access to secret intelligence to help in their assessment, they did have access to a great deal of open source information about events on the ground and were asked to use this in forming their judgments.

The exercise unfolds over eight stages, which ideally take up to 3 hours to complete in total. The composition of each stage is as follows.

Stage 1

A facilitated discussion with the class is held on the question of diagnosticity of evidence, working through some examples. One of the examples I use is that discussed

above concerning the Iraq case, and the specific piece of evidence that officials at suspected weapons sites were being obstructive to UN officials who were trying to carry
out inspections. Which hypotheses might this individual piece of evidence support?
What might be the explanation or explanations for the behavior of the Iraqi officials?
(Here, brainstorming can usefully be deployed to allow the students to think creatively
about possible scenarios.) Having established the possible scenarios, how diagnostic do
we think this piece of evidence is in helping narrow down our assessment? The correct
answer here is "not very diagnostic"!

Stage 2

Having discussed diagnosticity of evidence, the format of the ACH matrix is introduced (see below) and the question of diagnosticity is applied in terms of categorizing
information as either consistent, inconsistent, or ambiguous to any given hypothesis. In
the above case, the specific evidence was fairly ambiguous because it did not definitively
support or refute any particular hypothesis and could have applied equally to any number of situations. What other evidence, which we would have liked to have received,
would have been more helpful in helping us to narrow down the situation?

Stage 3

Here, a further element to the process is introduced, which is about "weighting"
of evidence, since not all pieces of information are equally valid. This is partly a recognition that, in intelligence, the question of denial and deception always has to be
considered. Indeed, Heuer initially developed ACH to specifically deal with this aspect
of analysis in counterintelligence operations in the CIA during the 1980s (Pherson &
Heuer, 2011, p. 161). The same principles of source evaluation should be applied to
open source information, and this may, in fact, be of growing importance given the
explosion of availability in open source information and the very variable nature of it.
In a situation of conflict, such as our Syrian example, there will be a great deal of fog
of war in the shape of deceptive and erroneous information designed to tilt opinion in
one way or another. Reports of casualty figures, for example, are a classic example of a
highly politicized and often very manipulated piece of information. A good analyst will
consider where information is coming from and how reliable it might be. In our Syrian
example, it is interesting to consider reports, purportedly on the same events, coming
from different sources: the Syrian Arab News Agency, for example, will report events in
very different ways from the mainstream Western media. To stimulate critical thinking,
the students are asked: Which source is likely to be more reliable and why?

In this example, the weighting will determine whether extra marks are accorded to
pieces of evidence during the final tally (see below).

Stage 4

Having introduced the way ACH works and the principles behind it, the students
are then given the batches of information on which they will work. There are two com-

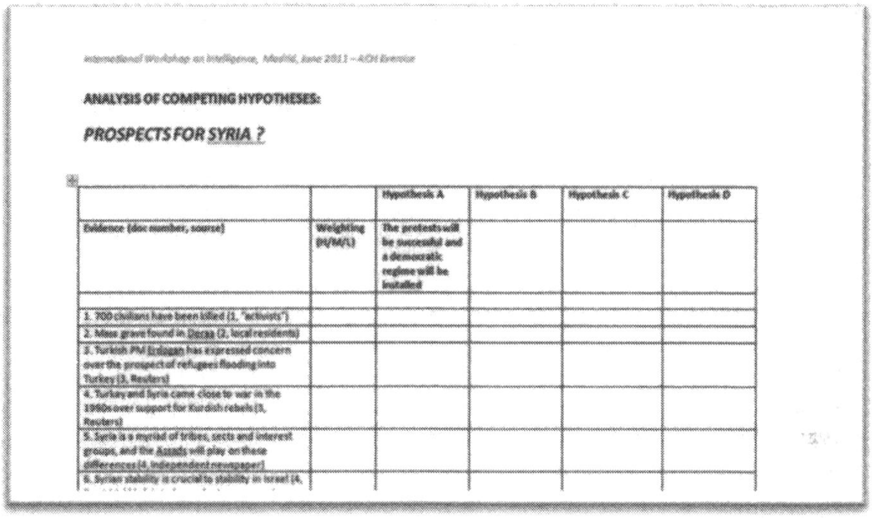

International Workshop on Intelligence, Madrid, June 2011 – ACH Exercise

ANALYSIS OF COMPETING HYPOTHESES:

PROSPECTS FOR SYRIA ?

		Hypothesis A	Hypothesis B	Hypothesis C	Hypothesis D
Evidence (doc number, source)	Weighting (H/M/L)	The protests will be successful and a democratic regime will be installed			
1. 700 civilians have been killed (1, "activists")					
2. Mass grave found in Deraa (2, local residents)					
3. Turkish PM Erdogan has expressed concern over the prospect of refugees flooding into Turkey (3, Reuters)					
4. Turkey and Syria came close to war in the 1990s over support for Kurdish rebels (3, Reuters)					
5. Syria is a myriad of tribes, sects and interest groups, and the Assads will play on these differences (4, independent newspaper)					
6. Syrian stability is crucial to stability in Israel (4,					

Figure 2.1.

ponents to this: a score sheet (matrix), an extract of which is shown in Figure 2.1, and a bundle of previously prepared open source pieces of information that they will use as their evidence. In this particular example, I use nine separate newspaper reports on the situation from a variety of different sources, ranging from BBC News to the Syrian Arab News Agency.

Stage 5

Having divided the students into groups, the first task they are allotted is to brainstorm potential hypotheses. These are to be recorded as A, B, C, and so on across the top of the score sheet. The first hypothesis is given ("the protests will be successful and a democratic regime will be installed"). The students are then asked to develop a range of other, mutually exclusive, hypotheses. A good way to start this process is to make hypothesis B an exact mirror image of A (in this case: "the protests will be crushed and the Assad regime will remain in power"). The groups are given 20 minutes or so to brainstorm potential outcomes to the situation and record these across the top of their score sheets. Although the sheet they are given has space for four hypotheses, they are told that they can have more or fewer than this number, depending on what they feel is appropriate.

Stage 6

Once the potential hypotheses are established, the groups are asked to consider each piece of evidence in turn, which are then present in the nine newspaper reports. These are recorded on the score sheet in the first column, with a signifier against each identifying the source and the specific document in which the evidence is to be found. For example, the first piece of evidence is: "700 civilians have been killed," and this is attributed to a group of activists, quoted in article 1. The students in each group must carefully consider each piece of evidence and decide on two things: First, they must agree on a credibility weighting for each piece of evidence, using a high, medium, or low credibility score, and record this in the first column of their score sheet. In our first piece of evidence, for example, the report that 700 civilians had been killed might be considered to be of low or medium credibility, given that it came from a group of activists opposed to the government. However, further careful analysis of the source report in question might shed some light on other information, which helps to make a more informed judgment on the source credibility (for example, the report could have been corroborated by a number of other sources). Second, the student must apply this piece of evidence to each of the potential hypotheses and consider its diagnosticity: Is it consistent, inconsistent, or ambiguous when considered against each hypothesis? This is then recorded in the relevant box on the score sheet as C, I, or A, respectively. There is an option here for considering whether a piece of evidence is *very* inconsistent with a hypothesis; these are to be recorded as II.

Here, some basic analysis is needed to deliver a judgment. In this particular example, the fact that the regime appears to have killed 700 civilians does not necessarily tell us how the situation will turn out in the end, but it does tell us that the regime is not minded to respond peacefully and democratically to the uprising. In fact, it is probably of a mind to deliver a robust and violent response to any challenge to its authority. This in turn might suggest that the uprising might turn out differently from how events unfolded in other countries such as Tunisia or Egypt, where the degree of violence against the demonstrators was less severe, if not altogether absent. Obviously one piece of evidence does not tell a story in itself, but it might be an important piece in the overall jigsaw.

Stage 7

The groups are given a good amount of time to work through and discuss their judgments on all of the evidence and fill in their score sheets. Usually there is a great deal of debate and "trading" about agreed judgments and evaluations. When the sheet has been completed to mutual agreement in each group, the students are asked to total up their scores. A spokesperson for each group is then appointed to report in plenary the result of their analysis.

The way the scoring works is that inconsistent pieces of evidence receive a score of two marks and doubled if they are rated as "very inconsistent." (Consistent and ambiguous pieces of evidence receive no marks.) For each of the pieces of evidence identified as inconsistent, the credibility weighting is then considered, and one extra mark is awarded if the weighting is "medium" and two extra marks if "high." At the bottom of each column, the scores are totaled, and the hypothesis with the lowest score is considered to be the most likely, by virtue of it having been assessed to have the least amount of inconsistent pieces of evidence applied to it. The spokesperson for each group is asked to report which hypothesis came out as the most likely (with the lowest score) and which the least likely (with the highest score).

Stage 8

This is a postmortem discussion stage, when the formal part of the exercise has been completed. Here, students are asked to reflect on the exercise and consider whether they can envisage ACH—or elements of it—being useful for future analytical situations in which they are likely to be involved. Prompt questions that can be asked include: Was the outcome of the analysis similar to what was expected beforehand? Do you agree with the outcome? If not, can you identify reasons why the outcome might be flawed? What would help, in your opinion, to deliver a more reliable outcome? Did the process of considering each piece of evidence in turn, and its credibility, force you to think about the question of diagnosticity and to take a more objective view of evidence?

CONCLUSION

It is important to observe that an exercise of this nature should be seen as just that: it is not a training course for how to use ACH and an injunction to use it in exactly this way henceforth. As Pherson and Heuer (2011, p. 167) noted, this technique should also not be seen as a mechanism for finding the "right answer" in any given situation, but merely a tool for helping with the process of analysis and judgment.

What the exercise does aim to do is to provide an experience and an environment in which analysts can consider some important issues of analytical weakness and bias and to consider how to mitigate these using structured techniques. In particular, the risks of confirmation bias, satisficing, prevailing wisdom, and a lack of imagination in considering alternative scenarios are all usefully highlighted in this exercise, and ACH is offered as a way of tackling such analytical pitfalls. The extra element of considering source credibility also allows analysts to think a bit more about source evaluation and the possibility of denial and deception. If the students go away from the exercise having reflected on these issues, then it has served its purpose.

How the tool of ACH could or should be used in the analytical environment is a question each student would need to consider within the context of the specific role and situation in which he or she is likely to find him- or herself. As discussed, analytical environments and objectives vary greatly, and there will never be one approach to suit every occasion. But if analysts understand the principles of the cognitive and analytical weaknesses and pitfalls that may trip them up and are armed with some ideas and tools for how to mitigate these potential problems, they will be well placed to consider what will work best in their own environment to ensure a good result.

In this case, a future-looking question involving the uprising in Syria was taken as the analytical question on which the students were asked to focus. Any number of other situations could be used, and potential scenarios are bounded only by the imagination of the trainer. In this case, a real situation using real open source evidence was used, but a completely hypothetical scenario using engineered evidence could also be used to illustrate the key elements of the analytical process and the pitfalls that the analyst may face. It is also possible to run the exercise "live" on an unfolding scenario, taking real evidence as it arises rather than previously prepared and formatted evidence. In all cases, the objective remains the same of providing a scenario in which analysts face a testing challenge over their generation of possible hypotheses and their objective analysis of evidence against them.

REFERENCES

George, Alexander. 1980. *Presidential decision making in foreign policy: The effective use of information and advice.* Boulder, CO: Westview Press.

Gladwell, Malcolm. 2006. *Blink: The power of thinking without thinking.* London: Penguin.

Hendrickson, Noel. 2008. Critical thinking in intelligence analysis. *Journal of Intelligence and Counterintelligence, 21*(4), 679–693.

Heuer, Richards J. Jr. 1999. *Psychology of intelligence analysis.* Langley, VA: Center for the Study of Intelligence.

Kahneman, Daniel. 2011. *Thinking, fast and slow.* London: Penguin.

Kent, Sherman. 1965. *Strategic intelligence for American world policy.* Princeton, NJ: Princeton University Press.

Lord Butler of Brockwell. 2004. *Review of intelligence on weapons of mass destruction.* London: TSO.

Pherson, Randolph H., & Heuer, Richards J. Jr. 2011. *Structured analytic techniques for intelligence analysis.* Washington, DC: CQ Press.

Richards, Julian. 2010. *The art and science of intelligence analysis.* Oxford: Oxford University Press.

3

Facing Intelligence Analysts with Ethical Scenarios

Fernando Velasco and Rubén Arcos

ABSTRACT

This simulation presents students of intelligence courses with a set of different ethical scenarios or situations that may pose a moral dilemma for intelligence analysts while carrying out their duties. Assuming and taking for granted that intelligence professionals must comply with the law, this simulation exposes participants to possible ethical dilemmas with which real intelligence analysts might be confronted, such as language and action, prioritization of competing principles, the ethics of responsibility, and the ethics of conviction. Divided into groups, participants address ethical scenarios and prepare ethical arguments for and against possible decisions. After having worked individually first, participants share and discuss their arguments in their team. Each team must determine a course of action by consensus and a list of arguments. Afterward, the facilitator asks a representative of each team to present his or her group's position to the class. Second, participants use what they have learned in the scenarios phase for designing a code of ethics as they role-play as practitioners policing their profession.

KEYWORDS

Analytic standards; codes of ethics; ethics of intelligence analysis; intelligence analysis; intelligence ethics; intelligence professionalism

Public debate and much of the discussion regarding intelligence services often focus on ethical or moral questions posed by intelligence-gathering practices and interrogation techniques. However, although moral dilemmas surrounding intelligence collection are

35

of utmost importance, collection is just one step of the intelligence cycle—the cyclical model that traditionally serves to depict how intelligence is produced for informing the decision-making process. Intelligence analysis (including interpretation) and communication or presentation of intelligence outputs to decision makers are also key steps of the intelligence process. This is valid both at the public policy level as well as the corporate level. That is to say, analysis and the communication of intelligence are determinant steps for national security intelligence as well as for competitive or business intelligence. For this reason, there is a need to address the role of intelligence analysts—as a key factor in intelligence services—from the point of view of ethics.[1]

Codes of ethics generally appear when occupations organize themselves into professions (Davis, 1991). Service orientation and a distinctive ethics are attributes inherent to a profession's normative dimension (Larson, 2013). And it is widely accepted that the professionalization of occupations produces practitioners "who are more aware of their responsibilities to the wider society and more concerned with the ethical nuances of their craft, business or trade" (Schultze, 1981, p. 64). The term *tradecraft* is widely used by intelligence community members to describe intelligence analysis (Johnston, 2005, p. 17). According to John C. Gannon (1997), the term was borrowed from the Central Intelligence Agency's clandestine service and then used to express the special skills and methods required to perform intelligence analysis. So, is intelligence analysis a skilled art, a trade or craft, or a profession? On the business side, can we use the terms *profession* and *professionals* when referring to competitive intelligence (CI) and their analytic tradecraft practitioners (Sawka, 2005)? Craig Fleisher (2003) elaborated five criteria or standards of CI professionalism with indicators for them that also can be applied to the intelligence field: collective service orientation; position of the occupation in the labor force; abstract (specialized) knowledge; generalized knowledge of other related fields; and active participation in a membership society. Independent of the conclusions derived from the test, the raising and maintaining of a code of ethics and standards of practice are clear indicators of the trail to professionalism. As Stephen Marrin and Jonathan D. Clemente (2006) pointed out, over the past years many improvements have occurred—both in national security and law enforcement, as well as in the private industry—in the process of turning intelligence analysis from an art or craft into a developed profession.

A remarkable achievement in this sense has been the enactment of Intelligence Community Directive (ICD) 203 that establishes the analytic standards that govern the production and evaluation of analysis (see Appendix G). As Robert Cardillo (2010) has highlighted, ICD 203, coupled with ICD 206, "Sourcing Requirements for Disseminated Analytic Products," forces analysts to inject rigor into analytic processes and products, holding the practitioners accountable for the results. Enabling the clients of intelligence to understand the quantity and quality of the information that sustains analytic products is especially important to strengthen the sense of responsibility of intelligence analysis professionals toward their clients, especially when most analysts rarely see the users of their products. In the words of Washington Platt (1957, p. 271) speaking about the peculiarities of the intelligence profession: "a Strategic Intelligence paper usually has many echelons of review through which it must pass after it leaves the original author or analyst before it reaches its primary user; namely, the 'ultimate consumer' in the National Security Council. The upper echelons of edit and review have probably never even heard the name of the original author."

THE SIMULATION

This simulation exercise[2] exposes participants to a set of different scenarios that present ethical dilemmas for intelligence analysts, both from the fields of national security and private industry. Participants are asked to put themselves in the place of the analysts involved in the narrative of each scenario and to face situations presenting a conflict of ethical principles or standards. The scenarios are inspired either entirely or in part by real events. They address dilemmas related to ethics of conviction and ethics of responsibility; prioritization of conflicting standards under certain circumstances; and the ethical significance of choosing words (Table 3.1).

The simulation exercise combines individual activities, group activities, and discussions. First, participants prepare ethical arguments for and against decisions or actions presented in each scenario. Later, participants share and discuss their arguments in their team. Each team has to come up with a decision or course of action by consensus and a list of arguments to justify their decision. Afterward, the facilitator asks a representative of each team to present the team's position to the class. Second, the exercise allows participants to use their outcomes in the scenarios phase for designing their own code of ethics as they play the role of practitioners policing their profession. The elaboration

Table 3.1. Summary of Scenarios Used in the Exercise (see Appendix B)

	Scenario 1	*Scenario 2*	*Scenario 3*
Context	Industry; Social Media Monitoring; Protests; Economic Crisis	Intelligence Service; Economic Intelligence; Trade Negotiations; Bargaining Position	Intelligence Service; Biological Weapons; Offensive Program
Ethical Issues and Intelligence Principles	Ethics of Conviction and Ethics of Responsibility Personal Convictions and Professional Ethics	Competing Values; Timeliness; Sourcing; All available sources; Objectivity; Excellence; others	Means and Ends; Politicization; Objectivity; Conveying uncertainty; others
Question	Should Claudia omit key information on the upcoming protest from her intelligence report?	Should your team send the intelligence report forward without these nuances to meet the deadline?	Should Robert assign a lower likelihood by using the words *even chance* (50 percent) instead of *likely deliberately* as a shield against analytic bias and politicization?

and presentation of a code of ethics by participants gives the instructor the opportunity to compare these results in the debriefing with codes of ethics standards currently in force in the world of intelligence services and in the field of competitive intelligence. The simulation exercise, and particularly the scenarios phase, allows instructors to facilitate participants' understanding of different applicable ethical frameworks and to suggest relevant readings for going into detail from the point of view of ethics.

BASIC DATA

Instructional Objectives

To experience the ethical dimension of analytic tradecraft; to encourage awareness of and stress the importance of the ethical aspects involved in the practice of intelligence analysis; to show the relevance of analytic standards and ethics for intelligence analysis professionalism.

Simulation Objectives

To address a set of ethical scenarios posing a dilemma and involving intelligence analysts; to prepare arguments for and against taking alternative decisions or actions; to design and propose a code of ethics for intelligence analysis.

Debriefing Format

The instructor explains ethical positions underlying each scenario and suggests relevant texts to the class for further detail. In the code of ethics phase, the instructor presents existing codes of ethics for intelligence professionals and analytic standards or principles and facilitates discussion of the differences among these codes.

Target Audience

Undergraduate or graduate students in basic or advanced courses in intelligence; students in master's programs in intelligence analysis; courses in competitive intelligence. The simulation exercise is suitable for any audience with an interest in intelligence.

Playing Time

3 hours

Debriefing Time

35–45 minutes

Number of Players Required

Between 9 and 35 participants. A minimum of three groups is required. Each group should integrate a maximum of five members for ensuring participation inside the teams in odd numbers so that potential discrepancies in each group do not lead to paralysis. A maximum of seven groups is recommended.

Participation Materials Included

See Appendices B, C, D, E, and F.

Debriefing Materials Included

See Appendix G.

Computer/Internet

Recommended.

Other Materials/Equipment Required

A large classroom; a whiteboard with erasable markers of different colors; a computer and a wall projector; large sheets of paper for each group. For more than three groups, two large classrooms (instead of one) are recommended with the aim of ensuring that the discussion inside each team does not interfere with the activities of the other groups.

FACILITATOR'S GUIDE

Materials

1. Appendix A: Facilitator Examples of Mission, Vision, and Values Statements
2. Appendix B: Scenarios
3. Appendix C: Scenarios Individual Worksheet
4. Appendix D: Scenarios Group Worksheet
5. Appendix E: Professional Codes of Ethics (Intelligence Community and Competitive Intelligence)
6. Appendix F: Code of Ethics for Intelligence Analysis Worksheet
7. Appendix G: Sherman Kent's Principles for Intelligence Analysis; ICD 203 Analytic Standards
8. Template 1: Global Results for Ethical Scenarios

PRESIMULATION BRIEFING

The facilitator starts by introducing the role of intelligence services in democracies, their main missions, and basic functions. A good way to begin the presentation while assessing participants' level of knowledge about intelligence is to ask questions such as: What is an intelligence service? How would you define intelligence? What are their missions and functions? Do you think intelligence professionals take ethics into account? Appendix A, "Facilitator Examples of Mission, Vision, and Values Statements," can be useful for showing the class examples of mission, vision, and value statements of some well-known intelligence organizations. Depending on the audience and on the simulation's context of use (undergraduate, graduate, business), the instructor can dedicate more or less time to this phase. For example, the facilitator can bring the exceptional character of secrecy in democracies to the attention of participants and call attention to the responsibility of administering secrecy in systems characterized by the principle of transparency.

The facilitator communicates to the participants that they are going to learn about the ethics of intelligence analysis and the key principles that should orient the conduct of analysts who work in intelligence agencies and also in the field of intelligence in business firms.

The facilitator informs the participants that they will be facing a set of different scenarios for which they have to prepare arguments in support of alternative decisions. Participants will work individually and in groups to analyze the situations, present and discuss arguments, and come to a consensus. The discussions and ethical arguments will provide participants with the basic tools for designing and presenting a code of ethics for intelligence analysts at a later stage, while they play the role of intelligence analysts concerned with the ethics of their tradecraft.

CONDUCTING THE SIMULATION

Simulation Step 1: Getting organized

Divide the class into groups. The number of members in each group depends on the total number of participants. The different groups will use different areas of the classroom to allow good communication among group members without disturbing the others. For more than three groups, it is advisable to divide the class into two contiguous classrooms. Next, the instructor hands out copies of Appendix B ("Ethical Scenarios") and Appendix C ("Scenarios Individual Worksheet") to participants. Each participant should have his or her own copy of the three ethical scenarios and the worksheet.

Simulation Step 2: Individual Reading and Preparation of Arguments
(30 minutes)

Participants will read the three scenarios and work individually in writing arguments for and against alternative positions using Appendix C. It is important to encourage the participants to put themselves in the place of the analysts described in each scenario. It is also important to stress that the objective of this step is to collect as many arguments as possible by working individually. Making comments and sharing arguments with other members of the group is not allowed in this step. Instruct participants to look at the issue from different perspectives. Even if a decision seems absolutely clear for them, they should look for supportive arguments for the alternative position. Remind the participants that arguments that may seem challenging at first glance can be very clarifying when they are discussed in a group session. *Stress that not bringing up arguments is worse than being wrong.*

Simulation Step 3: Group Discussion, Ranking of Arguments, and Decision on Group Position (30 minutes)

Deliver three copies of Appendix D "Scenarios Team Worksheet" to each group (one for each scenario). The Team Worksheet will be used to list the arguments for and against the positions from scenarios. The instructor tells the participants to share their arguments with the other members of their groups. Each group has to come up with an agreed-upon position on each scenario and a list of arguments—conveniently ranked according to the number of times that participants bring them up (e.g., three times, two times, etc.)—to be presented before the class. This rank is an indicator of its relevance for the discussion but not of the argument's strength. For example, if a certain Argument X is brought up by three members of the group while Argument Y is brought up only a single time, then Argument X should be ranked above Argument Y.

After all members of the group have shared their arguments and the relevance ranking has been done, the group should challenge the more relevant arguments to gain insights on their strength. Next, a round of discussion between members of the same group begins (NOTE: Participants should not criticize the arguments until all arguments have been shared). Participants present their positions one by one and engage in discussion. To avoid the discussion being monopolized by some participants and moving it forward, each member selects from the list the main argument that supports one or another position according to his or her criteria and gives way to the next member. Inform participants that, at the end of the presentation, the best argumentation will be elected. The round of discussions for each scenario ends when the groups reach a consensus on their position.

Simulation Step 4: Presentation of Group's Positions (30 minutes)

Each group selects a member to present to the class the position of the group on each ethical scenario and the arguments underlying that position. The overall results can be tabulated using a word processor and Template 1 (also downloadable at Rowman & Littlefield's website, https.rowman.com). The facilitator integrates (with the help of a member of each team) the global results for each scenario—position and should/should not arguments—and re-ranks the most recurring arguments for and against possible decisions. Next, the instructor displays the results using a wall projector for the entire class to see. These results can be printed and delivered to the participants for consideration during the next assignment of the simulation exercise.

Simulation Step 5: Design and Presentation of a Code of Ethics (60–80 minutes)

The facilitator can briefly introduce the issue of ethical codes and their relevance for professionalism. Next, the instructor assigns the task of preparing a code of ethics for intelligence analysis. The instructor explains that the aim of the code is that intelligence analysts agree to abide by this code. Depending on the number of participants, the instructor can put different groups together. The instructor distributes copies of Appendix E "Ethical Codes" and a copy of Appendix F "Intelligence Analysis Code of Ethics" to each group for use as a template for designing the code. Tell participants to consider the input from the scenarios phase when designing the code. Participants have to keep in mind the specific characteristics of intelligence analysis in relation to the codes of ethics for intelligence in Appendix E. Next, a representative of each group presents the code to the class.

The active phase of the simulation concludes when all groups have briefed their code of ethics for intelligence analysis.

DEBRIEFING

Debriefing plays an important role in experience-based learning by driving participants to a purposeful discussion of that experience (Lederman, 1992). A debriefing session should help participants reflect on their experience to extract meaningful insights (Thiagarajan, 1992). The debriefing session of the simulation exercise offers the opportunity for the instructor to provide insights to participants on the importance of ethics for intelligence analysis and the key ethical issues surrounding its practice. The session should help participants to understand the ethical frameworks underlying decisions on each scenario and to compare their codes with the existing analytic standards and the principles that should rule the practice of intelligence analysis. In the facilitation of the debriefing, the instructor can help participants reach an understanding from their experience on the implications of different ethical approaches (subjectivism, relativism, formalism, consequentialism, utilitarianism, virtue ethics, etc.) for the decisions.[3] Instructors can adapt the debriefing session to the distinctive features of their audiences and education or training necessities. The debriefing is structured as follows.

Scenarios Phase

- What did you think/feel when you were reading the three scenarios?
- Was it difficult for you to find arguments supporting alternative positions for each scenario?

- What were some interesting aspects of the experience of sharing and discussing the arguments within the groups?
- Did you find it difficult to achieve a consensus?
- Did you find the arguments that support positions for each scenario similar or different?
- How did you feel about the presentation of the position and arguments of other groups?

Scenario 1

Start by summarizing the global results for the scenario and the most recurring arguments underlying the positions. Identify and discuss the main issue as well as secondary issues in the scenario. The discussion should serve to examine intelligence analysts' responsibility to the intelligence customers, to the society, to the profession, and to other stakeholders. Cover the topic of ethics of conviction and ethics of responsibility. The key questions for moving the discussion forward are:

- Is the omission of information an acceptable conduct for intelligence professionals?
- Should personal convictions prevail over professional standards when there is conflict?
- To whom do intelligence analysts have a responsibility?
- How would you judge the behavior of Stakeout-Tech's management?

Reading Assignment: Instructors can refer participants to Webber's "Politics as a Vocation" (fragment) for reinforcing ethical concepts:

- Webber, Max. *The Vocation Lectures*, edited by David Owen and Tracy B. Strong, translation by Rodney Livingstone. Indianapolis: Hackett Publishing Company, 2004, pp. 80–94.

Scenario 2

Discuss the issue of prioritizing competing ethical principles or standards when situations involve conflict. Start by discussing sourcing issues and how documentation affects the credibility and transparency of intelligence analysis. Ask participants to place themselves in the role of decision makers and to assess how sourcing would affect their decision. Refer participants to Washington Platt's definition of intelligence as "timely truth well told" and think how these principles are connected and can affect outcomes. The discussion can also be stimulated by the use of ICD 206.

The key questions for discussion are the following:

- Which principles or standards are of most importance in intelligence analysis?
- How does timeliness affect the usefulness of intelligence reports?

- How does source reference citation influence insights?
- Should there be a hierarchy of analytic principles?
- Do you think intelligence services' managers favor secret over open sources of information? In affirmative case, can it potentially harm objectivity?

Reading Assignment: Instructors can refer participants to Scheler's fragment on "Higher and Lower Values" from his *Formalism in Ethics and Non-Formal Ethics of Value* for exploring in detail the issue of relationships of rank among values:

- Scheler, Max. *Formalism in Ethics and Non-Formal Ethics of Values: A New Attempt Toward the Foundation of an Ethical Personalism*, translated by Manfred S. Frings and Roger L. Funk. Evanston: Northwestern University Press, 1973, pp. 86–100.

Scenario 3

Discuss the significance of choosing the appropriate words when writing intelligence reports. Explain how analysts convey uncertainty to decision makers and highlight the ethical dimension of communication. Discuss the problems of sharing meaning and the importance of establishing standards for conveying uncertainty to policymakers in order to ensure a correct interpretation of the finished products by the client. Discuss the issue of politicization and how to prevent it through the use of appropriate instruments.

The key questions for moving the discussion forward are:

- Why do words matter in intelligence?
- How can analysts guard themselves against politicization?
- How can we bring transparency to the analytic process?
- Should words for conveying uncertainty be standardized?[4]
- Do you think that a string of edits and reviews blurs the responsibility for the intelligence outcome?

Reading Assignment: Instructors can direct participants to read Gorgias's "Encomium of Helen" as a relevant text on the ethics of persuasion and the power of speech:

- Gorgias of Leontini. "Encomium of Helen," in *The Greek Sophists*, edited and translated by John M. Dillon and Tania Gergel. London: Penguin Books, 2003, pp. 76–84.

Code of Ethics Phase

Provide each participant with a copy of Appendix G "Sherman Kent's Principles and ICD 203 Analytic Standards" and give a few minutes for participants to read it. Next, ask participants to compare these standards with the codes they have produced and ask them to what extent their codes reflect these values, principles, or standards. Questions suggested for conducting this step of the debriefing are the following:

- Does establishing a code of intelligence ethics make sense?
- What are the potential functions of a code of ethics for intelligence analysis?
- To what extent should analytic standards be different in the case of intelligence for the government and for the business sector?
- Do ethical codes have limitations?
- How can ethical codes be enforced?

Participants can be asked to: (a) compare their proposals of codes with the codes in force at their organizations; and (b) to assess the need of adding/changing anything if the opportunity arises.

ADDITIONAL ACTIVITIES

After finishing the exercise, and depending on time availability, instructors can require participants to do additional activities including reading assignments, viewing an intelligence or espionage film that addresses a relevant issue from the point of view of ethics, or improving the proposed code of ethics by looking at other professions.

The following texts are recommended to explore intelligence ethics in greater detail:

- Allen, George. "Professionalization of Intelligence," in *Ethics of Spying: A Reader for the Intelligence Professional*, volume 2, edited by Jan Goldman. Lanham, MD: Scarecrow Press, 2010 (1984), pp. 3–12.
- Gates, Robert. "Guarding against Politicization: A Message to Analysts," in *Ethics of Spying: A Reader for the Intelligence Professional*, edited by Jan Goldman. Lanham, MD: Scarecrow Press, 2006, pp. 171–184.

APPENDIX A: FACILITATOR EXAMPLES OF MISSION, VISION, AND VALUES STATEMENTS

	CIA	SIS	CSIS	ASIO
Mission/functions	We are the nation's first line of defense. We accomplish what others cannot accomplish and go where others cannot go. We carry out our mission by: Collecting information that reveals the plans, intentions, and capabilities of our adversaries and provides the basis for decision and action. Producing timely analysis that provides insight, warning, and opportunity to the President and decisionmakers charged with protecting and advancing America's interests. Conducting covert action at the direction of the President to preempt threats or achieve US policy objectives.	To give the UK advantage, acting secretly overseas to make the country safer and more prosperous. We do this by: Obtaining secret intelligence on critical security and economic issues to inform better policy decisions; Operating overseas to disrupt terrorism and proliferation and helping to prevent and resolve conflict; Using covert contacts overseas to shape developments and exploit opportunities in the UK's interests.	The people of CSIS are dedicated to the protection of Canada's national security interests and the safety of Canadians.	To identify and investigate threats to security and provide advice to protect Australia, its people and its interests.

Vision	One Agency. One Community. An Agency unmatched in its core capabilities, functioning as one team, fully integrated into the Intelligence Community.	To be an outstanding national intelligence organization dedicated to serving the people of Canada, through its Government, with effectiveness and integrity. This vision will only be achieved by employees who are guided by the principles of **excellence, integrity, and respect for the rights of all.**	The intelligence edge for a secure Australia.
Values	**Service**. We put Country first and Agency before self. Quiet patriotism is our hallmark. We are dedicated to the mission, and we pride ourselves on our extraordinary responsiveness to the needs of our customers. **Integrity.** We uphold the highest standards of conduct. We seek and speak the truth—to our colleagues and to our customers. We honor those Agency officers who have come before us, and we honor the colleagues with whom we work today.	**Integrity**. We act within our legal framework and with the highest ethical and professional standards. **Making a difference.** We judge ourselves by the value we add in our daily work and the difference we contribute to real world outcomes. **Teamwork.** We work as a team, across SIS, across Government, and with our international partners.	**Excellence:** producing high quality, relevant and timely advice; displaying strong leadership and professionalism; improving through innovation and learning. **Integrity:** being ethical and working without bias; maintaining the confidentiality and security of our work; respecting others and valuing diversity.

(continued)

	CIA	SIS	CSIS	ASIO
Values (*continued*)	**Excellence.** We hold ourselves—and each other—to the highest standards. We embrace personal accountability. We reflect on our performance and learn from that reflection.	**Innovation.** We use modern techniques, exploiting technology, working at pace, and being creative and intrepid in meeting our goals.		**Cooperation:** building a common sense of purpose and mutual support; using appropriate communication in all our relationships; fostering and maintaining productive partnerships. **Accountability:** being responsible for what we do and for our outcomes; being accountable to the Australian community through the Government and the Parliament
Source	https://www.cia.gov/about-cia/cia-vision-mission-values	https://www.sis.gov.uk/about-us/sis-strategy-and-values.html	https://www.csis.gc.ca/bts/mssnvsn-eng.asp	http://www.asio.gov.au/About-ASIO/Mission-and-Values.html

APPENDIX B: ETHICAL SCENARIOS

Scenario 1

Claudia has developed her professional career at Stakeout-Tech, a security services and consultancy firm based in Europe. She has been involved as an analyst in the production of a wide range of intelligence products on cyber security and organized crime–related issues for government and corporate clients. After years of dedication and successful analytic and writing work, Claudia has been promoted to senior analyst. The duties of her new position include managing a team of analysts that produces and delivers country risk reports. Claudia feels very lucky for this appointment, considering the economic situation that Europe is currently suffering. Particularly, Claudia's country is stuck in a prolonged economic crisis that has been getting worse over the past few years. The European Union has agreed to provide financial assistance contingent upon the implementation of economic measures in Country X. Government support to the banking system linked to austerity policies and budget cuts in public services have produced massive protests in the streets.

A Law Enforcement Agency (LEA) from Claudia's country has recently contracted with Stakeout-Tech services. This agency is especially concerned with the radicalization in social movements that has arisen from the economic crisis. Although most of the protests have been conducted in a civic way by unemployed workers, public servants, and housewives, recently there have been cases of protests using violent means. The unpopular economic measures and some political corruption scandals are fueling calls through social media for protesters to take to the streets. Claudia disagrees on the policies of her government and holds firmly that it is morally unacceptable to issue repossession orders against unemployed homeowners while, at the same time, government support is given to banks that asked for mortgage enforcement.

Stakeout-Tech's deliverables for this LEA include tailor-made reports on social movement radicalization in Country X for supporting police security operations. Stakeout-Tech has a reputation of being digitally savvy and a specialist in the monitoring of the Internet and social media. Claudia's team is charged with providing the best insights to this client, which in practice means regularly reporting on issues such as group profiling, calls for stopping evictions, protests in front of banking branches, and demonstrations. In practice, this means that Claudia's intelligence products can potentially influence her government's decisions on antiriot equipment, the number of personnel assigned to operations, budgeting for police operations, as well as the client LEA's strategy and tactics.

At the same time, there is a kind of informal pressure at Stakeout-Tech for exaggerating negative scenarios. Marketing management and sales personnel at the firm obtain better results and can persuade clients more easily to hire tools and services when their perceptions of insecurity and risks are kept high. However, Claudia has always managed to successfully avoid this corporate internal tendency.

As a result of her work, social protest against government policies in Country X has been successfully repressed, although quite a few people were injured in the last riot. The LEA is very satisfied with the services provided by the firm and is becoming Stakeout-Tech's best customer. Claudia's team has been congratulated on their work several times. However, Claudia is also conscious that, in the absence of protests, the government will perceive its policies as acceptable.

Social media monitoring and analytic work during the past few weeks have revealed the planning of an imminent protest. Claudia is confident that the upcoming protest will very likely destabilize the government.

Question

Should Claudia omit key information on the upcoming protest from her intelligence report?

Instructions

Examine this scenario and write arguments in favor of the should and the should not positions. Use the Scenarios Worksheet for this purpose.

Scenario 2

The effectiveness of your intelligence service has been put into question. It has repeatedly failed to provide a correct diagnosis of the intended economic policy actions of Country B, a Tier 1 foreign country. Your intelligence agency is responsible for providing economic intelligence on conditions and developments in foreign countries, and your country's national economic interests have been damaged by the inactivity of your country's economic policymakers regarding Country B. There are voices from within the government questioning the usefulness of your service engaging in economic intelligence, considering that there are other government departments that already gather economic information and deliver analysis to intelligence consumers.

In the context of a forthcoming round of negotiations on an important bilateral trade agreement, top management at the service feels there is an opportunity for changing perceptions of policymakers on the value added by the agency's analytical products in the economic field. Top management also believes that it is important to show the value of applying your service's "unique resources and capabilities" to economic intelligence collection.

The service, and especially your team, has a key role in informing the position of your country's delegation and its chief negotiator, which includes providing advance knowledge on the negotiating position of Country B regarding the agriculture sector. Such knowledge would affect the ability of your country to obtain the best possible deal in the negotiation from the potential partner while conceding the least. A better deal for your country means a worse deal for the other one. The chief negotiator requires the best intelligence on the bargaining ranges of Country B.

In the past, your team has experienced problems with a human source whose reliability was evaluated erroneously and is currently judged as C (fairly reliable). There has not been enough time to develop other primary intelligence sources, except for an expert close to Country B's delegation whose reliability cannot be judged (has not been used in the past).

Trade talks have kicked off. Information reported by the regular source contradicts the main judgment derived from open sources.

Suddenly, your team receives last-minute information from the second human source that is consistent with the information provided by the first one. However, there is not enough time to send the report forward and properly describe the quality and reliability of the sources.

Top management at the service is disappointed in your unit's incapacity to provide more than the other departments provide by just using open sources. Your agency's head of the Office of Economic Research and Analysis and the continuity of your office are walking a tightrope. However, an erroneous decision by the chief negotiator can damage a potential agreement and cost billions of dollars for the country and employment opportunities for many families.

Question

Should your team send the intelligence report forward without these nuances to meet the deadline?

Instructions

Examine the ethical scenario and write arguments in favor of the should and the should not positions. Use the Scenarios Worksheet for this purpose.

Scenario 3

Country Z is rapidly becoming the most serious concern for Country X's security. Country X has requested an assessment on the status of Country Z's biological weapons (BW) program. Policymakers believe that Country Z has violated the provisions the Biological Weapons Convention (BWC), to which Country Z is a state party. Country Z's possession of an offensive BW program would not only pose a significant threat to Country X but would also destabilize the whole area. More precisely, there is concern over a hypothetical secret program involving the use of the bacterium called *Bacillus anthracis* or anthrax. The rarest but most dangerous category of human anthrax is inhalation anthrax (skin and gastrointestinal anthrax are the other forms). The infection results from the direct exposure and breathing of pathogenic anthrax spores suspended in the air, being lethal in 99 percent of the cases. International organizations and states are seriously concerned about its potential as a biological warfare agent.[5] Although the president of Country Z has a history of being involved in the proliferation of weapons of mass destruction (WMD), he currently denies the existence of a secret program for developing pathogenic anthrax. He argues that research and development on the bacterium developed by his country are intended for peaceful use and has reminded his critics of the legitimacy of such program. Since the equipment and technology surrounding the BWC is intrinsically of dual use, there is a fine line between peaceful defensive and malicious offensive use.[6]

Country X's primary source of intelligence on Country Z's WMD programs has been a defector who has been providing information over the past few years. The last international inspections on Country Z's facilities did not find evidence of BW activities.

Robert is an analyst who works at Country X's main intelligence agency. He specializes in counter-proliferation analysis and BW. Robert agrees with outside, highly qualified experts in judging that the likelihood that Country Z is currently involved in developing anthrax for offensive intentions against Country X is "likely," which equates to 51 to 70 percent in the range of uncertainty. However, Robert is conscious of his intelligence service's mind-set and policymakers' views that Country Z has an active offensive BW program and has intentions to use it against Country X. There are a number of layers in the review process until the finished product is ready for dissemination, and, thus, there are also high chances that a reviewer will assign a higher confidence and a higher likelihood to the main judgment on Country Z's BW program.

Question

Given the current possibility that his analytic judgment will be modified in the review process toward this preexisting mind-set and policymaker's views, should Robert assign a lower likelihood by using the words "even chance" (50 percent) instead of "likely" deliberately as a shield against analytic bias and politicization?

Instructions

Examine the ethical scenario and write arguments in favor of the should and the should not positions. Use the Scenarios Worksheet for this purpose.

APPENDIX C: SCENARIOS INDIVIDUAL WORKSHEET

Scenarios		Should (reason why)	Should not (reason why)
Scenario 1			
Scenario 2			
Scenario 3			

APPENDIX D: SCENARIOS TEAM WORKSHEET

Scenario:		
Rank	**Should (reason why)**	**Should not (reason why)**

APPENDIX E: CODES OF ETHICS

Principles of Professional Ethics for the Intelligence Community

As members of the intelligence profession, we conduct ourselves in accordance with certain basic principles. These principles are stated below, and reflect the standard of ethical conduct expected of all Intelligence Community personnel, regardless of individual role or agency affiliation.

Many of these principles are also reflected in other documents that we look to for guidance, such as statements of core values, and the Code of Conduct: Principles of Ethical Conduct for Government Officers and Employees; it is nonetheless important for the Intelligence Community to set forth in a single statement the fundamental ethical principles that unite us—and distinguish us—as intelligence professionals.

Mission

We serve the American people, and understand that our mission requires selfless dedication to the security of our Nation.

Truth

We seek the truth; speak truth to power; and obtain, analyze, and provide intelligence objectively.

Lawfulness

We support and defend the Constitution, and comply with the laws of the United States, ensuring that we carry out our mission in a manner that respects privacy, civil liberties, and human rights obligations.

Integrity

We demonstrate integrity in our conduct, mindful that all our actions, whether public or not, should reflect positively on the Intelligence Community at large.

Stewardship

We are responsible stewards of the public trust; we use intelligence authorities and resources prudently, protect intelligence sources and methods diligently, report wrongdoing through appropriate channels; and we remain accountable to ourselves, our oversight institutions, and through those institutions, ultimately to the American people.

Excellence

We seek to improve our performance and our craft continuously, share information responsibly, collaborate with our colleagues, and demonstrate innovation and agility when meeting new challenges.

Diversity

We embrace the diversity of our Nation, promote diversity and inclusion in our workforce, and encourage diversity in our thinking.

Source: Office of the Director of National Intelligence: http://www.dni.gov/index.php/intelligence -community/principles-of-professional-ethics [Last accessed: 4 August 2013]

SCIP CODE OF ETHICS FOR CI PROFESSIONALS

- To continually strive to increase the recognition and respect of the profession.
- To comply with all applicable laws, domestic and international.
- To accurately disclose all relevant information, including one's identity and organization, prior to all interviews.
- To avoid conflicts of interest in fulfilling one's duties.
- To provide honest and realistic recommendations and conclusions in the execution of one's duties.
- To promote this code of ethics within one's company, with third-party contractors, and within the entire profession.
- To faithfully adhere to and abide by one's company policies, objectives, and guidelines.

Source: Strategic and Competitive Intelligence Professionals. http://www.scip.org/About/content.cfm?ItemNumber=578&navItemNumber=504 [Last accessed: 4 August 2013]

APPENDIX F: INTELLIGENCE ANALYSIS CODE OF ETHICS

General Ethics	Practical Ethics	Reasons
Our Professional Values	Principles of Ethical Practice	Intent

APPENDIX G.1: SHERMAN KENT'S NINE PRINCIPLES FOR INTELLIGENCE ANALYSIS

1. Focus on Policymaker Concerns
2. Avoidance of a Personal Policy Agenda
3. Intellectual Rigor
4. Conscious Effort to Avoid Analytic Biases
5. Willingness to Consider Other Judgments
6. Systematic Use of Outside Experts
7. Collective Responsibility for Judgment
8. Effective Communication of Policy-support Information and Judgments
9. Candid Admission of Mistakes

Source: Davis, Jack. (2002). "Sherman Kent and the Profession of Intelligence Analysis," in *The Sherman Kent Center for Intelligence Analysis Occasional Papers*, Volume 1, Number 5; https://www.cia.gov/library/kent-center-occasional-papers/pdf/OPNo5.pdf [Last accessed: 4 August 2013]

APPENDIX G.2: ICD 203 IC ANALYTIC STANDARDS

a) Objectivity
b) Independent of Political Considerations
c) Timeliness
d) Based on All Available Sources of Intelligence
e) Exhibits Proper Standards of Analytic Tradecraft, Specifically:
   1) Properly describes quality and reliability of underlying sources
   2) Properly caveats and expresses uncertainties or confidence in analytic judgment
   3) Properly distinguishes between underlying intelligence and analysts' assumptions and judgments
   4) Incorporate alternative analysis where appropriate
   5) Demonstrates relevance to U.S. national security
   6) Uses logical argumentation
   7) Exhibits consistency of analysis over time, or highlights changes and explains rationale
   8) Makes accurate judgments and assessments

Source: Intelligence Community Directive Number 203, "Analytic Standards," http://www.fas.org/irp/dni/icd/icd-203.pdf [Last accessed: 4 August 2013]

APPENDIX G TEMPLATE 1: GLOBAL RESULTS FOR ETHICAL SCENARIOS (NOTE: ASSIGN A COLOR TO DIFFERENT GROUPS FOR HIGHLIGHTING THEIR CONTRIBUTIONS)

Scenario:		
Rank	**Should (reason why)**	**Should not (reason why)**

NOTES

1. For exploring intelligence ethics, we refer the reader to: Andregg (2007), Goldman (2006 and 2010), and Olson (2006). For a detailed work on ethics and competitive intelligence, see Fehringer and Hohhof (2006).

2. The design of the simulation exercise has been partially inspired by Trefry, Woodilla, and Gumbus (2006).

3. Instructors may want to hand out a summary of ethical frameworks for participants for facilitating the debriefing. For an example, see White and Taft (2004). Also see Trefry et al. (2006, pp. 369–370). It is also recommended to refer students to Rachels and Rachels (2012).

4. Instructors can hand out copies of existing systems for conveying uncertainty. See ODNI (2012, p. 13). Also refer to the British uncertainty yardstick at DCDC (2011, pp. 3–23).

5. World Health Organization. Guidance on anthrax: Frequently asked questions. www.who
.int/csr/disease/Anthrax/anthraxfaq/en/; and Anthrax Vaccine Immunization Program, www.anthrax
.osd.mil.
    6. United Nations Office at Geneva. Disarmament. www.unog.ch/80256EE600585943/(http
Pages)/7CD9879E9CE09EFDC1257AC500309AA7?OpenDocument.

REFERENCES

Andregg, Michael M. (Ed.). 2007. *Intelligence ethics: The definitive work of 2007.* St. Paul, MN:
    Center for the Study of Intelligence and Wisdom. Available at: www.gzmn.org/pdfonline/
    IntelligenceEthics2007-MA.pdf.
Cardillo, Robert. 2010. A cultural evolution. *Studies in Intelligence, 54*(3), Extracts. Available at:
    www.cia.gov/library/center-for-the-study-of-intelligence/csi-publications/csi-studies/studies/
    vol.-54-no.-3/a-cultural-evolution.html.
Davis, Michael. 1991. Thinking like an engineer: The place of a code of ethics in the practice of
    a profession. *Philosophy and Public Affairs, 20*(2), 150–167.
Development, Concepts and Doctrine Centre (DCDC). 2011. *JDP 2-00,* 3rd ed. *Understanding
    and intelligence support to joint operations.* Shrivenham: UK Ministry of Defense. Available at:
    www.gov.uk/government/uploads/system/uploads/attachment_data/file/33704/20110830JDP
    2003rdEDweb.pdf.
Fehringer, Dale, and Hohhof, Bonnie (Eds.) 2006. *Competitive intelligence ethics: Navigating the
    grey zone.* Alexandria, VA: Competitive Intelligence Foundation.
Fleisher, Craig S. 2003. Are competitive intelligence practitioners professionals? In Craig S.
    Fleisher and David L. Bleckhorn (Eds.), *Controversies in competitive intelligence: The enduring
    issues* (pp. 29–44). Westport, CT: Praeger Publishers.
Gannon, John C. 1997. Foreword. In Jack Davis, *A Compendium of analytic tradecraft notes,* Vol.
    I (Notes 1–10). Available at: www.au.af.mil/au/awc/awcgate/cia/tradecraft_notes/contents.htm
    #contents.
Goldman, Jan (Ed.). 2006. *Ethics of spying: A reader for the intelligence professional.* Lanham, MD:
    Scarecrow Press.
Goldman, Jan (Ed.). 2010. *Ethics of spying: A reader for the intelligence professional,* Vol. 2. Lan-
    ham, MD: Scarecrow Press.
Johnston, Rob. 2005. *Analytic culture in the US intelligence community: An ethnographic study.*
    Washington, DC: CIA Center for the Study of Intelligence. Available at: www.cia.gov/library/
    center-for-the-study-of-intelligence/csi-publications/books-and-monographs/analytic-culture
    -in-the-u-s-intelligence-community/analytic_culture_report.pdf.
Larson, Magali Sarfatti. 2013. *The rise of professionalism: Monopolies of competence and sheltered
    markets.* New Brunswick, NJ: Transaction Publishers.
Lederman, Linda Costigan. 1992. Debriefing: Toward a systematic assessment of theory and
    practice. *Simulation & Gaming, 23*(2), 145–160.
Marrin, Stephen, and Clemente, Jonathan D. 2006. Modeling an intelligence analysis profession
    on medicine. *International Journal of Intelligence and Counter Intelligence, 19*(4), 642–665.
Office of the Director of National Intelligence (ODNI). 2012. *Global water security.* ICA 2012-
    08, 2 February. Available at: www.dni.gov/files/documents/Special%20Report_ICA%20Global
    %20Water%20Security.pdf.
Olson, James M. 2006. *Fair play: The moral dilemmas of spying.* Washington, DC: Potomac Books.

Platt, Washington. 1957. *Strategic intelligence production: Basic principles.* New York: Praeger Publishers.

Rachels, James, and Rachels, Stuart. 2012. *The elements of moral philosophy* (7th ed.). New York: McGraw-Hill.

Sawka, Ken. 2005. Analytic tradecraft. *Competitive Intelligence Magazine, 8*(4), 43–44.

Schultze, Quentin J. 1981. Professionalism in advertising: The origin of ethical codes. *Journal of Communication, 31*(2), 64–71.

Thiagarajan, Sivasailam. 1992. Using Games for Debriefing. *Simulation & Gaming, 23*(2), 161–173.

Trefry, Mary, Woodilla, Jill, and Gumbus, Andra. 2006. Dialogues and decisions: Moral dilemmas in the workplace. *Simulation & Gaming, 37*(3), 357–379.

White, Judith, and Taft, Susan. 2004. Frameworks for teaching and learning business ethics within the global context: background of ethical theories. *Journal of Management Education, 28*(4), 463–477.

4

Spies and Lies: The Perils
of Collection—A Simulation

Kristan J. Wheaton and James Breckenridge

ABSTRACT

The collection of information is a core part of the intelligence process no matter how that process is defined. This exercise is designed to allow students to experience not only some of the issues involved in planning and executing collection operations (particularly HUMINT [human intelligence] operations) but also to experience how poorly structured collection systems can seriously impair the quality of the overall collection effort as well as the accuracy of the ensuing analysis.

The simulation is designed for a class of 6 to 30 students and takes approximately 1 hour to run. The simulation puts teams of students in the roles of intelligence operatives collecting information for one of six Balkan nations. To begin the simulation, students receive a single sheet of paper that contains background information on their country and a list of 10 discrete "facts" to which that country alone is privy. The different nations (Bulgaria, Greece, Serbia, Albania, Turkey, and Macedonia [FYROM]) have been arrayed such that each country has two allies and one enemy with the remaining two countries marked as neutral. The simulation instructions force allies and enemies to interact under time pressure with predictable results.

This simulation has been used in introductory intelligence theory and application classes at the graduate and undergraduate levels for over 8 years. It is typically one of the students' favorite exercises.

The body count was a measurement of the adversary's manpower losses; we undertook it because one of Westy's [General Westmoreland's] objectives was to reach a so-called crossover point, at which Vietcong and North Vietnamese casualties would be greater than they could sustain.

—Robert S. McNamara (1995)

Ah les statistiques, your Secretary of Defense loves statistics. We Vietnamese can give him all he wants. If you want them to go up, they will go up. If you want them to go down, they will go down.

—An unidentified South Vietnamese officer (Schonfeld, 1995)

The collection of information is a core part of the intelligence process no matter how that process is defined. Teaching entry-level students of intelligence to appreciate the difficulties inherent in most collection activities is one matter, but getting them to understand the opportunities for and consequences of deliberate deception is quite another matter.

Most entry-level intelligence professionals have an idealized understanding of the collection process informed primarily by movies and television. Case studies and lectures typically only make the smallest of dents in this pervasive image of information retrieval systems that are able to precisely locate the exact piece of information required at the exact time it is needed. It is even more difficult to teach an appreciation for what a carefully orchestrated deception plan (like World War II's *Mincemeat* [Montagu, 2001] or the Cold War's *Farewell* [Farewell Dossier, 2012]) can do to analysis and operations.

This simulation is designed to allow students to experience not only some of the issues involved in planning and executing collection operations (particularly HUMINT operations) but also to experience how poorly structured collection systems (such as the body counting efforts in Vietnam) can seriously impair the quality of the overall collection effort as well as the accuracy of the ensuing analysis.

BASIC DATA

Instructional Objectives

The primary objective for this simulation is to give students and entry-level intelligence professionals an appreciation for the difficulties of conducting intelligence collection in an interconnected and hostile environment. As a secondary objective, this simulation should give students and entry-level intelligence professionals an understanding of the role that the collection system plays in creating incentives for collectors and how poor choices of incentives can corrupt collection activities. Although this simulation focuses on HUMINT collection activities, the lessons learned should be generalizable to other collection disciplines. Due to the mild deception that the instructor perpetrates on the participants during the exercise, this simulation is a particularly good lead-in to a more formal discussion of intelligence collection. Students should have little or no exposure to intelligence collection theory or practice prior to this simulation.

Simulation Objectives

Participants work as small teams of HUMINT collectors for different nations attempting to gather information on a target country from allied, neutral, and enemy countries. The simulation takes place in a time-constrained and information-constrained environment where quantity is rewarded over quality of information and where collectors do not understand the underlying purpose behind the collection activity. Participants are left to develop their own strategies for acquiring the information needed, and deceptive practices naturally arise as a way of coping with the lack of information available to the participants coupled with the pressure to acquire as much information as possible.

Debriefing Format

Debriefing is instructor led, guided by key questions (see Appendix D).

Target Audience

Undergraduate and graduate students in intelligence studies programs or in introductory or advanced courses about intelligence. It is also appropriate for political science, international relations, or security studies courses. Finally, this simulation would work well with entry level intelligence professionals in the national security community and, with some minor modifications, in the law enforcement and business areas as well.

Playing Time

Typically about 40 minutes for the simulation itself

Debriefing Time

Approximately 20–30 minutes

Number of Players Required

The simulation requires a minimum of six players, one for each country represented. The simulation works well with up to 24 players (four per team). The simulation has not been tested with groups larger than 27, but, due to the finite amount of information available in the simulation, groups larger than 30 would likely be unwieldy and lead to a diminished learning experience.

Participation Materials Included

See Appendices A through C.

Debriefing Materials Included

See Appendices C and D.

Computer/Internet

Not required.

Other Materials/Equipment Required

This simulation typically takes place in a single classroom. However, because of the nature of the exercise and the students' perception of a need for secrecy for both planning and for conversations with other teams, it is wise to allow students to utilize several rooms or a long hallway in order to facilitate the simulation.

FACILITATOR'S GUIDE

Materials

Appendix A: Instructions and Intelligence
Appendix B: Country Badge Template
Appendix C: Collection Evaluation Chart (Example)
Appendix D: Debriefing Questions

Presimulation Briefing

The simulation begins by dividing the class into six roughly equal groups. Teams should be placed around the room such that they have as much privacy as space will allow. Each group then receives a single sheet of paper with country-specific information on it (see Appendix A) and a set of name badges that clearly identify the country to which the individual belongs (see Appendix B). The instructor should reinforce the idea that the single sheet of paper each team is given is *only* for that team and contains special information available only to that team. It should be strongly reinforced that they are never to show this piece of paper to other teams, only teammates.

Each team has roughly the same instructions. Each country has exactly one enemy country (for example, Albania's "enemy" is Serbia) and one or two allies (Albania's allies, for example, are Bulgaria and Turkey). The mission is the same for all countries: to collect as much information about the enemy country and its plans as possible.

The relationships between countries define under what conditions countries will trade information. Allies will always give participants what they ask for and will expect nothing in return. Enemies will never willingly give participants information. Neutrals will barter with other participants for the best possible information trade. In order to get all the information available regarding a country, it quickly becomes obvious to participants that they must devise a plan to get information from their enemy. Since this is not possible directly, it drives participants to begin actively trading information with others who do have access. This information exchange activity drives, in turn, the simulation.

What not to say: All countries have exactly 10 "facts" about the other five countries in the simulation. It is important that the instructor and the students only divulge the exact number of facts in the simulation or the exact number of facts given to them initially in writing once the simulation is complete. Although this admonition is on each of the individual country handouts given to each of the teams, the instructor should reinforce this orally as well. The number of facts actually in the possession of each country is "top secret" information—other teams may never see the actual list, only be told what is on it.

Once the teams have been formed, physically separated such that they can have some privacy, and the instruction sheets handed out and explained, the instructor should begin the simulation in earnest.

CONDUCTING THE SIMULATION

Step 1: Initial Planning Phase

Participants should be given approximately 5 minutes to plan their collection activity. This activity does not need to be supervised by the instructor, but the instructor can heighten the sense of espionage by circulating throughout the room and occasionally making comments or asking questions that serve to heighten the tension. Once participants have had a chance to come up with a plan (and even if they have not), the instructor should allow all teams to begin collection.

Step 2: Initial Collection Activities Phase

This phase is deliberately unstructured, and instructors should expect some hesitation on the parts of the participants. Participants should be encouraged to "go out and collect" by contacting allies for free information and cutting deals with neutrals. Participants should also be told that beyond the rules on the sheets of paper they have been given, that there are no rules; eavesdropping, for example, is permitted, even encouraged, and the instructor should make this clear to the participants early in the exercise.

Step 3: Initial Evaluation Phase

After approximately 5 minutes, the instructor should stop the exercise and instruct all participants to move back to their starting areas. The instructor should ask how many pieces of information, how many "facts," each team has collected. These numbers should be placed on the Collection Evaluation Chart (see Appendix C). The instructor should loudly praise the team with the most information and encourage other teams to "do better" and "collect more."

Step 4: Combined Planning and Collection Phases

Once the initial evaluation phase is complete, the instructor should allow the teams to go back to collecting more information.

Step 5: Interim Evaluation Phases

Every 5 minutes or so, the instructor should stop the collection exercise and update the Collection Evaluation Chart. As in step 3, the instructor should praise the efforts of the team collecting the most information and encourage those that "aren't collecting enough." The instructor should repeat steps 4 and 5 until all or most teams claim to have collected more than 10 pieces of information on their target country, at which point the simulation will end. (NOTE: It is not necessary that all teams collect more than 10 pieces of information, although it helps make the deception point in the debriefing.)

DEBRIEFING THE SIMULATION

Objectives

The objectives of this simulation are twofold. First, the simulation exposes participants to some of the attributes of real-world HUMINT work. Planning, targeting, strategy, deception, and tradecraft all are part of this collection exercise and are appropriate topics for discussion in the debrief.

The second objective is to discuss the role of deception in collection activities. If the simulation has been run properly, virtually all of the teams should be claiming to have collected more than 10 discrete pieces of information from their allies and neutral countries regarding their enemy. This is impossible because there were only 10 pieces of information available regarding each country. The realization that some of the information each team has received must be lies is the launching point for a discussion regarding the second major topic—deception. Topics appropriate for discussion here include, but are not limited to, when and why deception became a "weapon" in the team's collection arsenal, what role the instructor's encouragement to "collect more" played in the exercise, and how the presence of deceptive information impacts analysis.

The instructor should use a free-form discussion format to elicit answers to some or all of the questions below. Instructors should feel free to deviate from this script, however. This exercise typically creates a number of ad hoc learning opportunities.

Step 1: Collection Strategy

- How well did the initial plan work? (It is unlikely that the teams stuck to their initial plan.) Why and when did the plan fall apart?

- How did the strategy change during the course of the exercise?
- How did the teams use their allies? Neutrals?
- What techniques did the teams use to get access to enemy information? (In addition to more traditional means, some teams might confess at this point to making up information to get access to other information. The discussion of why they did this and what the impact of it is, should be deferred to step 2.)
- What would the teams do differently?

Step 2: Deception

- How many legitimate pieces of information existed concerning each country?
- What does it mean that each country (or at least the majority) has collected more than 10 pieces of information?
- Was deliberate deception part of your initial collection plan? (This is rarely if ever the case. A good follow-up question is "Why not?")
- When did the idea occur to you to lie in order to get more information?
- Did it ever occur to you that others in the class were lying to you? (Be honest)
- What was it about the way the exercise was run that encouraged this behavior?
- Has this dynamic ever happened in real life (NOTE: body count data in Vietnam)?
- How would the presence of deceptive information impact the quality of your analysis?
- How would you devise a system to encourage quality over quantity and to check for deception?

CONCLUSION

Specifically designed to introduce newly hired intelligence professionals and intelligence studies students to the world of collection, this simulation introduces a variety of important concepts including the value of collection planning, the difficulties inherent in HUMINT collection activities, and the possibility and impact of deception.

Requiring only about an hour to conduct and debrief, the simulation is dynamic and can involve as few as 6 and as many as 30 participants, making it ideal for classroom use. It is best used at the beginning of a section on collection, before students know too much about the discipline, as it requires the instructor to create an environment of exigency that might not generate reliable outcomes if used with more experienced students.

The simulation also typically generates a good deal of out-of-scope questions, such as, How do intelligence professionals deal with these kinds of problems in the real world? These questions will provide an astute instructor unique teaching opportunities where he or she can capitalize on student interest to take on new topics or can use these opportunities to reinforce concepts already covered or to foreshadow concepts that will arise in later stages of the course.

APPENDIX A: INSTRUCTIONS AND INTELLIGENCE

Collection Exercise

You are a member of ALBANIAN INTELLIGENCE. ALBANIA is worried about aggressive moves by SERBIA. Your first target is your enemy, SERBIA. Your mission is to find out as much about SERBIA and its plans as you can. You *will never* knowingly give useful information to SERBIA.

Your friends are BULGARIA and TURKEY. You will give them information even if they have no information that is useful to you.

You are neutral toward MACEDONIA and GREECE. You will only give information to them if they give information to you.

You know the following information that might be useful to other countries. *You may tell this information to other countries and they may write it down, but you cannot show them this information.*

1. Turkey's military is decisively engaged against terrorists in the Southeast.
2. Turkey wants to protect the human rights of the Turkish Cypriots.
3. The major foreign investor in Macedonia is the United States.
4. Macedonia needs financing for a major highway project.
5. Bulgarians think of Macedonia as "western Bulgaria."
6. Bulgarian officials believe that Macedonian officials can be bribed.
7. Albania has been given a large batch of U.S. combat equipment. It will arrive in 6 months.
8. Albanians are proud of their country.
9. Current members of the Greek government are all successful businessmen.
10. The Greek people feel passionately about Cyprus.

Collection Exercise

You are a member of BULGARIAN INTELLIGENCE. BULGARIA wants to become a regional economic power in the Balkans. In order to do this, you know that the country needs to expand its economic influence into other neighboring countries. Your first target is your economic competitor (ENEMY for the purpose of this exercise), MACEDONIA. Your mission is to find out as much about MACEDONIA and its plans as you can. You *will never* knowingly give useful information to MACEDONIA.

Your friend is ALBANIA. You will give them information even if they have no information that is useful to you.

You are neutral toward SERBIA, GREECE, and TURKEY. You will only give information to them if they give information to you.

You know the following information that might be useful to other countries. *You may tell this information to other countries and they may write it down, but you cannot show them this information.*

1. Albania's army is weak and poorly trained.
2. Albania's terrain is difficult to traverse.
3. Serbia has 9 million people.
4. Serbia's army is on high alert.
5. Greece is worried about the future of Cyprus.
6. Greece is sponsoring Greek Cypriots in Greece's military schools.
7. Turkey is spending too much money to support the Turkish Cypriots.
8. Turkey wants to improve its image on the international stage.
9. Bulgarian businesses have recently increased the number of branch offices they have in the Macedonian capital.
10. The Bulgarian currency will likely strengthen in the near future against the Macedonian currency.

Collection Exercise

You are a member of SERBIAN INTELLIGENCE. SERBIA is tired of Albanian terrorists using Albania as a safe haven. SERBIA is contemplating large-scale military action to resolve this problem. Your first target is your enemy, ALBANIA. Your mission is to find out as much about ALBANIA and its plans as you can. You *will never* knowingly give useful information to ALBANIA.

Your friends are MACEDONIA and GREECE. You will give them information even if they have no information that is useful to you.

You are neutral toward BULGARIA and TURKEY. You will only give information to them if they give information to you.

You know the following information that might be useful to other countries. *You may tell this information to other countries and they may write it down, but you cannot show them this information.*

1. Bulgaria's army is in shambles.
2. Bulgaria is closely allying itself with the United States.
3. The Macedonian economy is severely depressed creating a number of buying opportunities.
4. The government of FYROM is corrupt and can be bribed.
5. Serbia's leadership is nationalistic and is territorially aggressive.
6. Serbia needs Albania's good ports for economic expansion.
7. Turkey's military has a large influence over most foreign policy decisions.
8. Turkey's government wants to negotiate a solution to the Cyprus problem.
9. Greece is waiting for many of the hardliners in Cyprus to be replaced or to die.
10. Greece cannot afford a war.

Collection Exercise

You are a member of MACEDONIAN INTELLIGENCE. MACEDONIA is concerned about the growing economic influence of BULGARIA. Your first target is your economic competitor (ENEMY for the purpose of this exercise), BULGARIA. Your mission is to find out as much about BULGARIA and its plans as you can. You *will never* knowingly give useful information to BULGARIA.

Your friend is SERBIA. You will give them information even if they have no information that is useful to you.

You are neutral toward ALBANIA, GREECE, and TURKEY. You will only give information to them if they give information to you.

You know the following information that might be useful to other countries. *You may tell this information to other countries and they may write it down, but you cannot show them this information.*

1. Macedonia is in negotiations with Serbia to sell its largest state-owned industry. The Serbs are offering $10 million.
2. Many Macedonians closely ally themselves with Bulgaria.
3. Turkey does not want Cyprus to become a part of Turkey.
4. Turkey's economy needs foreign investment.
5. Greece is trying to get the European Union to recognize Cyprus.
6. Greece does not want Cyprus to become part of Greece.
7. Serbia is angry about the border marking between Albania and Serbia.
8. Serbia has war plans for invading Albania.
9. Albania's special forces are well trained in guerrilla tactics.
10. Albania's ports are in disrepair.

Collection Exercise

You are a member of GREEK INTELLIGENCE. GREECE wants to try to negotiate a solution with TURKEY that will end the crisis between the two countries over Cyprus. GREECE needs to know if the time is now right for such negotiations. Your first target is your enemy, TURKEY. Your mission is to find out as much about TURKEY and its plans as you can. You *will never* knowingly give useful information to TURKEY.

Your friend is SERBIA. You will give them information even if they have no information that is useful to you.

You are neutral toward MACEDONIA, BULGARIA, and ALBANIA. You will only give information to them if they give information to you.

You know the following information that might be useful to other countries. *You may tell this information to other countries and they may write it down, but you cannot show them this information.*

1. Macedonian politicians are very worried about Bulgarian economic influence in Macedonia.

2. There are less than 2 million ethnic Macedonians in Macedonia.
3. Albanians have a strong fighting tradition.
4. Albania has a very weak navy.
5. The Serbian military has rearmed itself and is ready for war.
6. Serbia is not worried about international opinion.
7. The Greek navy is in need of repair.
8. The Greek army has not upgraded its equipment since the early 1990s.
9. Bulgarians believe that Macedonia controls the economic crossroads of the Balkans.
10. Bulgaria does not want to spend any more money on its military.

Collection Exercise

You are a member of TURKISH INTELLIGENCE. TURKEY wants to try to negotiate a solution with GREECE that will end the crisis between the two countries over Cyprus. TURKEY needs to know if the time is now right for such negotiations. Your first target is your enemy, GREECE. Your mission is to find out as much about GREECE and its plans as you can. You *will never* knowingly give useful information to GREECE.

Your friend is ALBANIA. You will give them information even if they have no information that is useful to you.

You are neutral toward MACEDONIA, BULGARIA, and SERBIA. You will only give information to them if they give information to you.

You know the following information that might be useful to other countries. *You may tell this information to other countries and they may write it down, but you cannot show them this information*.

1. The Macedonian language is very similar to the Bulgarian language.
2. Most Macedonians don't care who owns the companies as long as they have jobs.
3. Serbs think that, with the current population growth, Albanians will soon overrun the Balkans.
4. Serbia has long-range artillery capable of reaching anywhere in Albania.
5. Bulgarian businessmen have made a list of possible takeover targets in other countries.
6. Bulgarian infrastructure is improving.
7. The government of Turkey wants to cut a deal with Cyprus now due to international political reasons.
8. Turkey is under a good bit of international pressure on the Cyprus issue.
9. Albania's bridges cannot support the weight of tanks.
10. Albania's cell phone network can be easily jammed.

APPENDIX B: COUNTRY BADGE TEMPLATE

These labels can be printed on badges or taped or paper clipped to clothing. Each participant should have a badge, and it should clearly mark to which country that participant belongs. The template can be quickly modified for use with the other countries in the simulation.

APPENDIX B

Albania		Albania
Albania		Albania
Albania		Albania
Albania		Albania

APPENDIX C: COLLECTION EVALUATION CHART (EXAMPLE)

Team	1	2	3	4	5	6	7	8	9	10
Albania										
Bulgaria										
Greece										
Macedonia										
Serbia										
Turkey										

APPENDIX D: DEBRIEFING QUESTIONS

Topics to discuss in the after action review include:

Collection Strategy

- How well did the initial plan work?
  How did the strategy change during the course of the exercise?
  How did the teams use their allies? Neutrals?
  What techniques did the teams use to get access to enemy information?
- What would the teams do differently?

Deception

(NOTE: With each team having access to only 10 pieces of information, it is impossible for any team to gather more than 10 legitimate pieces of information about any country. Once teams claim to collect more than 10 pieces of information, it means that some team—perhaps many teams—has been lying in order to collect additional pieces of information. This is something most teams will acknowledge with a bit of pride until they realize they have also been the victims of lies.)

- How many legitimate pieces of information existed concerning each country?
- What does it mean for each country (or at least the majority) that has collected more than 10 pieces of information?
- Was deliberate deception part of your initial collection plan?
- When did the idea occur to you to lie in order to get more information?
- Did it ever occur to you that others in the class were lying to you? (Be honest)
- What was it about the way the exercise was run that encouraged this behavior?
- Has this dynamic ever happened in real life (NOTE: body count data in Vietnam)?
- How would the presence of deceptive information impact the quality of your analysis?
- How would you devise a system to encourage quality over quantity and to check for deception?

REFERENCES

Farewell Dossier. 2012. Wikipedia. Available at: http://en.wikipedia.org/wiki/Farewell_Dossier.

McNamara, Robert S., with Brian Vandemark. 1995. *In retrospect: The tragedy and lessons of Vietnam.* New York: Times Books/Random House.

Montagu, E. 2001. *The man who never was: World War II's boldest counterintelligence operation.* Annapolis, MD: Naval Institute Press.

Schoenfeld, Gabriel. 1995. In Retrospect, by Robert S. McNamara. *Commentary.* Available at: www.commentarymagazine.com/article/in-retrospect-by-robert-s-mcnamara.

5

Learning Intelligence Analysis: The Development of Cognitive Strategies

Dan Mazare and Gabriel Sebe

ABSTRACT

Leaving aside those programs aimed at *training* future intelligence professionals, one could note an increasing number of intelligence studies projects, in civil settings, aimed at *educating* by theorizing on intelligence-related topics. Such initiatives support the development of the intelligence culture, seen as an extension of a society's political culture. This simulation explores the boundaries between training and education by emphasizing the importance of *learning* intelligence analysis. Based on a case study defined as a "revolutionary crisis in Great Frusina," the exercise underlines the role that cognitive strategies play in solving intelligence analysis problems. The exercise was designed by taking into account Robert M. Gagné's developments on the conditions of learning and the theory of instruction.

KEYWORDS

Cognitive strategy; intelligence analysis; intelligence education; intelligence learning; intelligence training

There is currently a vivid debate on the manner in which the world of intelligence affairs could and should be better supported by the academic community. In a context defined by the emergence of the open source intelligence paradigm and the sociopolitical developments of the past few decades, democratization being the keyword, the world of intelligence affairs has increased its academic connectivity. As the limits of secrecy and openness in intelligence affairs started to be questioned and the puzzle-like problems to be solved inside intelligence communities required new dynamic approaches, academics entered the arena. Leaving aside those programs aimed at *training* future intelligence professionals, one could note an increasing number of intelligence studies projects, in civil settings, aimed at *educating* by theorizing on intelligence related topics. Such initiatives support the development of the intelligence culture, seen as an extension of a society's political culture.

Yet, there is a particular distance between the professionals' worries and the academics' responses. The social scientists' discourse on intelligence topics rarely tackles one of the most important problems of the professionals: the improvement of the intelligence analysis process per se. It seems that there is a rupture, leaving aside the parts of any integrative viewpoint on intelligence, as education, training, and practice are most often treated as completely decoupled activities. The effects of this rupture are limited in the short term, yet the long-term effects of such an approach hinder the development of the intelligence culture, which even the professionals claim is needed to foster a holistic view on intelligence.

Recent academic initiatives addressing the improvement of intelligence analysis are focused on achieving a cross-disciplinary perspective by seeking particular, targeted, solutions to specifically defined analytic problems, under the motto "learning from other disciplines." Such approaches draw upon principles and facts, scientific arguments and expertise, from scientific and practical domains alike (journalism, medicine, etc.). This is a meritorious approach as the possible solutions for the improvement of intelligence analysis are sought by avoiding the complexity of finding a general systemic mechanism in the intelligence ecosystem (intelligence community and the organizations approaching intelligence studies).

We are inclined to consider that a general solution to the problem of intelligence analysis improvement could come from a better understanding between practitioners and academics at the level of problem definition, segmentation, and communication: Who (says) What (to) Whom (in) What Channel (with) What Effect in the problem of intelligence analysis improvement. This translates into determining how practitioners could place into abstraction their requests for academic support, how academics could come from abstraction toward facts and time-constrained decision making in political and intelligence processes. It is a matter of developing better interfaces between practitioners and academics, not only in terms of defining procedures and roles but also in terms of a mutual conceptual interoperability.

Of equal importance to the improvement of intelligence analysis is the way in which education and training are pursued. We favor approaches that are developed by taking into account not only different arbitrary segments of the education and training processes, but also the learning process per se, the way in which a student learns and acquires new information. Therefore, from our point of view, an improvement in intelligence analysis could be achieved by employing to a greater extent the theories of learning when designing specific lessons and courses in intelligence analysis.

EXERCISE DESCRIPTION

General Description

Turning a student into a knowledge worker and a good intelligence analyst means that he or she was immersed in the above-described context, having gained the tools to place *him-* or *herself and others* in the right position among decision makers, other specialized analysts, and the supporting members of the academic community. The map behind this spatial process (which involves self-positioning) should not be conceived only as institutional, although this is a very important dimension, covered in detail by an existing legal framework. The positioning, as it is envisioned for this exercise, has to do with a multidimensional map, defined along the following axes: time, responsibility, argumentative capabilities, and ideological bias.

On the time axis, the student of intelligence has to be aware not only of the tyranny of deadlines and the real-life scenarios in which he or she, as an analyst, has to answer requests for intelligence initiated by managers under the motto: "I needed that report yesterday, you are already late." The time axis also involves taking into account the differences between concepts like retrodiction and prediction, and also the subjective feeling of time, the projection of the zeitgeist in a particular region of interest.

The responsibility axis usually triggers for any future intelligence analyst behaviors related to the established code of ethics in the intelligence field he or she aims to join. From the perspective of this exercise, it is also important to note the differences between risk and responsibility in politics, science, and intelligence in a holistic perspective.

Politicians, decision makers, scientists, and intelligence analysts are all constructing and delivering arguments, using, more or less, a structured approach: gathering evidence, pondering relevance and credibility, combining evidence, and entering recurrent formulas for the combination of evidence. Developed through training or education, the argumentative capabilities also empower the beholder with a reverse capability aimed at deconstructing argumentative constructs. This exercise is aimed at developing students' reflexes toward increasing their argumentative capabilities, both in constructing and deconstructing argumentative chains.

The intelligence literature usually covers those cases in which the analyst is the subject of psychological cognitive biases, of which he or she has to be aware during analysis. This exercise is aimed at emphasizing the complexity of an environment in which not only the analysts but also the scientists and decision makers are subject to ideological bias. The term here employed under the label of "ideological bias" covers a plethora of deviations in judgment that lead to an ideological interpretation of a particular decision-making process. Without being rooted in deep psychological mechanisms (as cognitive biases are), the ideological biases are envisioned as the result of the vast human value and belief systems, dependent on cultural and educational frameworks.

Uncertainty comes in shallow and deep forms, being more or less adequately addressed by probabilistic analysis. This exercise takes note of the fact that uncertainty analysis is a human-intensive activity, for which brainstorming and gaming can offer valuable insights, both in establishing alternatives and formulating strategies (Davis, 2012). The exercise places participants in one of three groups—decision makers, analysts, and consultants—and is aimed at emphasizing that, in order to achieve a balanced approach to the analytic practice, the interface among these groups has to be rooted in mutual understanding, what we call conceptual interoperability. It is our contention that such interoperability is mediated by a proper awareness of the outlined multidimensional map, each of the participants having to place him- or herself as accurately as possible on the map's four axes while addressing uncertainty's avatars.

In order to engage the student in a debate about the multidimensional map, the exercise addresses a phenomenon that has received wide coverage in the social sciences arena: the definition, explanation, and prediction of revolutions. Despite the fact that academics and dissidents alike failed in predicting the fall of the communist regimes in Eastern Europe in 1989, and despite the failure of academics and Western intelligence communities in gathering the right signals on the unrest that was to explode into popular uprisings in 2011 in the Middle East and North Africa,[1] the literature on forecasting instability and social movements has never been scarce.

This exercise establishes three groups of participants (particular roles being further attached to each group): decision makers, analysts, and consultants. The decision makers issue a request for intelligence, the analysts develop a report in response to this request, and the consultants deliver expert advice based on scientific approaches or prior direct experiences with the subject. According to our script, the request for intelligence is released by the decision makers because they need to prepare to deliver an official address concerning a national security issue. This address has to cover the large-scale uprising taking place in a neighboring country; the address represents the public expression of an effective policy-making process. As these incidents could trigger political violence and economic turbulence in the entire area, the group of analysts is asked for a situation assessment report.

Pedagogic Value

The exercise was designed by taking into account Robert M. Gagné's developments on the conditions of learning and the theory of instruction (Gagné & Driscoll, 2008). Gagné defined five categories of human performance obtained by learning, thus five learning outcomes: intellectual skills, verbal information, cognitive strategies, motor skills, and attitudes. This exercise aims at developing participants' cognitive strategies: the way in which they develop certain techniques of thinking and remembering, *ways* of analyzing and structuring problems in an interpretative context. Such an approach is rooted in our belief that most of the training and education in intelligence analysis is aimed at developing future analysts' intellectual skills ("know how" or having procedural knowledge) or verbal information ("know that," or having declarative knowledge), while the cognitive strategies for approaching intelligence-specific issues are rarely tackled. Moreover, we developed the exercise more like a learning experiment (being focused on the way in which the student acquires information) and less like a training lesson (being focused on the way in which the trainer delivers information).

In Gagné's theory, an external observer could recognize learning by noting behavioral changes that remain persistent over time, after learning occurred. Such a definition of learning favors the measurement of the learning performances achieved by a student. This exercise is not approaching evaluation; the debriefing stage is part of the learning process. A similar additional exercise would be needed to evaluate participants' learning performance.

BASIC DATA

Instructional Objectives

Much of the usual training received by future intelligence analysts is aimed at establishing competencies in analytical methods and tools through formalized and well-defined procedures and rules. However, authors place most of the blame for problems affecting intelligence activities not in use of the wrong approaches on the methods and tools, but rather in the lack of awareness of some of the fundamental concepts standing at the foundation of the regular analytic developments in intelligence. Therefore, the general objective of this exercise is the exploration of the conceptual area surrounding what seems to have become state of the art in the training of intelligence analysts. The specific objectives naturally unfold, being aimed at revealing the way in which the conceptual level triggers issues in the cooperation between intelligence producers (in the same institution and at community level), in the dialogue between intelligence consumers (decision and policymakers) and producers, and in the dialogue between intelligence consumers, producers, and the academy's representatives (the consultants).

Simulation Objectives

Being separated into three groups (decision makers, analysts, consultants), participants engage in the typical scenario that comes after a request for intelligence has been issued. Taking into account the specificity of the context as it is described by the facilitator (a revolutionary movement is about to break out in a neighboring country), each of the three groups has to produce what it knows best: a decision, an analysis report, and pieces of advice. There are many roles in each of the three groups, and the participants first have to obtain the results according to their role in a particular group and, second, contribute to that group's final product, when this is the case, by sharing their views with the others and through collaborative work.

Target Audience

Undergraduate or graduate students enrolled in a course that addresses issues of intelligence analysis and improvement in the functioning of the intelligence community.

Playing Time

At least 135 minutes. It is recommended to allocate three 45-minute class sessions to this exercise, taking into account the activities needed to set up the exercise and to pass through all the stages.

Debriefing Format

Using key questions, the instructor highlights the reasons behind each of the learning objectives, guiding the participants in reaching conclusions on the way in which the tasks have been completed. It is important that the instructor take into account the recommended reading list.

Debriefing Time

At least 45 minutes.

Number of Players Required

The participants are split into three groups, with two roles attached to each group. Therefore, it is recommended to start the exercise with a minimum of six persons; more than one participant can be assigned to a particular role in a group, yet there should be only one product (report) corresponding to a role.

Participation Materials Included

Each of the groups receives instructions concerning the activities to be performed and the expected outcomes; for each group, each of the corresponding roles is described in terms of the fundamental principles guiding the activities to be conducted by the participants.

Debriefing Materials Included

A list of references supporting the instructor with additional background information on the themes, subjects, and concepts to be employed during the debriefing stage.

Computer/Internet

Not required.

Other Materials/Equipment Required

The room should be large enough to allow each group to engage in debate, deliberation, and decision making without interfering with other groups. Since each group defines some distinct roles, the space should be further allocated to the particular roles.

EXERCISE: STEPS AND TIMING

Presimulation Briefing

The instructor informs the participants about the general objective of the exercise and gives them a description of the learning stages, underlining that the simulation is intended to deal with a process that takes place in the national security environment and that the case under consideration depicts a crisis in the international arena. Thus, each participant is reminded that the tasks of the exercise are intended to capture and address the complexity of real-world scenarios and that there are key questions to be asked at the end of the simulation, questions aimed at highlighting both principles and lessons to be learned. Therefore, participants are encouraged to pay attention not only to the details of the scenario but also to the way in which they make decisions when completing their tasks according to the role they have been assigned.

Exercise Step 1: Getting Organized (20 minutes)

1. The instructor reads in a loud voice the description of the scenario as it is depicted in Appendix A; each participant is given a copy of Appendix A.
2. The instructor reads in a loud voice the mission of each of the three groups to be formed: "Decision Makers," "Intelligence Analysts," and "Consultants." The instructor presents the list of roles attached to each group and the brief description for each role.
3. Participants are asked to join one of the three groups and to choose one of the existing roles. There can be more than one participant with the same role in a group. If this is the case, participants with the same role will act like a subgroup, reaching a common position, according to their mission. It is better to have the groups and subgroups distributed as much as possible in the room, so that each group's discussions will not interfere with those of the other groups.
4. Once the subgroups are formed and distributed in the room, participants are given a copy with the role description, according to their role. Therefore, each participant receives a copy of the scenario description, and there is at least one copy of the role description in each subgroup. See Appendices B through D for the roles' descriptions.

Exercise Step 2: Starting the Exercise (25 minutes)

The instructor invites the participants to assess the events, according to their group and role (subgroup in case there are more participants with the same role).

- *Decision makers* are called to come to a decision concerning the position to be taken by the government they are representing at the international level. Concerning the events under scrutiny, they have to draft a request for intelligence to the analysts. The request for intelligence (RFI) is defined as a list of three questions to be answered by the analysts. *At the end of this step, the decision makers will have assessed the situation, preparing an internal report on the events, and also an RFI.*

- *Intelligence analysts* are called to develop an assessment of the situation according to their role. *At the end of this step, the intelligence analysts will have assessed the situation and produced an internal report on the events, at the role-subgroup and at the group level. The group level report will be developed by the analysts whose role makes specific instructions on this task.*
- *Consultants* are called to deliver comments on the situation; they have to prepare a list of comments on the scenario, according to the role-subgroup. *At the end of this step, the consultants will have assessed the events and produced a report at the role-subgroup level (no group level report is needed).*

At the end of the allocated time, the instructor checks the completion of tasks: verifies that the decision makers and the intelligence analysts have produced group reports and that there are reports from each role-subgroup of consultants.

Exercise Step 3: Approaching Details (25 minutes)

The instructor invites:

- Decision makers to hand out their group's RFI to the subgroup of intelligence analysts whose role is to make specific instructions on this task.
- Consultants (randomly select a particular subgroup of consultants) to send their list of comments to the decision makers. Similarly, the instructor designates a subgroup of consultants (could be the same subgroup of consultants or a different one) to deliver comments to the designated subgroup of intelligence analysts.

Next, the instructor invites the participants to complete their tasks as follows:

- *Decision makers:* While waiting for the response to the RFI, the decision makers are called to continue the assessment of the situation based on the comments received from the consultants. There must be a dialogue between the subgroups of decision makers, as the role description establishes. *At the end of this step, the decision makers and the intelligence analysts will have completed reading and assessing the comments received from the consultants.*
- *Intelligence analysts:* They are called to respond to the RFI they received. There must be a dialogue between the subgroups of analysts, as the role description establishes. *At the end of this step, the designated subgroup of analysts (according to role description) will have digested the comments of the consultants and will have established a response to the RFI.*
- *Consultants:* They will choose a representative to support the delivery of the written report (just in case misunderstandings emerged when reading the comments). All the consultants will continue to assess the situation and add new comments to the existing ones. *At the end of this step, the consultants will have supported the other two groups when asked for support and will have extended the list of written comments on the developing events.*

At the end of the allocated time, the instructor checks the completion of tasks: verifies that the intelligence analysts prepared a response to the RFI, while the decision makers and the consultants extended previous results.

Exercise Step 4: Completing the Exercise (20 minutes)

The instructor asks the intelligence analysts to present their group's response to the RFI (actually, the subgroup of intelligence analysts whose role makes specific instructions on this task).

Next, the instructor invites:

- Decision makers to complete their final statement on the events, based on their previous draft and on the report received as feedback from the intelligence analysts. *At the end of this step, the decision makers will have completed an "official public statement" concerning the event.*
- Analysts and consultants will list five key points concerning the possible pitfalls in their activity. *At the end of this step, both the analysts and the consultants will have prepared a list of possible pitfalls.*

At the end of the allocated time, the instructor asks the intelligence analysts and the consultants to deliver the list of possible pitfalls and invites the decision makers to deliver the "official public statement" on the events.

Figure 5.1 summarizes the activities that have occurred during the simulation.

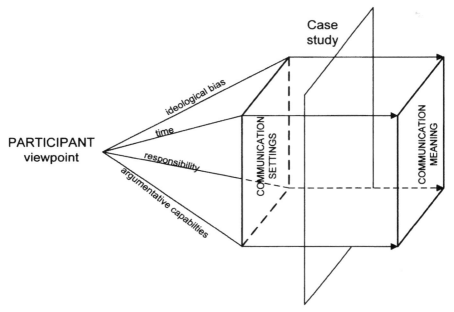

Figure 5.1. Four-Dimensional Mapping

DEBRIEFING

Objectives

The exercise is aimed at revealing the way in which the conceptual and institutional levels trigger issues in the cooperation between intelligence producers (in the same institution and at community level), in the dialogue between intelligence consumers (decision and policymakers) and producers, and in the dialogue between intelligence consumers, producers, and the academy's representatives. Thus conceived, it is assumed that the exercise could shed light on an intelligence analyst's intellectual and professional development paths. The four-dimensional map (time, responsibility, argumentative capability, ideological bias) serves as a projection space for the questions to be answered during debriefing (as seen in Figure 5.1).

There are two directions of investigation:

1. Communication settings: The scenario defines a *particular protocol of communication* between the participants, precisely establishing "Who (says) What (to) Whom (in) What Channel." The debriefing tackles the consequences that a particular communication protocol might have on the effectiveness and efficiency of the intelligence community and its members. It offers the participants an example of why such evaluations are needed periodically, at the personal and organizational levels, always questioning the status quo for the betterment of the ensemble.
2. Communication meaning: The scenario defines a *particular case study*, centered on a revolutionary moment characterized by a huge amount of risk, uncertainty, and ignorance. The debriefing is aimed at questioning the "What and What Effect," more the meaning and less the setting of communication. In such a context, the chosen four-dimensional map becomes a key for the assessment of the participants in terms of decisions they made and the intelligence and consultancy produced. It is a viewpoint aimed at revealing to the future knowledge worker or intelligence analyst the specificity of his or her activity.

This exercise is summarized in Table 5.1.

Debriefing Communication Settings

This exercise is based on the assumption that the event being analyzed is not radically unfolding while the protocol of communication between the participants takes place. Noticing this rather static approach, we analyze the protocol of communication by taking into account the four dimensions.

Time

The time frame of the exercise was defined by the particular sequence of communication activities between the participating entities. Outside the classroom, the timing and the associated communication protocols are defined by the existing written legal frame-

Table 5.1. Summary of Activities

		GROUPS		
STEP	TIME	Decision Makers	Intelligence Analysts	Consultants
1.	20 m	• Establish group • Assign roles, define subgroups	• Establish group • Assign roles, define subgroups	• Establish group • Assign roles, define subgroups
2.	25 m	• Draft report—situation assessment • Prepare and issue request for intelligence (RFI)	• Prepare report at subgroup level • Prepare report at group level	• Prepare consultancy report at subgroup level
3.	25 m	• Have an internal debate on the consultancy received	• Prepare a response to the RFI	• Deliver consultancy • Extend consultancy report at subgroup level
4.	20 m	• Prepare and deliver the official public statement on the events	• List five key points concerning the possible pitfalls in their activity	• List five key points concerning the possible pitfalls in their activity

work and by the norms that the members of the intelligence community are expected and systemically conditioned to follow. From this point of view, the debriefing is aimed at strengthening participants' reflexes toward questioning not only their own position in the timing mechanism but also the timing mechanism per se and the ensuing communication protocol. Sample questions:

- As a decision maker, you started the exercise by issuing an RFI when facing decision making. Name a topic on which you would have performed differently if intelligence early warnings on the case under scrutiny had been available before you issued the RFI.
- As an intelligence analyst in the exercise, when do you think you needed scientific consultancy: prior, during, or after an intelligence report development?
- What do you think about the reasons behind the randomness in the procedure aimed at selecting the consultant who delivers advice to decision makers?

Responsibility

The exercise makes specific instructions concerning participants' roles during the simulation: not only *when* (the time axis) but also *what is to be done* in the selected scenario. This approach mimics the democratization and bureaucratization of the modern intelligence communities. Even though a comprehensive definition of individual and collective responsibility in our modern democracies is still an open problem for social scientists and philosophers alike, the debriefing is aimed at revealing participants' compliance with the established rules of the exercise and thus the responsibility toward the settings of professional activity. Sample questions:

- How do you appreciate the description of the role you were assigned: Did it give you the necessary and sufficient amount of information on the tasks you had to complete?
- How would you change the description of your role to better approach your tasks?
- Is there an additional role you find necessary in the exercise? If your answer is positive, list the tasks that would be attached to the new role, for the better coverage of the case study.

Ideological Bias

This exercise was developed as an algorithmic sequence of activities within a fixed time frame to enforce specific educational goals. In this endeavor, we have left aside any personal ideological preferences that could have impacted the scenario modeling. In democratic institutional settings, the plurality of values and belief systems must be sustained and constrained through various checks and balances. From this point of view, the debriefing is aimed at questioning the way in which the proposed scenario could be altered, in terms of the communication settings, by ideological biases. Sample questions:

- Would the proposed communication protocol be altered if the intelligence services were supporting the ruling coalition or the opposition?
- How might communication in the group of analysts be affected if the covert agent, trained during the Cold War period, did not turn into a supporter of the open source intelligence paradigm?
- Which criteria are used when selecting a political consultant?

Argumentative Capabilities

Gathering evidence, constructing arguments, and making decisions are just some of the tasks a person routinely performs. The proposed simulation lists evidence and specifies the number of concluding remarks to be drawn by each of the individuals/roles involved in the exercise. For educational purposes, the pieces of the puzzle fit together to form a complete picture of the event, a situation that is not often available in intelligence affairs. From this point of view, the debriefing is aimed at outlining the way in which the exercise favors the gathering of evidence. Sample questions:

- How did you obtain the piece of evidence (piece of information) that proved to be decisive in shaping your approach to the case study: Was it the result of the intergroup communication or did it emerge out of the intragroup debates?
- Did you receive contradictory (mutually excluding pieces of evidence) or conflicting (pieces of evidence that can occur jointly but favor different possibilities) pieces of evidence from the other participants?
- As an intelligence analyst, please attach the "Need to Know" or the "Need to Share" labels to the pieces of evidence you own, according to the way in which you

think these pieces of evidence should be managed. How would the communication protocol be changed due to the labeling?

Debriefing Communication Meaning

Managing the tasks of the exercise, the participants exchange content (requests, reports, and decisions) and meaning based on the established communication protocol. On the same four dimensions, both participants' efforts in content production and the emergence of meaning were analyzed, thus enhancing the underlying richness of the conceptual framework supporting the exercise.

Time

Within the established time frame (*after* violent social movements challenged the regime in Great Frusina; *before* the international community took a stand), the participants are called to make decisions specific to their role. First, the debriefing has to enhance the difference between retrodiction and prediction, as both of these probabilistic activities are fundamental in decision making. The revolutionary event is considered the most appropriate scenario not only because there is a vast literature specifically addressing retrodiction and prediction in relation to revolutionary movements, but also due to its strong interaction with human perception ("war" is another concept/phenomenon that triggers strong human reactions). Second, the debriefing has to make participants aware of the different segmentation of time (a spatial viewpoint on time) by decision makers, intelligence practitioners, and scientists. Sample questions:

- Is it true that the available background information supports retrodiction more than prediction?
- As an analyst, could you select two pieces of intelligence specifically adding insight to your predictive goals in this exercise?
- As a politician and decision maker, would you have acted differently if the electoral campaign had not been approaching?
- To what degree do the participants agree that, because of time constraints, scientific analysis is not always possible?

Responsibility

For the established roles, the scenario defines various decision-making alternatives. The debriefing has to reveal these alternatives, emphasizing the differences between the *grand responsibility* associated with a group of participants and the responsibility as it is projected in each and every circumstance (a condition or fact that determines or must be considered in determining of a course of action). Thus, the debriefing is aimed at revealing the mechanism that projects the *grand responsibility along the course of action*, when approaching it from the position of a particular role in the revolutionary scenario under scrutiny. Sample questions:

- As decision makers/analysts/consultants, define your *grand responsibility* (group level).
- As intelligence analyst/decision maker/consultant, name two facts/conditions in your role description (among tasks to be performed, case study specific information) you have evaluated during the exercise by making reference to your grand responsibility (role level).
- List two topics specific to the way in which a revolutionary event challenges your grand responsibility (group level).

Ideological Bias

The roles were defined to emphasize the *potential for ideological bias,* understood as the result of the vast human value and belief systems, which are dependent on the cultural, educational, and professional frameworks in which an individual is embedded. The debriefing is aimed at revealing whether *this potential ideological bias came into actuality,* manifested during the exercise, perhaps affecting the course of action. Sample questions:

- Name the main item in the role description that fundamentally shaped your arguments when completing the associated tasks. Is this item in contradiction to your personal values and beliefs?
- Is there a role that might match your profile better than the role you had during the exercise?
- When writing your report, how did you manage the use of the particular vocabulary specific to your role description?

Argumentative Capabilities

A revolutionary moment includes a huge amount of risks, uncertainty, and ignorance. The classic definitions associate revolutions more with physical violence and bloodshed and less with the complexity of argumentation employed in the context. This exercise places participants in relation to a presumably revolutionary context and asks for arguments and decisions that might eventually interfere with the unfolding of the events. The debriefing is aimed at revealing the concept of relevance and the idea that information/knowledge/intelligence/evidence is relevant if it has some force in allowing us to change our beliefs during a particular inference task, in a well-defined context. Sample questions:

- You are an intelligence analyst. Order the available pieces of evidence by their force in supporting/rejecting the idea of a revolutionary event. Which of these pieces of evidence would not have been of any interest if the hypothesis of a revolution were not present?
- You are a decision maker. Which of your line items in the final public statements on the event are aimed at the internal context (the coming elections) and which are aimed at the international context (the social unrest in Great Frusina)?

• You are a consultant. Name the pieces of evidence that led you to consider that your abstract model of reasoning (as it is described in your role description) is suited to the context under scrutiny.

CONCLUSION

This exercise is aimed at extending participants' exposure to the world of intelligence affairs through role playing and a particular defined scenario of revolutionary context. A revolution has never been an easy case, neither for those directly involved in the unfolding of the events nor for the social scientists trying to understand them through explanation or prediction. An intelligence analyst is confronted with both of these worlds—the mundane world of practice (experiment) and the high realm of thought (theory). First, intelligence is rooted in tradition, the second-oldest practice in the world one would say. Second, intelligence analysis developed a special connectivity with social sciences since Sherman Kent (1949) laid out an agenda for the development of U.S. intelligence analysis after World War II. More than a half century later, the Kent–Kendall debate (Davis, 2007) is still of high actuality, reverberating throughout this exercise.

This exercise is also aimed at placing the participants in direct contact with some of the open problems currently challenging intelligence studies. The instructor and the participants are called to operate in a conceptual space, with much of the conceptual entities and limits being defined in other social sciences and domains of research, which reflects the plight of intelligence analysts and intelligence studies academics (nevertheless a challenging situation). This is not an easy task, as these domains have their own struggles to define concepts in such a way as to avoid the endless recurrence of inquiries and to assist in the accumulation of scientific knowledge.

A safeguard could be the fact that "most intelligence community (IC) analysts do not learn their trade primarily from books, training manuals, or courses but rather 'in the heat of the shop floor,' under the supervision of experienced managers and mentors" (George & Bruce, 2008, p. 213). This exercise draws on findings in learning theory and sets the foundation for a project aimed at exploring the process of *concept formation* in intelligence analysis (a process deemed not only relevant for practice but also for training and education in this particular area).

APPENDIX A: GREAT FRUSINA

Overview

Great Frusina is one of the countries neighboring the state you are representing. Starting a week ago, large and violent popular uprisings (demonstrations, marches, acts of civil disobedience, and labor strikes) have been taking place in the capital and other important cities of Great Frusina. While protesters of all socioeconomic, ethnic, and religious backgrounds are asking for the immediate demise of the incumbent president and for free elections, the state security services have been responding with force, protecting city halls and state institutions and the current authoritarian regime. The situation could escalate in unpredictable ways.

Contextual Information

1. The winter has just arrived in your region; temperatures will drastically drop in the coming 3 months; snowstorms are part of the forecast and a regular phenomenon in this part of the year.
2. Great Frusina is an important exporter of fossil fuels and provides most of the energy resources that your country's economy needs, especially during the winter season.
3. Economic realism has always been the key to the political and economic relationships your country has developed with Great Frusina. During the current term, the ruling coalition in your country signed important economic agreements with the regime in Great Frusina concerning not only the import of fossil fuels but also exports of industrial and high-tech products from your country to Great Frusina.
4. Economic realism helped you to deal with the endemic corruption in Great Frusina and the vast network of patronage backed by the incumbent president.
5. In Great Frusina's border region, once part of your country, a minority of inhabitants have the same ethnic roots as the inhabitants of your country. Due to the good economic relations developed over time with Great Frusina, your country has succeeded in providing this minority with fair treatment from the authoritarian regime in Great Frusina.
6. In a rush of exuberance, the authoritarian leader of Great Frusina has recently declared his admiration for your country. According to the latest polls, the public opinion in your country responded favorably to his statement; a majority of people in your country do not consider him a threat to regional stability.
7. In your democratic country, free elections are scheduled for the coming spring; the electoral campaign will start in a few weeks.
8. The international community has always supported your country's political role in the region and favored mediated meetings with Great Frusina's authoritarian regime when addressing human rights or democratic development issues.
9. Your ambassador to the United Nations announced through diplomatic channels that the situation in Great Frusina is under international scrutiny and that there are voices unofficially asking for United Nations sanctions and a possible military intervention in Great Frusina.

APPENDIX B: DECISION MAKERS

Mission

As members of the ruling coalition in your country and part of the executive, you are decision makers in this case. Preparing for the elections to come and willing to run for reelection, you have to manage the worsening crisis in Great Frusina, which is threatening to trouble internal, regional, and international politics. Unfortunately, this issue emerges as the main point on your coalition and executive agenda at the end of a successful mandate. The opposition is willing to play upon the subject, and each of your decisions could turn against you in the electoral campaign that is about to begin. Internally, the Greens could turn your decisions into leverage for the opposition, exploiting your possible line of arguments based on energy security. Regionally, the possibility of a mass movement of refugees from Great Frusina should be taken into account. At the international level, a resolution of the UN Security Council concerning Great Frusina is expected soon. As a nonpermanent member of the Security Council, you have a vote but not the right to veto (preventing the adoption of a proposal no matter the number of affirmative votes).

Chief of the Executive

You are the chief of the executive and the principal representative of your country in international settings.

Tasks

You are called to deliver a public statement on the unfolding events, addressing the following issues:

1. The popular uprising in Great Frusina as the media talks about the "revolution in Great Frusina."
2. Your country's position on the events, by taking into account internal, regional, and international constraints and interests for yourself and your country.

Instructions

1. Good decisions will bring you reelection.
2. Formulate your statement using five phrases, at most.
3. Ask for any piece of advice and intelligence you may find useful in covering the issue; the consultants and the representative of the intelligence community (the intelligence analysts) are ready to help you.

Minister of Energy

You are the chief of the Ministry of Energy and directly involved in any revision to your country's energy strategy. During your term of office, you have supported a project aimed at identifying alternative sources of fossil fuels in the regional and global market, while strengthening "green" public and private initiatives in energy production.

Tasks

You are required to prepare a report concerning your area of activity. Energy security issues are the main topics as possible fluctuations in fossil fuels imports from Great Frusina may appear.

Instructions

1. Good decisions will support the chief of the executive and your position in the government to be established after the elections.
2. Formulate your position statement using three phrases, at most.
3. Ask for any piece of advice and intelligence you may find useful; the consultants and the representative of the intelligence community (the intelligence analysts) are ready to help you.

APPENDIX C: INTELLIGENCE ANALYSTS

Mission

Your mission is to support the decision makers by providing them with valuable intelligence while serving with integrity the national intelligence system as an intelligence analyst or covert agent.

Intelligence Analyst

You have completed your training as an open source intelligence analyst, in addition to your bachelor's degree in political science. You have joined your country's Central Office for Open Source Intelligence after picking up all important security clearances. Your job is to add value to collection, processing, and analysis; you also fuse intelligence reporting by the other intelligence units into a single product. As a proof of your capabilities, most of the reports your superiors send to decision makers are based on the results of your assessments, on your daily work. The unfolding events in Great Frusina are part of a scenario you have been following for a couple of months. Based on the multisource capabilities of the office, the existing early warning system started to record information on this scenario more than a year ago. Some pieces of information recorded in the early warning system are available below:

- A newly developed oil pipeline and dedicated refineries started production in the region. Great Frusina lost some of its traditional markets. There were public statements regarding the authoritarian position adopted by Great Frusina's vocal president during negotiations concerning the development of the regional pipeline.
- A couple of tycoons in Great Frusina decided to restructure their businesses, closing production lines from various industries, including some media outlets. Some

argued that these actions were the result of the global financial crisis, while others pointed out the particular financial problems in Great Frusina as the likely cause.

- The media reported on a number of recent acquisitions by rich citizens of Great Frusina in the luxury real estate markets in London and Paris.
- A couple of foreign diplomatic representatives talked about people igniting themselves in front of police stations in the poorest region of Great Frusina to protest for the terrible living conditions and the lack of qualified medical assistance.
- A concert at the Opera City Concert Hall in Great Frusina was interrupted when one of the spectators started to sing a traditional revolutionary song directed at corruption, scarcity of goods among the people, and blaming the "the crazy buffoon" in Great Frusina for this situation. Part of the audience applauded this brazen instance of civil disobedience.

Tasks

Prepare and deliver an intelligence report concerning the general context of the events in Great Frusina.

Instructions

1. Take into account the details listed above, the content, and the goals of the decision makers' request for intelligence.
2. Issue a need-to-know request for other intelligence colleagues, if needed, and fuse their responses into the final intelligence report.
3. Conceive your response using five phrases, at most.

Covert Intelligence Agent

You completed your training in intelligence operations during the Cold War period, being directly involved in undercover operations in most of the countries in the region. Your degree in architecture, your linguistic abilities, and a good background in the region's historical and cultural developments have helped you establish a network of contacts as you traveled and worked in various construction sites all over the region. You were involved in the development of important oil terminals and other public and private infrastructure projects in the region. As a senior covert intelligence agent, approaching retirement, you are still engaged in covert intelligence collection, regularly providing reports on particular subjects in the region. You favor an open source intelligence approach since you started to support the intelligence services.

Concerning the situation in Great Frusina, some pieces of information you gathered from your contacts are available below. You have checked the information, fusing evidence from many sources; as a result, you believe that the information below has a high degree of certainty.

- The important oil pipeline to be developed in the region was originally designed to cross Great Frusina. However, the hard line adopted by Great Frusina's president during the initial closed-door project negotiations led to a deadlock, as he conditioned Great Frusina's participation on his personal patronage of the project, infuriating the others. Finally, the plans were redesigned so that the pipeline would not cross Great Frusina.
- In retaliation, Great Frusina was confronted with a loss of its traditional regional markets and it incurred direct financial and economic consequences.
- A few important business owners in Great Frusina question their president's strange mental condition and ask for a change, even though they do not seem to criticize the authoritarian regime—only the president.
- In a private message received from one of your old-time friends in Great Frusina's army, you learn: "The great dam shows signs of erosion more than ever before, and I don't know if the army is going to cement it anymore."

Tasks

Prepare and deliver an intelligence briefing on the general context of the events in Great Frusina.

Instructions

1. Take into account the details in the role description above.
2. Take into account the content and goals of the request for support, and any *need-to-know request* issued by the other analysts.
3. Conceive your response using three phrases, at most.

APPENDIX D: CONSULTANTS

Mission

Your mission is to offer expert advice according to your professional background, as a representative of the academy or as a representative of the corporate world.

Academic Consultant

As an academic representative, you favor scientific arguments, according to your intellectual and professional background (professor). You have been previously engaged in research projects addressing the study of revolutionary movements. You are one of those academics who value the scientific truth more than anything, always ready to engage in a research project to cast light on unanswered questions and to retest available results. Based on your wide knowledge in the area of social movements, you consider that the study of revolutions remains much like the study of earthquakes. The next one that occurs still surprises everybody.

Considering revolutions, you are seen as a structural theorist; you try to avoid both narrow definitions of revolutions (comparing social movements with the great revolutions of the past, searching for regularities and similitude) and wide ones (comparing social movements with more than just a few great revolutions of the past and trying to establish a theory of collective political violence). As a structural theorist of revolutions, you consider that:

- There are states that have a political structure more likely to fail: states that are centralized, seeking not only to extract resources from the society but also to permeate it, to reconstruct it symbolically, and to mobilize it. Such states maintain elite monopolized political institutions.
- One particular case is represented by those states that have a structure with a high degree of patronage: the chief executive maintains power through an informal system of personal rewards and patronage, reaching people in all the institutions, including the military.
- In case of an economic downturn affecting the entire society but especially the flow of resources from the top chief executive to the pillars supporting the regime, a contestation of the status quo is likely to occur.
- The leaders of the contestation movement generally aim first at replacing the chief executive. The systemic change is less likely to occur in the short term, even though the popular uprisings ask for such changes and the complete renewal of the political system.

Tasks

You provide consultancy services, when asked for them.

Instructions

1. Take into account the details of your role description.
2. Take into account the content and goals of the request for consultancy service.
3. Conceive your response using three phrases, at most.

Senior General Manager

You are a retired general manager, having a background in economics and management. You act as a senior consultant in the energy security area, after leading for more than two decades one of the largest gas and oil companies in the region. In addition to a very good understanding of the global energy market, you have gained a deep understanding of the social and political landscape in the region. Most of your reasoning tools have roots in economics, while your viewpoints usually emerge in terms of costs and benefits. Yet, during your years in service, you have become familiar with the dismal record of prediction in social and political contexts, as surprises are unavoidable.

You are inclined to consider that, on any given issue, a person has a private preference and a public preference (what is revealed to others). Individuals engage in preference falsification whenever the costs of participation in a particular cause seem to be much higher than the expected benefits. Thus, a society could be on the verge of a revolution even if its members claim it is quite stable. On the other side, even if a political regime is shaking under popular pressure and there are elites supporting such social movement, it is difficult to have a clear understanding of the elites' intentions toward the toppled regime's inner principles.

As a trained economist, you are aware that, when economists predict a rise in unemployment, they may contribute to a recession that would not have emerged if they had kept silent. This sort of situation always reminds you that social predictions may interact with the phenomena they predict.

Tasks

You provide consultancy services, when asked for it.

Instructions

1. Take into account the details in the role description.
2. Take into account the content and goals of the request for consultancy service.
3. Conceive your response using three phrases, at most.

APPENDIX E: SUPPORT FOR DEBRIEFING

The simulation is defined as a laboratory in which the participants use various concepts as operating tools. A participant's performance should not be assessed by taking into account the way in which he or she deals with the theoretical background employed when developing the tools of the laboratory, but rather should be judged by his or her versatility during daily operating procedures, when conducting experiments with the tools, according to their operating manuals, and adherence to instructions. It is up to the instructor to reveal to the participants various facets of the historical and philosophical background of the concepts under scrutiny in such a way that participants succeed in "operating" the concepts, according to their role. A list of supporting references is provided to assist instructors to perform this role. One could note that we did not choose references from a particular domain, but instead approached ideas in philosophy, sociology, political science, economy, history, and law. It is the goal of academic intelligence studies to *adapt* concepts to contexts where intelligence issues arise.

NOTE

1. For example, the U.S. senators questioned intelligence agencies' anticipation of the Egypt uprising, with the principal deputy director of the Office of Director of National Intelligence, Stephanie O'Sullivan, asserting that the intelligence community

warned of instability in Egypt without knowing precisely the "triggering mechanism" (Miller, 2011).

SUPPORTING REFERENCES

Time

Ancona, Deborah G., Okhuysen, Gerardo A., & Perlow, Leslie A. 2001. Taking time to integrate temporal research. *Academy of Management Review, 26*(4), 512–529.
Shackle, G. L. S. 1959. Time and thought. *British Journal for the Philosophy of Science, 9*(36), 285–298.

Responsibility

Garrath, William. Responsibility. Internet Encyclopedia of Philosophy. Available at: www.iep .utm.edu/responsi/.
Giddens, Anthony. 1999. Risk and responsibility. *Modern Law Review, 62*(1),1–10.

Ideological Bias

Herzon, F. D. 1980. Ideology, constraint, and public opinion: The case of lawyers. *American Journal of Political Science, 24*(2), 233–258.
Sartori, Giovanni. 1969. Politics, ideology, and belief systems. *American Political Science Review, 63*(2), 398–411.

Argumentative Capabilities

Anderson, T., Schum, D., & Twining, W. 2005. Evidence and inference, some food for thought. In *Analysis of evidence.* Cambridge: Cambridge University Press.
Salmon, Wesley C. 1989. *Four decades of scientific explanation.* Pittsburgh, PA: University of Pittsburgh University Press.
Schum, D. A. 1987. *Evidence and inference for the intelligence analyst* (2 vols.). Lanham, MD: University Press of America.

Retrodiction and Prediction

Veyne, Paul. 1984. Causality and retrodiction. In *Writing history: Essay on epistemology.* Middletown, CT: Wesleyan University Press.

Revolutions

Goldstone, Jack. 2001. Toward a fourth generation of revolutionary theory. *Annual Review of Political Science, 4,* 139–187.
Kuran, T. 1995. The inevitability of future revolutionary surprises. *American Journal of Sociology, 100*(6), 1528–1551.

REFERENCES

Davis, J. 2007. The Kent–Kendall debate of 1949. *Studies in Intelligence, 35*(2), 91–103.

Davis, Paul K. 2012. *Lessons from RAND's work on planning under uncertainty for national security.* Santa Barbara, CA: Rand National Defense Research Institute.

Gagné, R. M., & Driscoll, M. P. 2008. *Essentials of learning for instruction* (2nd ed.). Upper Saddle River, NJ: Prentice-Hall.

George, R. Z., & Bruce, J. B. (Eds.). 2008. *Analyzing intelligence: Origins, obstacles, and innovations.* Washington, DC: Georgetown University Press.

Kent, Sherman. 1949. *Strategic intelligence for American world policy.* Princeton, NJ: Princeton University Press.

Miller, Greg. 2011. Senators question intelligence agencies' anticipation of Egypt uprising. *Washington Post.* Available at: www.washingtonpost.com/wp-dyn/content/article/2011/02/03/AR2011020305388.html.

6

Kim's Game: Developing Powers of Observation and Memory

William J. Lahneman

No volume of this kind would be complete without including Kim's Game among its offerings. Kim's Game is an enjoyable way for participants to assess their own powers of observation, their short-term memory capabilities, and their retention of information while giving them the opportunity to compare their own performance to that of their classmates in a noncompetitive setting. By playing Kim's Game several times over the course of a term, participants have the opportunity to improve their performance in these areas. All of these traits are important and valuable skills not only for intelligence professionals but also for anyone whose job requires a need for attention to detail and retention of facts. The game only takes about 10 minutes to play.

Kim's Game takes its name from Rudyard Kipling's 1901 novel *Kim*, in which the hero, Kim, plays the game as part of his training to become a spy.[1] An excerpt from the 1950 film *Kim* is available on YouTube[2] and is useful for demonstrating to students how the game is played. Electronic versions of the game are available for purchase.

INSTRUCTIONS

1. The instructor assembles a number of small objects, places them together on a table or some other kind of flat surface, and then covers them so that students cannot see them. An alternative approach is to photograph a collection of objects—or select any photograph that displays several objects—and display the photograph on a classroom projector or document camera. This obviates the need to carry the objects to and from class. NOTE: The U.S. Army Sniper School uses a variation on Kim's Game to train their snipers' ability to pick out anomalous details

in their surroundings. This is clearly an essential skill for any human intelligence operative. Accordingly, one variation of the game that would apply to intelligence courses would be to use a photograph of some location that possesses many details in place of a collection of small objects.

2. The instructor briefs the class that they are going to view several objects, and students must try to remember as many of them as possible. They cannot write anything down or document what they see in any way, but rather must rely exclusively on their memories. If the instructor is using a photograph of a location in place of the small objects, then students should be instructed to remember as many details about the location as possible.

3. The instructor uncovers the objects (or displays the photograph) and gives the students some set amount of time before covering them again. For example, "they would put different objects on the table: a bullet, a paper clip, a bottle top, a pen, a piece of paper with something written on it—10 to 20 items. You'd gather around and they'd give you, say, a minute to look at everything. Then you'd have to go back to your table and describe what you saw. You weren't allowed to say 'paper clip' or 'bullet,' you'd have to say, like, 'silver, metal wire, bent in two oval shapes.' They want the Intel guys making the decision [about] what you actually saw" (U.S. Army Ranger, recounting how the game is played at Sniper School [Valdez, 2013]).

4. After the objects (or photograph) are no longer in view, the instructor requires students to write down as many of the objects (or location details) they can recall. If the game is being run multiple times over the course of a term as a way to improve students' memories and powers of observation, the instructor can vary the time that objects are exposed for viewing as well as the time period before students are asked to write down what they remember. For instance, at the beginning of the term, students should list what they have seen immediately following the viewing of objects. As the term goes on and additional rounds of the game are played, the instructor can increase the number of objects on the table and increase the time period between when students view the objects and when they write down what they have seen.

CONCLUSION

Kim's Game is a proven way to give students an opportunity to assess their memories and powers of observation, including their attention to detail. The game is fun to play and does not take up much class time. Repeated playing of the game allows students to improve their performance in these areas.

NOTES

1. See the Wikipedia site on Kim's Game for more background information. http://en.wikipedia .org/wiki/Kim's_Game.

2. www.youtube.com/watch?v=0uVKSK818bI.

REFERENCE

Valdez, Robert. 2013. How military snipers work. Available at: http://science.howstuffworks.com/ sniper10.htm.

Part II

ONE- TO TWO-WEEK SIMULATIONS

7

Cyber Attack on the Office of Intelligence Production: A Collaborative Simulation

Randolph H. Pherson and Vaughn F. Bishop

ABSTRACT

This simulation, called CyberSIM, is designed for students who are working in large organizations to help them learn how to communicate and collaborate more effectively with their peers in other offices or agencies. The primary objective of CyberSIM is to explore the key components of collaborative behavior and practice building more robust collaborative systems. The simulation also helps students develop more effective interpersonal communication skills by forcing them to determine which functions are most and least valued within their organization. Students make these decisions by working collaboratively in groups comprising representatives from all the various parts of their organization.

CyberSIM assumes that most large organizations have stovepipes that work largely autonomously and that those working in each stovepipe believe their function is one of the most, if not the most, critical function of their organization. The simulation gives students a better understanding of what other parts of their organization do every day and the value each part contributes to the overall mission performance. Students also learn more effective means of communicating with their peers and how best to fashion a truly collaborative work environment.

The simulation takes a full day to conduct and requires little preparation by instructors and participants. It is a valuable addition to courses on the intelligence process, organizational behavior, collaboration, and interpersonal communication. It is most effective when the students are drawn from various parts of a large intelligence organization or government bureaucracy that handles sensitive information. It can also be modified for use with a large business or major academic institution. The simulation is targeted at the general workforce but can easily be modified as a tool to teach managers how to improve communication and collaboration within their organizations.

KEYWORDS

Collaboration; interpersonal communication; small group dynamics; intelligence production; intelligence process; cyber; critical infrastructure; organizational behavior; stovepipes; out-of-the-box thinking; mutual trust; mutual benefit; mission criticality; incentives; access and agility; common understanding; common lexicon

Most large intelligence organizations are divided into units that perform different but equally critical functions such as collection, information processing, analysis, research and development, information technology (IT), and logistic support. Similar patterns are often mirrored in the commercial world in companies with different divisions for manufacturing, sales, marketing, human resources, IT, and administrative support. In academia, the workforce is usually divided according to various disciplines, schools, or programs as well as recruiting, alumni relations, IT, and administrative support. In most large organizations, workers know a lot about what colleagues in their units are doing but often little about work being done in other parts of the organization. All assume that the role their unit plays is vital to the overall performance of their core mission and that their unit's contribution is often underappreciated by those in other parts of the organization.

In the intelligence world, much the same pattern applies at the interagency level. In the United States, the director of national intelligence oversees the work of 16 different agencies, with each making a unique contribution to the overall mission of protecting U.S. national interests. In the United Kingdom, intelligence functions also are performed by many different organizations including MI-5, MI-6, the Cabinet Office, Government Communications Headquarters (GCHQ), and the Ministry of Defence. In order to perform their mission well, it is essential in both the United States and the United Kingdom that these different agencies share their information and work collaboratively to address national security concerns.

This dynamic is not unique to intelligence. Particularly in these times of shrinking budgets, the key components of any intelligence community, large corporation, or university must learn how to do more with less. The world is becoming more globalized and the challenges more complex, but resources are diminishing and difficult trade-offs will increasingly be required to optimize productivity—or even simply to stay afloat. Stovepipes are no longer inviolate; CyberSIM was designed to show the growing need for workers to understand how they and their particular unit fit into the broader scheme. This requires effective communication across the stovepipes at the personal, organizational, and even interagency levels.

IMPROVING COMMUNICATION

An inescapable reality in almost every large organization is the meeting. Some organizations—mostly in the private sector where time is money—have perfected the skill of holding effective meetings, but far more organizations fail miserably at this task. Key characteristics of poor meetings are that they lack focus, have no clear agenda, have the wrong mix of people, lack leadership, shift focus to tangential topics, generate no final decision or product, and require no follow-through. A good meeting, on the other hand, has a clear purpose, maintains its focus, and generates an actionable product. Attendees know why they are meeting, come prepared with ideas, share the same expectations, work collaboratively, contribute appropriately, and are mutually accountable for the results. CyberSIM is designed to help instill these good work habits for conducting meetings in all participants.[1]

An even greater challenge than learning how to hold effective meetings is to learn how to create robust collaborative environments (Figure 7.1). Extensive research conducted in the U.S. intelligence community suggests that the key to establishing a robust collaborative environment lies primarily in focusing attention on human factors—not IT systems.[2] Collaboration is fundamentally about behaviors and interactions among individuals working toward a common objective enabled by technology, organizational policies, and underlying cultural norms. The rapid growth of social networks is creating new opportunities for more effective collaboration but also poses some obstacles.[3]

- The correct nexus for collaboration is the human interface with other minds, not the human interface with IT.
- Robust social networks serve as an essential underpinning of collaboration and ensure that communities can come together to put more eyes on the target, promote analytic excellence, and facilitate informed decision making.
- Achieving a robust collaborative environment requires sustained commitment on the part of the senior leadership.

The obstacles—cultural, structural, and managerial—in institutionalizing collaborative practices across a diversity of cultures run much deeper and go to the heart of how

---

Why Do We Need to Collaborate?

• In today's increasingly complex and interdependent world, no one person or organization has a monopoly on what is needed to get the job done.

• Expertise is increasingly distributed as the boundaries between analysts, collectors, and operators become ever more blurred.

• In organizations with a relatively inexperienced workforce, the need to connect new officers with more experienced experts is a critical need.

• It is more efficient to engage the full spectrum of key players at the start of a project and to generate consensus on how to proceed than to wait until the end of the process and fight over what is right.

Figure 7.1. The Need for Collaboration

the community has traditionally conducted its affairs. Although technology is an important multiplier in promoting better collaboration, collaboration is unlikely to become embedded in the operating culture until work processes take advantage of its potential power. Senior leaders need to demonstrate their support for collaboration by "walking the walk" if they "talk the talk." More important, senior leaders must empower their workforce to integrate collaborative work processes into daily work, hold subordinates accountable for fostering analytic transformation, and accept or even encourage the risk inherent in change.

Successful, sustained collaboration is most likely to occur when members foster a collaborative environment that promotes positive participation. The following characteristics, which we have dubbed the Six Imperatives, are key to creating and sustaining such an environment.

Mission Criticality

Members of a collaborative community must see their participation as essential to their core activities and not as a "nice-to-have" activity or as a resource to exploit when they have extra time. For example, if several organizations decide to collaborate in creating a joint database, the data should only reside in the shared space; no one should enter data into their "home system" and then enter it again into a "shared" database.

Mutual Benefit

Participants must derive benefits from one another's knowledge and expertise in ways that help them perform their missions. They must recognize that they will not succeed—or their product will be inferior—if they work alone. Participants should possess a shared sense of mission and articulate a common set of goals and objectives for the "collective good."

Mutual Trust

True collaboration is a personal process that requires the willingness to share partly formed opinions and insights, risk being wrong, and adopt new collaborative business practices. For these reasons, people feel the need to trust those with whom they collaborate. A good way to develop such trust is to organize face-to-face meetings. As trust develops, participants become more willing to engage in collaborative behavior.

Incentives

Collaborative work practices must save participants time over the long run and increase the impact of their analysis. The most important, and often overlooked, incentive for collaborating is the psychic reward that comes from solving a hard problem, making a unique contribution, or contributing a profound insight. Effective collaboration at the start of a project almost always leads to faster coordination at the end.

Access and Agility

Collaboration requires that users be able to quickly connect with one another and, given the pace of world events, coalesce into virtual work groups or add new members to their group within hours, if not minutes. Policies and collaboration tools must enable innovation, "public" thinking, broad dissemination, and the tracking of information sources, but also permit compartmented and confidential small group collaborations. Achieving the necessary degree of agility requires business processes that foster the organic shaping and reshaping of collaborative communities.

One innovative approach is to establish "trust bubbles" comprised of interlocking cells of six to eight colleagues. A high level of trust is easier to maintain in such small cells. Individuals who belong to two or three cells are much more efficient human sharers of information. They know exactly how much information their colleagues can absorb when transferring information or insights from one group to the other. They also know what is most appropriate to share given that group's culture and work style.

Common Understanding

A concerted effort to understand cultural differences across multiple organizations and to develop a common lexicon and transparent rules of engagement can reduce misunderstandings. Given the wide variety of organizational cultures, the chances for miscommunication abound. Anecdotal evidence derived by the authors from decades of working with interagency teams and task forces suggests that the amount of miscommunication that occurs in such settings is consistently underestimated. Similarly, the need for lists of common terms, acronyms, and definitions cannot be understated. The development of mutually agreed-upon "rules of engagement" for a collaboration initiative or environment can promote a common understanding and build mutual trust.

CORE PRINCIPLES

Overcoming the many obstacles to collaboration will require that senior leaders—and the entire workforce—understand and embrace a new doctrine composed of three core principles.

Responsibility to Provide

Analysts should not be at the mercy of information "owners" who must give them permission before they will be allowed to share information with others who need it to do their jobs. The traditional culture and mind-set of "need to know" must be replaced with a culture in which everyone accepts responsibility to share information with those who need it to perform the mission. As the workforce takes more responsibility to share knowledge, management must also take responsibility to provide clear guidelines and training on the characteristics of a good sharing environment.

Empowerment to Participate

People should be empowered to engage with others and share their insights, information, and work in progress (within preestablished and clearly communicated guidelines) without having to first seek the permission of their superiors. Empowerment also carries responsibility. Guidelines are essential to establish what can be shared, how, and with whom.

User-Driven Environment

Collaborative communities should be self-defining, self-creating, agile, and adaptive. The users should effectively own their work environments. This principle simply acknowledges the complexity and fluidity of the world in which we now must function.

CRITICAL ENABLERS

Successful implementation of a robust culture of collaboration requires proactive engagement by all participants to ensure that the leadership is committed, the technical and human support infrastructure is in place, and organizational policies are aligned.

Engaged Leadership

Virtually every study of successful transformation of a business culture includes a key finding that change must be led from the top. If CEOs do not practice what they preach, then their employees will view pronouncements about the need to collaborate as empty rhetoric or just another fad.

Collaboration Support Cells

Collaborative systems are almost certain to fail in large bureaucracies if the participants do not have access to "human enablers" or facilitators who can advise on how to work best collaboratively and assist in tailoring a set of collaborative tools to specific work objectives.[4]

Consistent Policies

Policies must support collaboration and be consistent across all participating organizations and adjusted when they are not. Managers should be particularly alert to situations where oft-cited "policies" turn out to be better described as deeply encrusted traditions. In many cases, when collaboration collides with bureaucracy, closer scrutiny will reveal that what was asserted as dogma is no more than common practice that can be changed by managers who value collaboration.

Technical and Administrative Infrastructure

One of the quickest ways to discourage an employee's desire to collaborate is to make collaboration software difficult to obtain, too difficult to use, or much-needed technical support too hard to access when difficulties arise.

THE SIMULATION

This ready-to-use simulation offers an opportunity for students to practice communicating skills in a small group setting and to better understand how collaborative work practices can contribute to a more effective work environment and mission accomplishment. CyberSIM has been run many times mainly with mid-level officers and managers working at a large intelligence organization, but it can be adapted for use with nonintelligence bureaucracies or large corporations. (Ways in which it can be adapted are discussed at the end of this chapter.) After-action responses to the simulation indicate most students come away from the experience with a better understanding of both their personal communication strengths and weaknesses and a more sophisticated understanding of what it takes to work effectively in small groups and collaborate across multiple components that often share different cultures, perspectives, and interests.

Students are given a situation where a sudden, unexpected event (a cyber attack) has an immediate and major deleterious impact on their agency or company. The exercise is designed to allow students to play themselves in their workplace environment (rather than playing another role) and to represent the culture, equities, and personality of their unit or the larger functional organization. The setting is one in which they are expected to work together to achieve a consensus solution, deal with conflict and competing interests/agendas, know when to listen and when to speak, and understand the importance of questioning assumptions and being sensitive to other cultures. The simulation requires that the class include a mix of participants who work in different organizational units such as collection, analysis, research and development, information processing, human resources, infrastructure, or IT support.

The simulation itself is divided into four broad phases and can be completed in 1 day. The times assigned to the various phases are based on this design but can be adapted and modified to meet other requirements or demands. Our experience suggests that the simulation has greater impact if, before introducing the scenario, the instructor engages the students in an interactive discussion of characteristics of effective and less than effective meetings (see Appendix A).

- In Phase 1 (approximately 1.5 hours), the instructor outlines the simulation, provides students with the background and details of the cyber attack, reviews student tasking, assigns students to their teams, reviews the simulation schedule, and offers broad guidance on how best to approach the simulation. This phase ends with students breaking into functional groups to begin discussing the impact of the cyber attack on their component or function.

- In Phase 2 (approximately 3.5 hours), the students meet in teams made up of representatives from all of the functional areas represented in the class. Students remain in these groups to brainstorm solutions, build a consensus, and prepare a briefing on their deliberations. This phase ends with each team providing their briefing to the director of the organization—or his or her surrogate.
- In Phase 3 (approximately 1 hour), the students reconvene as teams to review the day's experience, focusing on the behaviors observed during the morning meeting and how well they believe they performed. Each team prepares a short briefing on lessons learned and best practices observed.
- In Phase 4 (approximately 1 hour), the exercise concludes with each team briefly presenting its lessons learned to the rest of the class. This is followed by a facilitator-led discussion that focuses on the keys to developing and sustaining collaborative work environments.

Phase 1: Setting the Scene

CyberSIM begins with a brief PowerPoint discussion (Appendix A). A copy of the PowerPoint presentation can be obtained at www.pherson.org/publications/Occasional Papers/PapersonCollaboration.

Phase 1: Setting the Stage

The simulation formally begins with the instructor handing out a short excerpt from a fictitious *New York Times* report (dated January 1, in the future) that describes a cyber attack on the Office of Intelligence Production (OIP) and the extent of the damage

---

Massive Cyber Attack Knocks Out Power at Key Government Agency

(1 January, the future) The Headquarters of the Office of Intelligence Production (OIP) was hit yesterday with what is being called a "massive, sophisticated, multi-pronged" cyber attack. The full extent of the damage is still being assessed but early indications are that the attack focused on OIP's electrical power grid.

Many media pundits are saying it was only a matter of time before such an attack on a critical government agency took place. They noted that OIP was a tempting target for cyber attackers given its critical role in providing national intelligence. The government has launched an investigation, but no group or individual has yet claimed credit for the attack.

Sources at OIP are estimating that it will take at least six months to fully restore power. A spokesperson for OIP issued the following statement: "While the damage done is significant, the entire OIP workforce is committed to responding to the challenge. All of OIP's customers can be assured that we will continue to provide the timely, relevant, and accurate intelligence support critical to ensuring the nation's security. Our highest priority is supporting all of our partners."

Figure 7.2. *New York Times* **Report of Cyber Attack**

Situation Report, 1 January

The Office of Intelligence Production (OIP) has experienced a major cyber attack. As a result, the main power grid has been severely damaged and is non-functional. Only the quick response of engineers and IT specialists prevented all the back-up generators from being taken down as well. Most of the back-up generators are working but are capable of supplying only 60 percent of OIP's overall power needs. An initial damage assessment has raised the possibility that the attackers built in multiple follow-on attacks, or possibly introduced "worms," designed to be triggered when repairs to the system begin to be made. Given this risk, engineers have determined that it is not possible to bring the main grid back on line gradually. New generators will have to be ordered and none currently are available in inventory. As a result, for the next six months the workforce will be dependent on non-infected back-up generators capable of meeting only 60 percent of OIP's total power needs.

Figure 7.3.   OIP Office of Public Affairs Situation

done to the building and its operations (Figure 7.2). The article can be adapted and either shortened or lengthened to meet the requirements of the organization as necessary.

After students read the article, the instructor asks if they have any questions. Then the instructor provides the students with a Situation Report prepared by the Office of Public Affairs that was distributed to all employees reporting to work on January 1 (Figure 7.3).

Students are told that their senior management has asked them to participate in one of several agency-wide teams being assembled to provide initial input and recommendations on how OIP can best respond to the crisis. The instructor informs them that they have been selected because of their unique expertise, experience, and insights. The teams' findings will be incorporated into a comprehensive mitigation strategy communicated to the entire OIP workforce. Students are informed that all teams are receiving the guidance presented in Figure 7.4.

Following this general guidance, the instructor announces the team assignments; experience suggests that the optimal size of each team is 8 to 10 students. (The instructor should determine the composition of each team before the simulation begins.) For phase 1, the students should be grouped by function with students who work in the same functional unit in the same group.

The instructor then quickly reviews the PowerPoint slides describing what the simulation is and what it is not, tips for maximizing the value of the simulation, and the day's schedule (Appendix B). A copy of the PowerPoint presentation can be obtained at www.pherson.org/Publications/OccasionalPapers/PapersonCollaboration. From this point forward and to the extent possible, instructors should allow teams to establish their own procedures, practices, and outcomes, hopefully drawing from the material presented earlier in the course on how to run effective meetings. Teams should decide when to take breaks and when to have lunch (see Appendix A).

TEAM TASKING AND GENERAL GUIDANCE

Thank you for agreeing to serve on this important team. The Director/OIP has asked each team to prepare a briefing to be delivered this afternoon at 1300 summarizing their recommendations for dealing with the crisis. Each team's briefing should include:

- A prioritized list of the mission critical functions OIP must continue to perform during this period.
- A prioritized list of functions that can be temporarily suspended or cut back.
- Any "out-of-the" box ideas the group may have generated for handling the crisis.

The Director has emphasized that the groups are not expected to draft the strategy itself. OIP's senior leadership is seeking input from the entire workforce; you have been selected to participate because you have unique perspectives, expertise, and experiences. Your team's task is to provide a concise, well-organized, coordinated presentation that will help OIP leaders make more informed decisions.

The following additional information is provided to help frame your discussions:

- OIP must have a coordinated "whole of OIP" strategy that is transparent and has the buy-in of all components; a series of uncoordinated component solutions is not acceptable.
- OIP cannot expect significant additional funds to implement the mitigation strategy.
- There are no quick, "stop gap" technical fixes to the power outage.
- Think strategically. You are not expected to provide personnel numbers or specific budget recommendations.
- OIP leadership is committed to a robust, open, information-rich communication strategy.

Figure 7.4.   OIP Task Force Member Guidance

Phase 1 ends with students meeting with other students from their functional group. The purpose of these brief meetings (approximately 45 minutes to 1 hour) is not to develop a coordinated response for each functional area, but rather to allow students to share thoughts and ideas, as well as to share information, on how the cyber attack will impact their functional area's ability to perform its mission. For example, they may discuss what key tasks they believe their specific unit must maintain and what functions could be delayed or deferred. This session also allows students time to begin thinking about imaginative or "out-of-the-box" ideas for addressing the crisis. Experience indicates that these sessions are often key to building student confidence going into the team meeting phase of the simulation. Instructors do not observe or participate in these sessions.

Phase 2: Multidisciplinary Team Meetings

Following the functional meetings, students are reorganized into multidisciplinary groups and report to their assigned team to begin discussing how to respond to their taskings. Experience shows that it is important to emphasize that the only variable used in determining the teams is the need to ensure that each team has members from all of the components represented in the class.

At the beginning of the team meeting, an instructor tells the team that the director of OIP has assigned an additional task, as presented in Figure 7.5.

TEAM MEETING INJECT

Each team, in addition to the scheduled briefing, must provide by 1300 no more than two paragraphs for the Director on how the team believes the mitigation strategy being developed can be best communicated to the workforce and what means or mediums of communication will be most effective for conveying the message.

Figure 7.5. Team Meeting Inject

The purpose of this inject is twofold. First, it is designed to have students think more systematically about the importance of communication and means of communication in the workplace. Second, it provides a way to introduce into the meeting a common, "real-world" situation where tasking often is changed, revised, or expanded.

To the extent that resources permit, an instructor should act as a nonparticipating observer for each group. This aids in the facilitation of the after-action afternoon debriefs and discussions. As noted above, however, the instructor should attempt to limit his or her participation. If a team becomes stuck or confused, the instructor can suggest ways for getting the meeting back on track by reminding the students of tools and techniques to ensure effective meetings, as discussed earlier. If an instructor intervenes, he or she should inform the other instructors what information was provided to the team and whether the other teams should have or need the same information.

Phase 2 ends with each team delivering its briefing to the director of OIP. All teams should be present when the briefings are given; this often provides valuable feedback in the review sessions. The role of director of OIP can be played by the actual director, a senior official in the organization, or by one of the instructors. Each briefing should be limited to no more than 15 minutes, leaving the director with 5 minutes to respond to the briefing and ask questions of the team. The goal of the briefing is not to evaluate the briefing skills of the students or the content of the briefing but to explore the process and behaviors that led to the recommendations.

Phase 3: Team Debriefs

Teams reconvene following the briefing sessions to assess both their individual performances and their team's performance. The instructors can help facilitate these sessions, but the students should take the lead in identifying and evaluating both their performance and key takeaways from the morning session. The following questions may help guide and structure the team self-assessment process:

- What was your personal *reaction* to the exercise? How did you feel?
  - You may want to go around the room and ask each team member for his or her key takeaway.

- Were there particular *behaviors* you observed during the meeting?
  - Were there behaviors you thought were particularly effective in helping the team reach its goals? Were there behaviors you observed that worked against the group meeting its goals?
- What did you *learn* from the exercise? About yourself? About group dynamics?
  - How did your personal preferences for communication influence the discussion?
  - Did you try out or experiment with any new or different communication skills?
- How *effective* do you think the group was in reaching its goals or making decisions?
  - Was the sum greater than the parts?
- What could you have done differently?

Phase 4: Class Lessons Learned

The simulation concludes with teams reassembling as a class to share their insights, experiences, and best practices. When the team debriefs the class, the primary emphasis should be on the behaviors students observed and the dynamics of the team meetings and not just the specific outcomes or recommendations of the session. The objective is to draw on the day's experience and lessons learned to recognize the importance of communication patterns and behaviors in facilitating or hindering reaching workplace objectives.

Instructors can emphasize that in a "real-world" crisis situation, displaying and employing effective communication skills may have had an even greater impact because team members may not have had the advantage of knowing one another before assembling as a team. Instructors may choose at this point to lead to a more detailed, in-depth discussion of how the day's experience relates to building collaborative environments and how collaborative environments built on the six principles discussed above can facilitate critical thinking, build consensus, and lead to creative problem solving.

CONCLUSION

Developing effective communication skills—whether in face-to-face situations or in group environments—is critical to achieve an organization's mission objectives. Acquiring these skills, however, requires practice. The CyberSIM exercise offers students an opportunity to test and practice their communication skills in a scenario that has current, real-world relevance; it further allows them to test or "try out" and evaluate the effectiveness of communication tools and techniques that may fall outside "their comfort level."

A key element of the simulation is that it sets the stage for more in-depth discussions of the importance of collaboration and collaborative environments in an increasingly complex and interdependent workplace by providing students with examples from a realistic, current workplace scenario. Students have the opportunity to gain greater insight into how they communicate and how others see and interpret their communication behaviors and—through a practical experience—to better understand the challenges and the benefits of building and sustaining collaborative environments.

MODIFYING THE SIMULATION FOR OTHER AUDIENCES

The CyberSIM simulation is most effective when the students are drawn from various parts of a large intelligence organization or government bureaucracy that handles sensitive information. For most of the students, the challenge is trying to perform the mission when most of the work is classified or must be done at the headquarters complex and cannot be done over the Internet. This constraint forces the students to prioritize which functions must be protected as mission critical and which can be suspended or accomplished in new or more innovative ways.

CyberSIM can be modified for use in large businesses or academic institutions that have large departments or a variety of functional areas that are undergoing major downsizing or must compete for a piece of a rapidly shrinking resource pie. In such circumstances, outsourcing the work would be a prohibitively expensive option, leaving the students with little option but to set internal priorities and brainstorm more creative ways to perform the core mission of the organization.

CyberSIM is targeted at the general workforce but can be easily modified as a tool to teach managers how to improve communication and collaboration within their organizations. It can be transformed into a management training exercise with only minor modifications. The scene setter for a manager's CyberSIM exercise, for example, would be modified as follows:

Phase 2: Component Meetings

The students are told it is day one of the crisis and their senior management has asked them to participate on a task force to recommend how best to proceed. They need to develop a comprehensive mitigation strategy that must be approved by the director of OIP and then will be communicated to the entire OIP workforce. The class is divided into four to six groups based on the functions they perform for the organization. [*Delete the following:* The instructors tell the students they are *not* being asked to develop or draft the mitigation strategy itself but to provide a coordinated set of ideas or inputs that can better inform the strategy that senior management must devise.]

Phase 3: Multidisciplinary Teams

Revise the second paragraph as follows: The groups are told the director of OIP is seeking input from the entire workforce; they were selected because they have unique perspectives, experience, and management expertise. Their task is to develop a concise, well-organized, coordinated plan that will educate the director of OIP on the types of trade-offs that will be required and recommend a series of initial actions.

ACKNOWLEDGMENT

The authors declared no conflicts of interest with respect to the authorship and/or the publication of this chapter. The authors received no outside financial support for the research and/or authorship of this chapter. All statements of fact, opinion, or analysis expressed in this book are those of the authors and do not reflect the official positions of the Office of the Director of National Intelligence (ODNI), the Central Intelligence Agency, or any other U.S. government agency. Nothing in the contents should be construed as asserting or implying the authentication of information or the endorsement of the authors' views by the U.S. government. This material has been reviewed by the ODNI only to prevent the disclosure of classified material.

APPENDIX A: WHAT MAKES AN EFFECTIVE MEETING?

WHAT MAKES AN EFFECTIVE MEETING?

How to Make Sure a Meeting Fails!

- Do little or no advance planning
- Invite too many people, too few people, too many wrong people
- Do not make clear why you are meeting
- Forget to provide participants with an agenda
- Show no leadership
- Do not make clear who is accountable for what or discuss next steps

Follow these steps and failure is almost guaranteed!!!

On the Other Hand, If You Want a Successful Meeting...

- Make sure everyone knows the meeting's purpose and what we need to accomplish
- Set a meeting climate and tone that identifies expectations and clarifies meeting norms
- Stay focused and on track
- Employ effective facilitation tools
- Encourage and support collaboration
- Hold people accountable and establish follow-through mechanisms

In Sum, Good Meetings Require:

- Advance **P**lanning
- A clear **P**urpose
- The right **P**eople
- An achievable **P**roduct, goal, or outcome
- A meeting **P**rocess—key to reaching your objective

APPENDIX B: CYBERSIM OVERVIEW AND GUIDELINES

CyberSIM Sequence

Phase One
- Introduction/overview/tasking/team assignments/ general guidance (30 minutes)
- Functional area meetings (45-60 minutes)

Phase Two
- Team meetings (3.5 hours)
- Team briefings (15 minutes per team)

Phase Three
- Team debriefs (1 hour)

Phase Four
- Class lessons learned (1 hour)

CyberSIM OVERVIEW AND GUIDELINES

A Few Suggestions and Tips for the Exercise

- Remember this is not a test or a game— there are no winners and losers.
- Be yourself!
- Be an active participant!
- Be confident!
- Ignore the observers!

APPENDIX C: ACHIEVING A ROBUST
AND COLLABORATIVE ENVIRONMENT

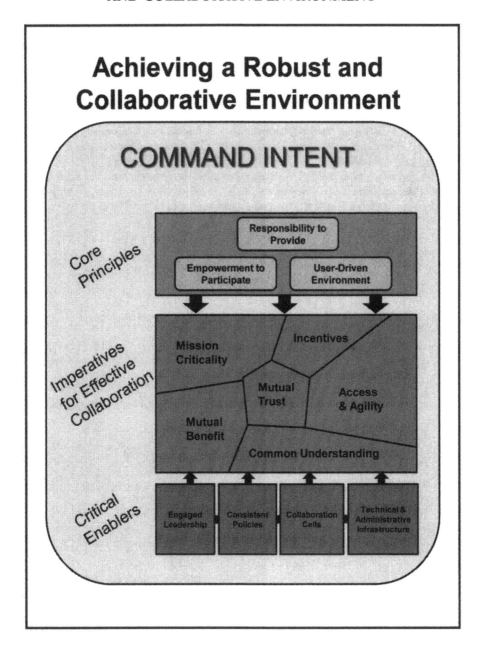

NOTES

1. These themes are discussed in more detail in the following articles: "Analytic Teams, Social Networks, and Collaborative Behavior" and "Small Groups, Collaborative Pitfalls, and Remedies" that can be accessed at www.pherson.org.

2. See Randolph H. Pherson and Joan McIntyre (2009). The article is part of a collection published by the Topical Strategic Multilayer Assessment (SMA), Multi-Agency/Multi-Disciplinary White Papers in Support of Counter-Terrorism and Counter-WMD in the Office of Secretary of Defense/DDR&E/RTTO. Other articles in the collection that have direct relevance to collaboration in the intelligence arena include: "Blueprints for Designing Effective Collaborative Workspace"; "Breaking the Mold in Developing Training Courses on Collaboration"; and "Transformation Cells: An Innovative Way to Institutionalize Collaboration." These articles can also be accessed at www.pherson.org.

3. Insights into how to build effective teams and avoid the common pitfalls of small groups can be found in Chapter 12, "Practitioners Guide to Collaboration," in Heuer, Richards J. Jr. and Pherson, Randolph H. 2015. *Structured analytic techniques for intelligence analysis*, Second Edition. Washington, DC: CQ Press.

4. For more information on this concept see Pherson (2009, note 2).

REFERENCES

Heuer, Richards J. Jr., and Pherson, Randolph H. 2015. *Structured analytic techniques for intelligence analysis*, Second Edition. Washington, DC: CQ Press.

Pherson, Randolph H. 2009. Transformation cells: An innovative way to institutionalize collaboration. In *Collaboration in the national security arena: Myths and reality*. Available at: www.yumpu.com/en/document/view/4572324/transformation-cells-an-innovative-way-to-institutionalize-.

Pherson, Randolph H., and McIntyre, Joan. 2009. The Essence of Collaboration: The IC Experience. In *Collaboration in the national security arena: Myths and reality—What science and experience can contribute to its success*.

8

Market and Competitor Analysis: Real Exercise

Luis Madureira

ABSTRACT

A well-designed market positioning is a critical part of today's successful business or government enterprise. Designing such a positioning implies being able to understand the external environment in all its vectors. Two critically important vectors are the market analysis and the competitor analysis. The market analysis will list the constraints the external environment puts on a player's strategic alternatives, while the competitor analysis will allow players to understand the likelihood, timing, nature, intensity, and ability of its initiatives. This is critical, particularly in highly competitive markets and situations of uncertainty.

This exercise first focuses on understanding the external environment and the industry in which players act. This reflects the fact that the industry players do not operate in a "vacuum," and their strategic decisions derive from the external environment's opportunities and threats. Second, it focuses on developing a competitor profile to deeply understand its drivers and key functional areas' modus operandi. Finally, it uses Porter's (1980) 4-Corner analysis to understand the current, and forecast the future, likely direction of a player, including the strategic risk mitigation of its competitor's strategic moves. The outcome of this exercise can be used as input to other tools or frameworks such as war games or scenario planning.

KEY TASKS

Understand the external and internal factors impacting any given market player strategy; identify opportunities and threats and strategic alternatives facing a company;

understand and develop a competitor strategic analysis; develop a competitor profile including past, present, and future likely directions (Porter's 4-Corner); and understand competitors and their strategies.

KEYWORDS

Analysis; intelligence; competitor profile; industry analysis; competitor analysis; external environment; PESTEL; intelligence process; intelligence simulation; teaching intelligence analysis; 4-Corner; real-life exercises; Intelligence Funnel.

This exercise is designed to help students acquire strategy development skills considering that the ultimate objective of competitive intelligence (CI) is to inform or help strategic decision making and thus inform or help deliver an effective strategy. Today's effective strategy depends in great part on a company's chosen positioning against the positioning of its competitors. In order to develop such positioning, a company must consider the environment and industry where it develops its activity, as well as its own internal idiosyncrasies and its competitor's strategy.

In this simulation, participants play the role of intelligence analysts. Their task is to produce a market and competitor analysis that will inform the development of the company's strategy for that market.

The simulation's subject matter adds to its pedagogic value in several ways. First, it reinforces the need to follow the intelligence cycle, which helps participants to understand intelligence development as a process that should be respected, going from identifying intelligence needs, through collection, to analysis and dissemination. Second, this simulation highlights the interactions and crossed impacts between the tools and frameworks and the different levels of analysis. Lastly, it addresses the need to derive actionable insights and strategic and tactical initiatives from the analysis. A final note should be made on the versatility of this exercise, which is not only applicable in the intelligence arena but also to business administration, marketing, strategic planning, and international business, especially when there is need to expand into new markets. This simulation can be a useful addition to any course that emphasizes students' briefing, critical thinking, problem solving, and strategic alternatives development abilities.

THE PROCESS

I coined the process used in this simulation as the *Intelligence Funnel*. This Intelligence Funnel starts by analyzing the external environment in its wider form through a PESTEL analysis (Political, Economic, Social, Technical, Environment, and Legal), and in its narrow scope through Porter's 5-Forces industry analysis. Next, it focuses on the internal environment of the players in the industry under analysis. This is done by building a competitor profile, which will inform a Porter 4-Corner analysis, which in turn, will help derive the current and future likely direction of this industry's players (see the competitor's profile structure in Appendix B for clarity). This process increasingly narrows the scope of the analysis to guide the analyst to deliver a comprehensive and sharp analysis that will allow the development of an efficient strategy for his or her company.

In order to guarantee the exercise's usefulness and veracity, a small amount of preliminary reading and research is needed. The preliminary reading allows participants to understand the topic, the frameworks, and tools, while also preparing them to participate in the simulation. The input will promote a collaborative approach within the group toward the development of the analysis and ultimately a shared vision for the players' future direction. The profile to be developed in the classroom is a real-life example, the kind of CI project a competitive intelligence manager might be asked to initiate in his or her career.

BASIC DATA

Instructional Objectives

To develop an appreciation for following the intelligence process while using an established tool or framework; to acknowledge the complexities involved in using several tools and to get to a comprehensive integrated deliverable; to show the difficulty in deriving competitor behavior and its strategic alternatives; to communicate efficiently the outcome to the intelligence consumers; to reveal the different perspectives of different players; to emphasize the challenge companies have to develop a strategy and act under an incomplete information background.

Simulation Objectives

The objective in this exercise is to deliver industry players' strategic alternatives derived from a Porter 4-Corner analysis. The simulation has several stages that mimic the actual process used by analysts to produce strategic recommendations for any given market. Participants first prepare a PESTEL (optionally can be a given), then a 5-Forces (optionally can be a given), and later a competitor profile, including a Porter 4-Corner to come up with the likely future direction of the players in the chosen industry. Several players should be assigned to different groups within the pool of participants. The simulation uses raw intelligence collected from open sources (except if PESTEL and 5-Forces analyses are given).

Debriefing Format

The different groups present the different players' likely future directions resulting from the 4-Corner analysis. The instructor then facilitates a class discussion among all participants in order to highlight and systematize the different strategic alternatives available.

Target Audience

Undergraduate and graduate students in an introductory or advanced course about intelligence. The simulation is also suitable for courses in business administration, marketing, and strategic planning.

Playing Time

1 day (NOTE: Instructors can conduct the simulation and debriefing in half a day if the external environment and industry analysis are provided: 1-hour introduction and framework, two 60-minute breakout sessions, and a 60-minute presentation and wrap up.)

Debriefing Time

60 minutes (or at least 20 minutes per group)

Number of Players Required

12+. The simulation requires a minimum of three groups or teams, each of which should contain a minimum of four persons.

Participation Materials Included

Appendix A: PESTEL Methodology and Template
Appendix B: Industry 5 Forces Methodology and Template
Appendix C: Industry Player Profile Structure Template; Competitor Profile Structure Template developed by Luis Madureira inspired by William L. Sammon and International Best Practices
Appendix D: Industry Player Porter 4-Corner Methodology and Template

Debriefing Materials Included

Participants can use the Appendix C template for presenting the findings and likely future direction of their assigned players.

Computer/Internet

At least one computer with Internet connection per group.

Other Materials/Equipment Required

Breakout rooms, depending on the number of groups, with markers and large sheets of paper for recording their insights and key assumptions (classrooms with adequate blackboard/erasable board space can be used instead).

FACILITATOR'S GUIDE

Materials

Preread

Porter (1980, Chaps. 1, 2, and 3); Appendix A: PESTEL Template; Appendix B: Industry 5-Forces Template; Appendix C: Industry Player Profile Structure Template; Appendix D: Industry Player 4-Corner Template.

Pen Drives

One pen drive per group containing the templates (PESTEL, 5-Forces, Profile, and 4-Corner) the participants will use during the exercise. Regarding Appendix C: Industry Player Profile Structure Template, it is best to copy and paste the headings into an Excel file column and allow a second column for groups to fill in.

Computers

I suggest asking the participants to bring their own computers in order to fill in the templates electronically as well as to present their conclusions. This will allow students to do some real-time research and validate their discussion or to answer questions that might arise.

Presimulation Briefing

The groups must be assigned distinct roles beforehand so they can do some research. On the day of the simulation, the facilitator explains the overall process to the participants and briefly summarizes the tools and frameworks that will be used, as well as gives direction on how the templates should be filled in (details are provided in the appendices).

RUNNING THE SIMULATION

Simulation Step 1: Getting Organized

On arrival, divide participants into at least three groups of four people according to the groups formed (as per the "Presimulation Briefing"). Each group's members should sit together (and a break room should be assigned to each group if possible). Next, hand out the pen drives containing the templates and advise the students to work with the templates from the pen drive (not copying them to the school's or venue's computer or to their own PC).

Simulation Step 2: Developing the External Environment Analysis (90 minutes)

Each group will start filling in the PESTEL and industry analysis. The facilitator should go from room to room (or table to table) to clarify any process doubts and other questions.

Simulation Step 3: Alignment on External Environment Analysis (60 minutes)

One of the groups presents the PESTEL and the others give feedback so that a global consensus is reached (please note that each group is impacted in different ways, but overall the PESTEL and industry assessment should be coherent and consistent among the groups).

Simulation Step 4: Developing the Competitor Profile (120 minutes)

Each group should now fill in the competitor profile (except to the strategic direction module) with the information they may already have or have extracted from the Internet. The most obvious resource is the players' website, so ensure that the industry chosen has well-known players that have corporate or branded websites. Because this is a simulation, advise the students to fill in as much as they can without going into much detail (this will also teach them the need to synthesize).

Simulation Step 5: Developing the 4-Corner Analysis (60 minutes)

This part of the simulation will help the group fill in the "Strategic Direction" part of the player's profile. This is a very important part of the profile, which needs to be filled in with the information from the rest of the profile. This means that the better the rest of the profile, the easier it is for the participants to derive the 4-Corner and the "Future Likely Direction" of the player being analyzed. *The most challenging part of the 4-Corners is the "Management Assumptions," which derive from the understanding of how the player acts, which in turn can be derived from the rest of the profile.*

Simulation Step 6: Deriving Industry Players' Likely Future Direction (30 minutes)

Having the 4-Corner as the background for this, consider Porter's 3 Generic Strategies and choose one of them as the overall "Strategic Umbrella." Next, develop the key "Strategic Initiatives" each of the player's will pursue. *Guaranteeing each group has a generic strategy identified (current and future) is absolutely crucial, especially when presenting to and discussing the outcome of the exercise with other groups.*

Simulation Step 7: Presenting, Discussing, and Reaching a Conclusion (60 minutes)

Each group presents its generic strategy, as well as its strategic initiatives, followed by an all-group discussion. The other groups can now assess their own blind spots. The sum of the group presentations on the strategic alternatives pursued by each player will result in the likely future market behavior.

DEBRIEFING THE SIMULATION

Objectives

An effective debriefing session (60 minutes) can help participants reach a better understanding of a number of factors that make intelligence analysis so challenging.

Information Gaps

Participants acknowledge that the raw information available for producing the several analyses is missing some important elements, which are not readily available, although most of it can be found or inferred. Participants realize that time constraints take a toll when it comes to information completeness and that collection is a continuous process that must be performed daily.

Uncertainty

Gaps in information constitute one source of uncertainty in an analysis. The impact of gaps is increased when participants combine the pieces of raw intelligence into a finished analysis.

Cognitive Biases

Participants are encouraged to avoid mirror imaging (assuming the players act according to their own set of values and beliefs instead of using the players' set; as stated earlier, these are part of the "Management Assumptions" corner of the 4-Corner model and are the biggest challenge in this exercise).

Deadlines/Timing

Participants have a limited time to obtain information and conduct the simulation. Insufficient time can produce an inconclusive analysis and misinformation for the other groups and thus an inaccurate market landscape in the end.

Briefing Skills

Participants' ability to extract meaningful insights from data to create their own set of actionable knowledge is critical in this exercise. Particular attention must be given by the facilitator to guarantee that debriefs add value to the analysis made. This is exactly the objective of the templates used.

The Role of the Intelligence Cycle, Tools, and Frameworks

The participants should understand that only by following the intelligence process (cycle) can they arrive at the most accurate conclusions while making their work easier and more structured, thus saving time and allowing for better analysis. In addition, participants should understand when to use the several techniques, tools, and frameworks within the cycle, its order, interactions, and the interrelationships among the different elements. This will structure their work and lead them to the best perspectives. Lastly, participants should use the different analyses to acknowledge blind spots that the players they represent might have, as well as blind spots other players might have, by comparing other players' conclusions with their own analysis.

CONCLUSION

This simulation exposes participants to key frameworks that every CI professional must master. Using real-life information and allowing time for participants to source their own information will make the simulation closer to reality while forcing the participants to come to terms with the difficulty, complexity, uncertainty, and ambiguity that CI professionals face on a day-to-day basis.

The strategic formulation and discussion that arises from this exercise are extremely rich, especially if well conducted, so a thorough preparation is advised, as well as running this exercise using an industry that the facilitator knows well. The overall idea, and something the facilitator should avoid at all cost, is to lead the groups into a strategy. Rather, instructors should allow the groups to discuss and formulate strategic alternatives that, although bound to logic, provide possible courses of action.

The simulation gives students firsthand experience with making difficult choices based on incomplete information, thus allowing them to understand the real-life challenges of positioning and running a business. As such, this exercise can also be run by courses in business administration or strategic marketing.

Acknowledging that well-made analyses produce the conclusions that allow businesses to shape the future of an industry, and be successful within it, will make the participants sensitive to the CI role in modern management. In parallel, the need to communicate the findings is as critical as the quality of the analysis itself. This brings the strategy versus execution dichotomy to the table and the inevitable balance between both (according to Sun Tzu's [1997] adage "It is enough, to adjudge the opponent correctly, to concentrate one's own strengths and win the people—that is all"); winning the people, or leadership, is built on the capability to communicate, and thus mobilize, the business toward the objective and course of action defined, which in turn is the result of the analysis.

APPENDIX A: PESTEL METHODOLOGY AND TEMPLATE

He, who is victorious because he knows how to change and fit the environment's needs, deserves to be called a genius.

—Sun Tzu (1997)

The goal here is to include all potentially relevant trends and developments, determine their possible influence, and develop the initial strategic courses of action applicable to them. It is especially important to discover the driving forces that can change the structure of an industry, a market, or a specific market segment.

Method

In accordance with the PESTEL analysis of Ambrosini, Johnson, and Scholes, six environmental aspects are to be differentiated. A one-by-one analysis of the different aspects should be initiated, and this should be a systematic process within the strategy development.

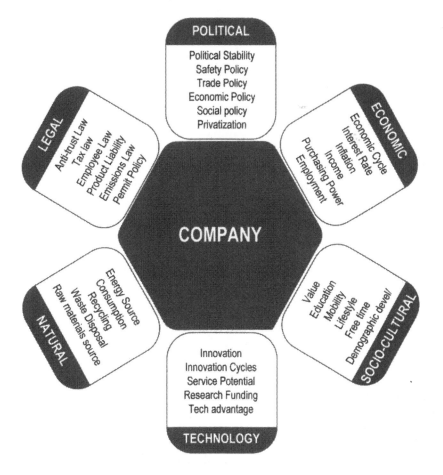

Template

Answer the following question based on the template below: Which external trends influence future success?

Analysis of the External Environment					
Environment	What trends are there?	What opportunities/risks are the result?	How big is the probability and influence?	What reactions are there in the environment?	How do we proceed?
Political					
Economic					
Socio-Cultural					
Technological					
Environment					
Legal					

APPENDIX B: INDUSTRY 5 FORCES METHODOLOGY AND TEMPLATE

When you know neither yourself nor your opponent, you endanger every single battle.

—Sun Tzu (1997)

The development of the strategy depends essentially on positioning the business in relation to its competitive environment and establishing sustainable advantages. The structure of each industry has a powerful influence on the rules of the game for our business and the competitors. Please note that intensity of competition can arise not only from the behavior of existing competitors but also from potential new competitors, existing and emerging substitutes, and the bargaining power of suppliers and customers.

Method

Porter's model for industry attractiveness is the most commonly used method for analyzing these issues.

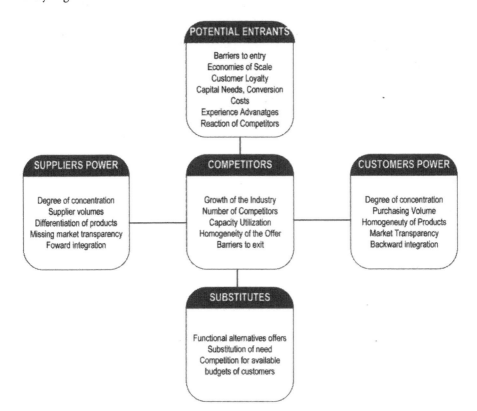

POTENTIAL ENTRANTS

Barriers to entry
Economies of Scale
Customer Loyalty
Capital Needs, Conversion
Costs
Experience Advanatges
Reaction of Competitors

SUPPLIERS POWER

Degree of concentration
Supplier volumes
Differentiation of products
Missing market transparency
Foward integration

COMPETITORS

Growth of the Industry
Number of Competitors
Capacity Utilization
Homogeneity of the Offer
Barriers to exit

CUSTOMERS POWER

Degree of concentration
Purchasing Volume
Homogeneuty of Products
Market Transparency
Backward integration

SUBSTITUTES

Functional alternatives offers
Substitution of need
Competition for available
budgets of customers

Template

Fill in by answering the questions within the template below.

Industry Analysis				
Competitive Force	What are the characteristics of the force?	How does the force develop?	What opportunities and risks are there?	How do we proceed?
Existing Competitors				
Potential Entrants				
Substitutes				
Power of Suppliers				
Power of Customers				

APPENDIX C: INDUSTRY PLAYER
PROFILE STRUCTURE TEMPLATE

© Luis Madureira 2010 (inspired in William L. Sammons + International Best Practices)

General Information
Profile Highlights
Website	Headquarters
Industries
Beverages Strategic Group
Business Description, Industrial Reputation & Market Position
Shareholders
Main Stakeholders
CEO	C Suite profiling
Company Culture (Past | Present | Continuity)
Business Development (M&A | Recent Trends Alliances | Investment | Divestments)
Recent Structural Changes
Corporate Social Responsibility
Business & Product
Production Volume (Last 5 years)
Business Volume per Business Unit (BU) per Market (last 5 Years | Domestic/Export)
Business Revenue per BU per Market (last 5 Years | Domestic/Export)
Business Profit per BU per Market (last 5 Years | Domestic/Export)
Product & Brand Volume Market Shares (last 3 Years)
Product & Brand Revenue Market Shares (last 3 Years)
Major Characteristics / Product
Brand Communications Model

Financial Analysis (last 5 Years)
Market Capitalization
Gross Sales | Revenue | EBITDA | EBIT | Operating Profit | Net Operating Profit | Net Profit
Free Cash Flow
ROI | ROA | ROE | ROS
Employees (Average | Year End)
Productivity
Assets Rotation
Debt Ratio
Value Chain Analysis by Product

Sales & Marketing
Head of Sales - Profile | Head of Marketing – Profile
Strategy & Goals
Portfolio Strategy
Brand Strategy
Advertising & Promotional Calendar
Marketing Capabilities (Size, Organization & Skills)
Market Coverage (ND & WD)
Route to Market Strategy
Market Coverage (ND & WD & Market Share)
Commercial Strategy
Sales Capabilities (Size, Organization & Skills)
Credit Policy

Export
Head of Exports – Profile
Strategy & Goals
Exports Countries & Shares
Volume Split per Country
Revenue Split
Profit Split
Operations
Head of Operations – Profile
Strategy & Goals
Organization
Factories Location
Production Capabilities
CAPEX
Group Resources / Partnerships
External Customers
Innovation
Head of Innovation – Profile
R&D Capabilities
Product/Service Description & Differentiation
Core Technologies
Patents
Investment

NPD Potential
Quality Observatory
Strategic Direction
Drivers and Goals
Current Strategy
Management Assumptions (Hot Buttons / Time to Reaction)
Capabilities (Organizational & Functional)
Future Likely Direction
People & Organization
Reputation Management
Recruitment Process (include Origin from people recruited)
Career Progression
Rotation
Organization Policy
Incentive Scheme

APPENDIX D: INDUSTRY PLAYER PORTER 4-CORNER METHODOLOGY AND TEMPLATE

Analyse your opponent, so that you may learn his plans. Learn from his successful, as well as, his failed plans.

—Sun Tzu (1997)

Many businesses fail to systematically gather information about their competitors. It is of utmost importance to have a profound knowledge of the strengths and weaknesses, as well as the behavior of one's main competitors. It is essential to conduct a detailed competitor analysis in order to carry out a comprehensive strategy formulation.

The competitor analysis is divided in three parts:

1. Determine the probable behavior of the competitor relative to changes in the industry and the expanded environment.

2. Evaluate the chances for success for the expected strategic steps of competitors.
3. Determine the potential reaction of the competitors to your business' strategic steps.

Based on this analysis, it is possible for an individual business to derive options for its strategic focus.

Method

Porter defined four elements to be taken into consideration:

1. Goals and drivers of the competitors' behavior that allow forecasting about a pending change in the competitor's strategy.
2. The current strategy gives the direction actually being followed by the competitor as well as clues to the future direction the competitor will pursue.
3. Identifying the assumptions that the industry has about the competitor and the competitor has about itself gives the paradigms on which a competitor bases its competitive behavior.
4. Identifying the abilities of competitors, their strengths and weaknesses, delimits the potential strategic steps a competitor can take.

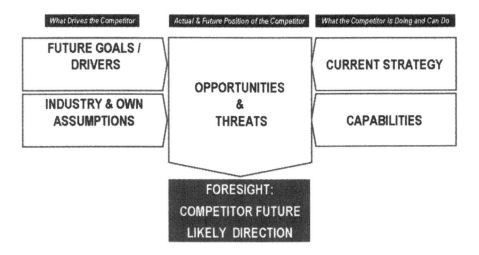

The development of your strategy essentially depends on positioning the business against competitors' foreseen future likely direction based on the present strategy, its strengths and weaknesses, its objectives and drivers, and finally the industry and one's own assumptions filtered by the external environment opportunities and threats.

*What Drives
the Competitor*

*What the Competitor
Is Doing and Can Do*

FUTURE GOALS
At all levels of management and in multiple
dimensions

CURRENT STRATEGY
At all levels of management and in
multiple dimensions

COMPETITOR'S RESPONSE PROFILE
Is the competitor satisfied with its current position?
What likely moves or strategy shifts will the competitor make?
Where is the competitor vulnerable?
What will provoke the greatest and most effective retaliation
by the competitor?

ASSUMPTIONS

Held about itself
and the industry

CAPABILITIES

Both strengths
and weaknesses

ACKNOWLEDGMENTS

The author declares no conflicts of interest with respect to the authorship and/or publication of this article. The author thanks the students of the Competitive Intelligence Masters course he teaches for providing him with greater insight into the process of running this exercise successfully, as well as his family for supporting him in this endeavor. A last brief note of thanks to all the competitive intelligence professionals around the world who, besides promoting the CI discipline, shared their wisdom with me.

REFERENCES

Ambrosini, V., Johnson, G., and Scholes, K. 1998. *Exploring techniques of analysis and evaluation in strategic management.* Prentice Hall Europe/Pearson, Harlow.

Porter, Michael E. 1980. *Competitive strategy: Techniques for analyzing industries and competitors.* New York: Free Press.

Sun Tzu. 1997. *Wahrhaft siegt, wer nicht kämpft: Die Kunst der richtigen Strategie.* Freiburg.

Wittmann, Robert G., & Reuter, Mathias P. 2004. *Strategic planning.* Redline Wirtschaft.

9

"Need-to-Share" Intelligence and Crisis Management in Fighting Terrorism and Organized Crime: The Need for Integrated Training Solutions

Gheorghe-Teodoru Stefan and Cristian Barna

ABSTRACT

Terrorism, along with its possible links with transnational organized crime such as money laundering, drug trafficking, and weapons smuggling, forms part of a complex set of new security challenges. The merging of organized crime and terrorism leads to the significant expansion of the financial, material, and purely operational capabilities of terrorist organizations, along with strengthening them.

Because of the internationalization of terrorism and crime by the spread of its typical characteristics, tendencies, and forms to other regions and countries, international cooperation is essential in the fight against drug trafficking, money laundering, weapons smuggling, and terrorism. This is the set of problems that international cooperation must resolve in the process of ongoing globalization, and this can be done only through international coordinating organizations and international legal resolutions together with academic research and training in the intelligence field. Effectively combating these asymmetric threats requires the presence of legal, organizational, and scientific support structures.

The recent evolution of terrorism distorts academic and organizational attempts to study this phenomenon. In the contemporary age, the connections between terrorist and organized crime groups represent the main threat to national and international security, a fact that requires the internationalization of the fight against these two evils.

International and regional institutions can play the role of a true transmission belt among states. Interpol, Europol, are Eurojust are just a few examples of institutions that possess the capability to contribute to ensuring an efficient dialogue among the states that are confronted with terrorist or criminal threats.

In this respect, special focus should be given to reaching a consensus at the international level regarding the instruments to be employed in combating terrorism and organized crime, the main purpose being to eliminate the hot spots, destroy the logistic bases of terrorist and organized crime groups, as well as prevent them from committing attacks.

The careful monitoring of financial activities suspected of being used to launder money resulting from drug trafficking or to finance the activity of terrorist groups can lead not only to a decrease in the aforementioned illegal activities but also to the identification of important representatives of these groups, their arrest, and the dissolution of the networks to which they belong.

This is the reason why international cooperation must represent a priority in combating terrorism and organized crime, taking into consideration that both the criminal organizations involved in drug trafficking and terrorist entities operate at the international level, their flexibility being an enviable trait.

The 9/11 terrorist attacks are a good example in this respect. The attacks showed the entire world that terrorists are better organized and more capable of acting on a global level than was initially believed. Moreover, a subsequent analysis of the data regarding the preparatory actions for the 9/11 terrorist attacks revealed the existence of interconnections between terrorism and drug trafficking.

In fact, the possibility of permanent links between criminal and terrorist entities is not considered a novelty (even though, in most cases, the two phenomena have been subject to separate investigations) as there is enough evidence of interaction between the two groups. The acceptance of this fact can be observed in the manner in which the new security strategies, adopted at the international level after 9/11, have tried to deal with this problem, giving an entirely new dimension to the relation between the two.

Looking back, we can see that recent history provides irrefutable evidence in support of the existence of strong connections between drug trafficking and terrorism. The links between terrorism and drug trafficking take various shapes: facilitation, protection, transport and collection of protection taxes, as well as the direct involvement of terrorist groups in drug trafficking with the purpose of self-financing their activity.

It is important to mention that drug traffickers and terrorists have the same logistical needs and are dependent on the illicit traffic of materials, persons, or money transfers. Conducting joint operations is advantageous for both criminal entities, the former having the opportunity of benefiting from the military capabilities of terrorist groups while the latter have at their disposal a reliable adviser concerning money transfers and money laundering. Moreover, drug traffickers can benefit from the protected transport routes in the region controlled or inhabited by terrorist groups.

Thus, the interaction between terrorist groups and the drug traffic networks from Colombia constitute an obstacle in the peace negotiations between the Colombian government and the Revolutionary Armed Forces of Colombia (FARC), which exchange cocaine for weapons or buy weapons with money acquired from drug trafficking.

In addition, after the 9/11 terrorist attacks, FARC started to be considered more of a terrorist group than a drug traffic network, the focus being on trying to stop its terrorist activity. FARC's involvement in drug trafficking is considered to be a method of financing its other activity.

Similarly, the Shining Path (Sendero Luminoso), a terrorist group from Peru, is strongly financed by the "taxes" it collects from drug traffickers, while in the border regions of Paraguay, Brazil, and Argentina (known as the Tri-Border Area), less controlled by the authorities, members of Islamic terrorist groups (HAMAS, Hezbollah) are involved both in drug trafficking and money laundering, counterfeiting, and weapons smuggling (Gray, 2009).

For example, in Lebanon, Hezbollah is involved in cocaine trafficking on the Latin America–Europe–Middle East route, exporting the opium cultivated in the Beka'a Valley, a region from southern Lebanon militarily controlled by this terrorist group. The involvement of Hezbollah in drug trafficking and other illicit activities could increase, considering the decline in financing from "sponsor states" such as Syria and Iran.

Also, prior to the 9/11 terrorist attacks, the link between drug trafficking and terrorism can be easily proven in the case of Afghanistan, through the taxes imposed by the Taliban regime on the illicit production of opium being financed by al Qaida activities (U.S. Senate, 2002).

In spite of the measures taken by the current Afghan government, which came to power after the fall of the Taliban regime, the income from opium traffic (and especially heroin) has resulted in a consolidation of criminal groups involved in these activities (which even possess their own armed forces). There is evidence that part of the local military and religious leaders maintain direct contact with these groups, supporting them in multiple ways in exchange for benefiting from significant financial advantages. Furthermore, there is an increasing concern regarding the possibility of direct links between the leaders of the drug traffickers from the region and al Qaida, which could hinder the operations of the international military coalition directed at annihilating the remains of the Taliban regime and of al Qaida, as well as other criminal groups involved in drug trafficking, which employ terrorist techniques against law enforcement personnel of the Afghan government and North Atlantic Treaty Organization (NATO) forces.

The complexity and volatility of the situation in Afghanistan and the fact that a large number of the members and supporters of al Qaida still find shelter in the region have led many analysts to say that the terrorists are involved in the trafficking of Afghan heroin to ensure the necessary funds for their survival and the continuation of the "holy war." This hypothesis is further supported by the fact that the Afghan government does not manage to exert a real and efficient control over the entire territory; in certain regions, the authority of religious leaders with Islamist views remains strong, a real problem considering their known ties with drug traffickers.

Consequently, there are voices who say that Afghanistan is a narco-state, an overstated assertion as proven by the measures taken by the Afghan regime to ensure internal stability and the rule of law. Although the eradication of poppy cultures and the stopping of heroin trafficking are important objectives for the Afghan government and the international community, achieving these objectives requires a long time.

It is true that the scale of drug trafficking accounts for the international community's fear concerning the financing of terrorism; it has become obvious that the money from the illicit drug trade plays an important part in financially supporting the organization of terrorist attacks.

There are no clear data on the involvement of the Taliban insurgents in drug trafficking, but British and American intelligence agencies have acquired a number of clues that prove the existence of strong connections between terrorists and the leaders of drug trafficking networks. One such piece of intelligence stated that Haji Juma Khan, one of the military leaders in Afghanistan, was the main coordinator of the traffic with Afghan heroin, having at his disposal an infrastructure that allowed its transport to the main European markets, through Pakistan, while a large part of the resulting funds were used to arm terrorist groups, active on the territory of this state.

In 2009, Haji Juma Khan was charged with narco-terrorism, conspiracy to fund and finance terrorism. He initially faced a single charge of conspiring to distribute narcotics with intent to support a terrorist organization. According to U.S. prosecutors, since 1999, Khan has led an international opium, morphine, and heroin trafficking group that arranged to sell morphine in the United States, and he was closely aligned with the Taliban, designated by the United States as a global terrorist group, since 2002.

Regarding international initiatives for combating narco-terrorism in Afghanistan, efforts of the international community and of the Afghan government to destroy the drug industry is one of the most pressing challenges to the democratic reconstruction of Afghanistan.

In this respect, we must conclude that the large amounts of money resulting from heroin trafficking represent an important incentive for criminal groups in Afghanistan. Since these groups are difficult for the Afghan authorities to annihilate, continued drug trafficking ensures the proliferation of criminal and terrorist activities in the region.

All the aforementioned elements enable terrorist groups with support centers in the region to continue to finance their activities over the short and medium term!

ROMANIA ON THE MAP OF
INTERNATIONAL NARCO-TERRORISM!

Romania is located on the main heroin traffic routes from central and southwest Asia to Western Europe. These illegal activities are conducted under the cover of either import–export activities (especially of fruit and vegetables) or of international transportation services. The criminal groups involved in these activities, with the complicity of fellow nationals who have migrated to various European states, have created true support centers in the territory of the transit states, including Romania, consisting of places where the drugs can be temporarily deposited or of "cloak companies" for the illegal activities in which they are involved.

The main gate of entrance for Afghan heroin on the European continent is still Turkey, closely followed by the so-called Balkan Route, as most criminal groups involved in transportation activities are composed of Turkish and Albanian ethnics.

The Afghan heroin reaches Turkey by car via Iran. The most frequently employed covers for these types of illegal activities are merchandise or people transport. From Turkey, following the Balkan Route, the heroin transits through the states of the Balkan Peninsula, with almost 80 percent of the total quantity reaching the drug consumer markets in the western and northern parts of the European continent (the Netherlands, Sweden, Denmark, etc.).

The statistical data on heroin captures made by the authorities from the states in this region point to the existence of three branches of the Balkan Route, which are alternatively or simultaneously employed by drug traffickers depending on the geopolitical developments in the region. One of these routes starts from Turkey, transits Bulgaria, Romania, Hungary, and Austria, from where the drugs reach the Western European markets. The second branch starts from Turkey and transits the Balkan states from the south shore of the Danube River, reaching Austria with the same final destination. The third branch transits Turkey and Greece, from where it reaches Italy by sea and from there to the western part of the European continent (Agenției Naționale Antidrog, 2011).

An example of an international Afghan heroin trafficking criminal network that operated on Romanian territory is one that was coordinated by an Iranian citizen living in Romania. The network's activities were monitored for a year and a half by the Romanian border police and officers from the Foreign Intelligence Service from Romania, with the cooperation of authorities from the United States, the Netherlands, Turkey, Great Britain, and Germany. Based on intelligence sharing, over 200 kilos of heroin were confiscated in 2007 and several dozen members of the international network producing and distributing heroin were arrested.

An Iranian citizen in Romania coordinated the criminal network, which was active in the territories of several states from Europe, Asia, and America (the Netherlands, Germany, Great Britain, Turkey, Afghanistan, Iran, Canada, and the United States). The network was composed of hundreds of individuals of various nationalities and was structured in various specialized cells, from those of the opium poppy cultivators to that of the final distributors.

The operation of dismantling the criminal network was conducted in cooperation with the Drug Enforcement Administration (DEA), the Athens office, under the direct supervision of a representative of the U.S. general attorney; the Netherlands National Police; the UK's Serious Organized Crime Agency (SOCA); the German National Police; the Turkish National Police; the Foreign Intelligence Service of Romania; the General Inspectorate of the Romanian border police; and Romanian judiciary authorities. Cooperation among these institutions started in late 2005, when it became clear that all of them were investigating elements of this operation, the common link being the Iranian citizen residing in Romania (Stoleru, 2007).

Another case involved a Romanian citizen who masterminded six illicit heroin transports to Western Europe between April 2002 and May 2003, the drugs being brought into Romania by two Kurdish nationals suspected of ties with the Kurdistan Workers Party (PKK). The Romanian citizen was arrested in 2004, when Romanian authorities discovered 112 kilos of heroin in his trailer. The drugs were to be distributed through different networks, including some subordinated to the PKK, in European Union states (Ghergut, 2011).

An additional example of direct financing of the PKK through funds acquired as a result of conducting drug trafficking operations is that of two Turkish citizens of Kurdish origin residing in Romania. These individuals were arrested in 2007 at the Turkish–Bulgarian border in conjunction with the capture of 58 kilos of heroin disguised in the cargo of an auto-train. The capture was a result of an international joint operation conducted by Romanian judiciary authorities together with judiciary authorities in Turkey and Bulgaria. The intelligence acquired by the Turkish authorities revealed that two of the members of the criminal network were regional leaders of the PKK (Topala, 2010).

PREVENTING AND COMBATING TERRORISM AND RELATED ACTIVITIES IN ROMANIA: THE LEGISLATIVE AND INSTITUTIONAL FRAMEWORK

The cooperation among national law enforcement and intelligence entities, in a common effort directed toward preventing and combating terrorist activities as well as blocking their financing sources—drug trafficking, arms smuggling, and illegal migration—represents the main element in the fight against these illegal phenomena.

According to the Romanian National Security Strategy (n.d.), the monitoring of activities conducted on Romanian territory by terrorist or criminal groups is composed of:

- Identifying, gaining control over, and restricting the actionable capabilities of terrorist groups that are active on Romanian territory and directly or indirectly challenge national security;
- Monitoring the activities conducted on national territory by international terrorist organizations, with the purpose of putting an end to their propaganda and proselytism activities, as well as to those activities that contribute, legally or illegally, to gathering funds for terrorist organizations;
- Identifying existing/potential links between terrorist groups and organized crime entities, both national and transnational;
- Ensuring a conceptual, institutional, and organizational interoperability to facilitate cooperation with partner intelligence services in order to improve monitoring transnational threats and limiting or eliminating the risk they pose to national security.

The actions directed toward reaching these objectives take place in the entire Romanian territory and involve law enforcement, the judiciary, intelligence, counterintelligence, and military organizations.

The legal framework for these activities is composed of Law 535 on preventing and combating terrorism, which was ratified by the Romanian Parliament on November 25, 2004. This law was used as the basis for the National Strategy for Preventing and Combating Terrorism. Taken together, these two documents ensure an efficient implementation of the legal provisions in this field in order to operationalize the exchange of data and intelligence at the interinstitutional level.

With this purpose in mind, Romanian authorities designed the National System for Preventing and Combating Terrorism (NSPCT), an institution that includes the following entities involved in the prevention and combating of terrorist actions and related activities:

- The Romanian Supreme Defense Council, as a strategic coordinator;
- The Romanian Intelligence Service, as a technical coordinator;
- The Foreign Intelligence Service;
- The Protection and Guard Service;
- The Special Telecommunications Service;
- The Prosecutor's Office attached to the High Court of Cassation and Justice, co-ordinating the judiciary activity;
- The Ministry of Administration and Interior;
- The Ministry of Defense;
- The Ministry of Foreign Affairs;
- The National Office for the Prevention and Control of Money Laundering;
- The National Commission for the Control of Nuclear Activities.

The NSPCT achieves its mission of preventing and combating terrorism through these types of activities:

- Intelligence operations, conducted both inside and outside the national territory, which support the other types of missions of the system;
- Operations directed against the recruiting efforts of terrorist organizations, conducted both inside and outside the national territory;
- Operations directed against the financial, logistical, and intelligence resources of terrorist entities, conducted both inside and outside the national territory (*Strategia națională de prevenire și combatere a terorismului*, 2002).

To fulfill its role as the technical coordinator of the NSPCT, the Romanian Intelligence Service created a Center for Antiterrorist Operational Coordination (CAOC), which includes representatives from the other institutions belonging to the NSPCT. CAOC is mainly concerned with:

- Controlling the implementation of the National Strategy for Preventing and Combating Terrorism;
- Analytical processing of the data received from NSPCT partners and ensuring an adequate dissemination, on the basis of integrated documents regarding the terrorist phenomenon;
- Management of the common databases;
- Ensuring the sharing of intelligence about terrorist groups with foreign partners;
- Ensuring a permanent framework of dialogue at the expert level in order to optimize the activity of the system;
- Ensuring, in the case of a terrorist crisis, the logistical and operational support required to operationalize a National Centre for Antiterrorist Action, which would be

integrated into the general system for crisis management, according to Law 535 from 2004 concerning preventing and combating terrorism (Official Monitor, 2004).

It is important to mention that the CAOC meets in regular session at the beginning of every month (and in extraordinary session whenever is necessary). The representatives of all the institutions taking part are consulted on the agenda of the meeting, as one of the permanent tasks of this entity is to analyze data and information gathered by the members of the NSPCT with regard to threats and vulnerabilities to Romanian national security generated by terrorist activities.

THE SIMULATION

Basic Data

Instructional Objectives

The scientific community must offer academic and training expertise in order for intelligence, security sector, defense, and foreign policy specialists to be fully prepared to deal with the asymmetric threats mentioned above. The emphasis must be put on the "need-to-share" intelligence cycle combined with efficient crisis management.

Simulation Objectives

The objective of this simulation is to put students in the situation of playing the role of representatives of the public order, defense, national security, and foreign affairs institutions from the Center for Antiterrorist Operational Coordination (CAOC) to effectively manage a potential terrorist threat to Romania in accordance with the legal framework that regulates the activity of the CAOC.

This exercise can be conducted whenever and as often as the instructor desires, since the real CAOC meets whenever extraordinary circumstances occur. Also, the team can be composed of any number of students, with the condition that the educational objective is attained.

In our case, we propose a training cycle in which students will be divided into operational teams, based on the necessity of integrated crisis management. A team must have from six to eight members, with different academic backgrounds (e.g., sociology, intelligence, defense, security law studies, and international relations).

After selecting the operational team, the members (according to their academic and professional background) will be asked to analyze a piece of intelligence that will be put at their disposal. The instructor will state that this raw intelligence material is the main topic on the agenda of the monthly meeting of the CAOC.

Debriefing Format

Several times during the simulation, the instructor facilitates the dialogue among the members of the operational team by asking several key questions to guide the discussion to ensure that the class discusses the operational objectives. At the end of the simulation, there will be free discussion among the students, based on the instructor's observations. First, the discussions take place among the members of the same team and then among members from different teams (according to the role played by each student—intelligence, law enforcement, diplomacy, security, defense, judiciary, etc.).

Target Audience

Undergraduate and graduate students in courses on intelligence, national security, law enforcement, and international relations.

Playing Time

4 to 6 hours. Instructors must conduct the simulation in two parts consisting in briefing and discussions among team members, based on the raw intelligence materials put at their disposal at the beginning of the two sessions (two 50-minutes class sessions) and one session to put together an integrated strategy to deal with the identified threat (2-hour class session).

Debriefing Time

Two sessions (first of 60 minutes and second of 45 minutes)

Number of Players Required

24+. The simulation requires a minimum of four groups/teams, each of which should contain a minimum of six persons.

Participation Materials Included

Appendices A and B (raw intelligence)

Computer/Internet

Required.

Other Materials/Equipment Required

1. Four different classrooms
2. Appendix A: Raw intelligence. Appendix A is an initial intelligence report gathered by the Romanian Intelligence Service and put on the agenda of the monthly meeting of the CAOC in September 2012.
3. Appendix B: Raw intelligence. Appendix B comprises additional intelligence provided by other members of the CAOC, following the request made by their representatives, after the monthly meeting of the CAOC from September 2012.

Presimulation Briefing

The facilitator informs the participants that they will be learning about intelligence analysis and crisis management by serving as representatives of law enforcement, defense, national security, and foreign policy from the CAOC as they reunite, at the beginning of September 2012, in the ordinary meeting. The students are informed that their objective is, in accordance with their expertise, to play the part of one of these representatives and act accordingly in order to perform the tasks they have within the CAOC.

Taking into consideration that the students to which this type of exercise is addressed are in the course of becoming potential experts in intelligence and crisis management (in law enforcement, national security, defense, and foreign policy institutions), we consider that it is important for them to understand the manner in which the CAOC works and to become capable of acting as representatives of the member institutions. The objective is for them to prove that they can work on the basis of the "need-to-share" principle and to demonstrate that they have analytical capacity, control, efficiency, team spirit, and respect for the principle of legitimacy in identifying, preventing, and combating terrorist activities on Romanian territory.

For this purpose, the students will be provided with a set of documents that comprise Law 535 from November 25, 2004, on preventing and combating terrorism, in which the attributions of the CAOC are clearly specified, as are the regulations of the institutions that participate in the CAOC.

Simulation Step 1: Getting Organized (15 minutes)

Divide students into at least four groups. Each of these operational teams should sit in a different classroom so that members of each group cannot overhear the discussions of the other groups. The facilitator hands out to each member of the four operational teams the raw intelligence contained in Appendix A. The facilitator cautions the students to be as objective as possible regarding the raw intelligence and to show their capabilities to identify a possible threat to the national security.

Simulation Step 2: Developing Individual Assessments (15 minutes)

Students work individually during this step. The facilitator tells the students that this phase of the simulation is meant to examine their own individual analysis of the raw intelligence. The students are asked to analyze the raw intelligence and to provide their own judgment regarding a possible threat to national security.

Simulation Step 3: Preparing Operational Team's Intelligence Product Regarding a Possible Threat to National Security (20 minutes)

Once students have constructed their own intelligence products, they will be asked to read it to the colleagues from their operational team. The facilitator will explain that this is necessary in order to go further to the process of intelligence fusion.

After reading it, all the students from the operational team will be asked by the facilitator to list their intelligence products in a location where all members of their team can view them.

At this point, the facilitator will ask the students to discuss the individual intelligence products and to deliver a team intelligence product, which will represent the operational team's assessment regarding the identified threat to national security (if there is one in their opinion!).

After this simulation step, the students will be offered a break (10 minutes). *The facilitator should pay attention as the students from different operational teams must not to talk to one another!*

Simulation Step 4: Preparing Operational Team Positions (10 minutes)

Students now work as team members within their operational teams. If any operational teams identify a possible terrorist threat, the facilitator will instruct the students in these operational teams to reach agreement (consensus) among themselves in assigning a position in the team (e.g., one could be the representative of the Romanian Intelligence Service [SRI], one could be the representative of the Ministry of Defense [MApN], another could be the representative of the Ministry of Foreign Affairs [MAE], etc.). This measure encourages the members of each operational team to identify themselves as team members, taking into consideration their academic expertise (as previously mentioned).

Simulation Step 5: Identifying the Intelligence Needs of the Members of the Team. Providing the Information Required in Conformity with Appendix B (10 minutes)

The facilitator must require that the students act in conformity with the role played by the operational team and act in accordance with the need-to-know principle in order to gather more information on the Pakistani citizen, taking into consideration the legal attributions and the intelligence capabilities of the institutions they represent in the CAOC.

It is important to mention that the facilitator will tell the students within the same operational team that they must act based on the need-to-share principle! This means that if the representative of one of these institutions does not request information, he or she could have received it from another institution, but if another member of the team does, the requested information should be provided to the other member. For example, if the student representing the Ministry of Interior and Administration does not request information on the visa and the circumstances in which the Pakistani citizen had acquired it, but this information is requested by another member of the team (e.g., the one acting as a member of the Romanian Intelligence Service), the requested information should be given to this person!

Based on the information requirements of the members of the operational team, the facilitator will provide the additional intelligence included in Appendix B. *It is important that the facilitator gives only the information from the agencies from which students request it and only to those who have requested it (each member of the team receives only the information he or she personally requests)!*

Simulation Step 6: Establishing the Analytical Capacity of Each Member of the Team in Respect to the Role Played (15 minutes)

Students work individually during this step. The facilitator will request the members of the team to analyze the intelligence received and to produce an analytical product (if one of the members of the team wishes to also use the primary intelligence received, he or she will be allowed to do so). Each member of the team is asked to read his or her analytical product and then post it on the board of the team, next to their first analytical product.

Simulation Step 7: Acting on the Need-to-Share Principle of the Intelligence Process (15 minutes)

In this stage, the facilitator will ask each member of the team to put together the primary intelligence received from Appendix B (on the basis on which they had written the second analytical product). The students will be required to jointly analyze and establish the level of terrorist threat and associated risks generated by the Pakistani citizen and to write an intelligence product on behalf of the operational team.

After this simulation step, the students will be offered a break (10 minutes). *Again, the facilitator should pay attention that the students from different operational teams do not talk to one another!*

Simulation Step 8: Decision Time for Crisis Management Team (20 minutes)

The facilitator will ask the students to consult with one another and choose a team coordinator who will be responsible for managing the crisis that could be generated by the identified terrorist threat and decide the roles each member of the team will play in managing the crisis.

The facilitator will tell the students that in solving these tasks they must consider the desire of each member and also the legal framework that regulates the activity of a crisis management operational team within the CAOC.

Simulation Step 9: Planning Time for Crisis Management. Developing a Strategy to Deal with the Terrorist Threat (60 minutes)

The facilitator will ask the team coordinator to act together with his or her team to develop a strategy directed toward preventing and combating the terrorism-related activities identified as a result of the intelligence analysis of the primary intelligence from Appendices A and B.

After this simulation step, the students will be offered a break (10 minutes). *Again, the facilitator should pay attention that students from different operational teams do not to talk to one another!*

Simulation Step 10: Briefing to Policymakers (30 minutes)

The facilitator directs each of the four operational teams to prepare an intelligence briefing for the policymakers. Students will be asked to pay particular attention to the fact that they also must be able to present their crisis management strategy (having 10 minutes at their disposal) in front of the policymakers (in an extraordinary session of the Supreme National Defense Council). This concludes the active phase of the simulation.

DEBRIEFING THE SIMULATION

Objectives

An effective debriefing (two sessions, first of 60 minutes and second of 45 minutes) can help participants reach a better understanding of a number of factors that make need-to-share intelligence and crisis management in fighting terrorism and organized crime so challenging.

Debriefing Session 1: Comparing Results (60 minutes)

At this stage, the facilitator will reunite the four operational teams in the same class-rooms and ask the coordinators of each team to consult with the members of their team in order to present the intelligence product elaborated by the team, as a result of the intelligence analysis made from the primary intelligence comprised in Appendices A and B and the action strategy each team developed. The facilitator will give each team 10 minutes for this presentation.

The facilitator will ask students to talk about the briefings and the problems encountered in trying to write with such concision. Furthermore, the facilitator will ask students to place themselves in the role of the policymakers and assess how they would interpret the intelligence products and the action plan presented.

After this simulation step the students will be offered a break (10 minutes).

Debriefing Session 2: Comparing Intelligence Products. Group Dynamics in Dealing with Need-to-Share Intelligence and Crisis Management (30 minutes)

The facilitator will ask students to look at the intelligence products made by their colleagues in order to see the way their colleagues had worked (first separately and second as a team) in producing intelligence products.

The key questions to be asked to the students, after doing this, are the following:

1. What are the main factors that led students individually to arrive at their estimates?
2. Did individual students assign significantly different values to the same piece of raw intelligence? Was the teamwork better?

Students should be encouraged to raise issues associated with group dynamics and deadlines during these discussions. The key questions to be asked are:

1. What were the major factors involved in reaching agreement during operational team sessions?
2. Was the initial view adopted by each student the one that made it into the final briefing?
3. How did students persuade colleagues who disagreed with their position?
4. Did anyone feel pressure to conform to another colleague's views? How was this issue resolved?
5. Was there evidence of groupthink, dominant leader, or layering? Were any group members excluded from discussions because they held unpopular views?
6. During the final group session, did students in each operational team prove reluctant to change their team's views?
7. Did students feel pressure because of time constraints? How did these constraints affect individual and team performance?

The facilitator should conclude the debriefing by asking students to assess how they would rate their operational team's use of need-to-share intelligence and crisis management tools. This should lead to a discussion about whether students would do anything differently if given another chance.

CONCLUSION

One of the conclusions of the analysis of the causes that led to the "failure" of the U.S. intelligence community to prevent the 9/11 terrorist attacks was that insufficient attention was given to the issues related to the intelligence paradigm and the manner in which intelligence services cooperated with other institutions from the national security system. In particular, the 9/11 terrorist attacks tragically illustrated the fact that we are now dealing with a new type of terrorist threat, which we were not ready to face.

The solution identified by intelligence services in order to strengthen their capabilities of preventing and combating transnational terrorism was changing the intelligence paradigm from "need to know" to "need to share" while promoting joint operations at the international level, mainly through military campaigns based on the "preemptive strikes" strategy.

But it became clear that military institutions and intelligence agencies were not prepared to provide a full solution for the threat of international terrorism, in spite of the military campaigns against the terrorist bases in Afghanistan and Iraq, as terrorist attacks continued to claim victims in the Western world.

From an institutional point of view, intelligence agencies have implemented strategies for preventing and combating terrorism on their national territories, through which they tried to prepare and specialize intervention units and optimize the methods of collecting intelligence from within the terrorist cells.

But these action plans were not complete without an operational dimension focused on countering the terrorist threat, to which all law enforcement and defense institutions must contribute. The solution is the integrated management of the terrorist crisis. An important question was how to operationalize a strategy for the integrated management of the terrorist crisis—apart from legal and informational issues—with a focus on training the human resource.

In this respect, the objective of this training simulation is for students from academic fields such as intelligence, security, diplomacy, law enforcement, and public policy studies to realize the importance of teamwork and capabilities sharing in order to efficiently address security threats that require integrated crisis management.

APPENDIX A: RAW INTELLIGENCE

The Romanian Intelligence Service has information that a Pakistani citizen, who came to Romania from Germany 3 months ago, is suspected of involvement in activities of gathering funds for terrorist groups in Afghanistan and Pakistan.

After coming to Romania, the Pakistani citizen showed himself to be a deeply religious person, participating daily at the religious service from the Bucharest mosque and following the Koranic principles. At the end of each religious service, the individual in question argues, in small circles composed solely of Pakistani and Afghan citizens, in favor of helping the "suffering Muslim brothers" and "punishing those guilty for the suffering of the brothers and sisters from Afghanistan and Pakistan."

During these conversations, the Pakistani citizen showed interest in gathering an important sum of money for charitable purposes from other Pakistani nationals residing in Romania and other European Union states. Through this process he managed to gather a considerable sum of money. During a private conversation, he mentioned that the money will be used to "pay for the medical treatment of fellow Pakistanis with precarious financial situations and who require surgical interventions in private clinics in Turkey."

With regard to this issue, the Romanian Intelligence Service has acquired information indicating that this money is used for the medical treatment of Taliban insurgents in Afghanistan and the tribal area of Pakistan, who were wounded in confrontations with the International Security Assistance Force (ISAF) forces.

APPENDIX B: RAW INTELLIGENCE

1. Primary information provided by the Romanian Office for Immigration, a body within the Ministry of Administration and Interior, collected after analyzing databases regarding the legal situation of the Pakistani citizen:

In 2012, the Pakistani citizen came to the Romanian Office for Immigration to demand a visa with the purpose of conducting business in Romania. When asked about his purpose for residing in Romania, the Pakistani citizen mentioned, at that date, that he was coming from Germany where he worked in the resort business. He now wanted to dispose of a large sum of money destined for the opening of a fruit and vegetables warehouse.

Following in-depth study of the databases, it was ascertained that, before 2012, the Pakistani citizen had traveled several times to Romania as a tourist, for short periods of time, coming from states such as Germany and the Netherlands.

2. Primary intelligence gathered by the General Police Inspectorate in Romania, an entity within the Ministry of Administration and Interior concerned with commercial activities conducted by the Pakistani citizen in Romania:

The Pakistani citizen owns a company specializing in retail commerce dealing with the "import and sale of fruit," which conducts its activity in Bucharest.

Since 2012, the Pakistani citizen has been a Romanian resident, when he founded a company, as a unique associate, being interested also with initiating and developing import-export and national distribution of agricultural and food products.

In the time he has spent in Romania, the Pakistani citizen has managed to create a large circle of acquaintances, including several among the ranks of civil servants belonging to the local and central administration.

3. Primary intelligence concerning the Pakistani citizen provided by the Federal Intelligence Service of Germany (Bundesnachrichtendienst), at the request of the Romanian Intelligence Service on the basis of the cooperation protocol in the field of preventing and combating terrorism, signed by the two intelligence agencies:

The Pakistani citizen left from his native country illegally in 2011 with the destination of Germany, through an illegal migration network believed to be connected with members and sympathizers of al Qaida and insurgent Taliban groups from Afghanistan and the tribal region of Pakistan.

German authorities suspected the Pakistani citizen of acting on the territory of their state on the behalf of the illegal migration network for bringing Muslim citizens, including members of terrorist groups, to the European continent. He was being monitored by the Office for the Protection of the Constitution in Germany. As a result of this monitoring, in the period 2011–2012, they determined that the Pakistani citizen frequently makes telephone calls to individuals who were under observation by the German and Dutch intelligence services because they were suspected of terrorist activities. This conduct led them to believe that he was acting in support of the aforementioned criminal network.

Moreover, German authorities managed to acquire from the National Spanish Police data ascertaining that the Pakistani citizen was arrested in Spain in 2008 for involvement in drug trafficking. Also, in the period 2005–2007, he was arrested several times in Italy, being charged with forging travel papers, drug trafficking, and the smuggling of stolen cars.

4. Primary intelligence regarding the Pakistani citizen provided by the Directorate for Combating Organized Crime within the Ministry of Administration and Interior:

In the Bucharest region, there is a drug trafficking network, which, for sums of money varying between 80,000 and 100,000 euros, ensures the transport of significant quantities of narcotics from Afghanistan via Iran and Turkey to states in Western Europe. It is suspected that a part of the money resulting from these activities is being transferred (by using informal fund transfer systems) into the accounts of insurgent Taliban groups in Afghanistan.

The members of this network have their roles set in advance and act in various directions, from introducing the drugs on Romanian territory, transiting the territory of this country, to passing the drugs over the border (disguised as transports of fruits or persons) and transporting them to western states (Germany and the Netherlands).

One of the members of this network is the Pakistani citizen about whom the CAOC requested data. There seems to be evidence indicating that the illegal activities he is currently conducting in Romania are meant to support the transit of drugs coming from the Middle East and Afghanistan through Romania as well as to identify companies that could be used as "cover companies" for transporting the drugs to Germany and the Netherlands, as well as taking out of the country the money resulted from the drug trafficking.

For the transport of drugs to the Western European countries, the Pakistani citizen has recruited several Romanian citizens who are employed as drivers for the auto-trains that transport fruits. One of these drivers has stated, among his circle of friends, that he must leave for the Netherlands on September 28, 2012, at 05:00 a.m., to deliver a large quantity of fruits coming from Turkey and that his boss, the Pakistani citizen, promised him a "bonus" if "things go okay."

5. Primary intelligence on the means of communication and data transfer employed by the Pakistani citizens, provided by the Special Telecommunications Service:

The Pakistani citizen currently under investigation by the CAOC uses several mobile phones with prepaid phone cards that he exchanges frequently (both the cards and the phones), probably with the purpose of avoiding investigation from the law enforcement and judiciary authorities.

In addition, the Pakistani citizen seems to use a disguised contact system in his relations with other individuals, avoiding to speak at length on the phone or making very short phone calls with his mobile phones (with the exception of extraordinary circumstances). There is also evidence that the person under investigation keeps contact with his acquaintances by sending e-mail messages (changing the addresses periodically, on a monthly basis) or through direct conversations by messenger.

6. Primary intelligence on the Pakistani citizens from the Foreign Intelligence Service:

On August 25, 2012, the Dutch authorities made a drug capture of 250 kilos of heroin, which were hidden in 10 metal barrels that were part of a tomato transport of 100 barrels. The transport was destined for a Dutch company and belonged to a fruits and vegetables import–export company from Turkey. The driver of the auto-train making the transport, which was registered in Romania at the company where the Pakistani citizen in question is the unique associate, was a Romanian citizen. He was detained for questioning by the Dutch authorities and released, as it could not be proven that he knew of the existence of the drugs in the transported merchandise.

The subsequent investigations made by the Dutch authorities showed that the transport of food products from the Turkish company to the Netherlands is done almost monthly with the help of auto-trains, which are registered in Romania, on the name of the Romanian company where the Pakistani citizen is a unique associate.

REFERENCES

Agenției Naționale Antidrog. 2011. Raportul național privind situația drogurilor în România 2011: Noi evoluții, tendințe și informații detaliate cu privire la temele de interes european a REITOX—Rețeaua europeană de informații privind drogurile și toxicomania. Available at: www.ana.gov.ro.

Ghergut, Ondine. 2011. Romanii care traficau drogurile drogurile columbienilor sunt foști șoferi de TIR. January 19. Available at: www.romanialibera.ro.

Gray, Mike. 2009. Drugs & terrorism. July 16. Available at: www.narcoterror.org.

Official Monitor. 2004. LEGEA nr. 535 din 25 noiembrie 2004 privind prevenirea și combaterea terorismului. *Official Monitor, 1161* (December 8).

Romanian National Security Strategy (SSN). n.d. România Europeană, România Euro-Atlantică: pentru o viață mai bună într-o țară democratică, mai sigură și prosper. Available at: www .presidency.ro.

Stoleru, Bogdan. 2007. Unul dintre cei mai mari traficanți de heroină din lume, stabilit în România de 15 ani. Amos News. May 16.

Strategia națională de prevenire și combatere a terorismului, Anexa la Decizia CSAT n no.36 din 5 aprilie 2002. Președintele României. Available at: www. presidency.ro.

Topala, Andi. 2010. Traficanți de droguri periculoși, eliberați de instanțe. În ultimii ani, mulți narcotraficanți care au adus în țară sute de kilograme de stupefiante au dispărut fără urmă sau se plimbă în voie grație judecătorilor. September 20. Available at: www.puterea.ro.

U.S. Senate. 2002. *Narco-terror: The worldwide connection between drugs and terrorism.* Hearing before the Subcommittee on Technology, Terrorism, and Government Information of the Committee on the Judiciary, United States Senate, 107th Congress, 2nd session, March 13. Available at: www.judiciary.senate.gov.

10

A 3D Intelligence Analysis on Migration as Security Threat: From Data to Intelligence

Irena Dumitru and Ella Magdalena Ciupercă

ABSTRACT

This simulation aims to improve students' or future analysts' ability to analyze intelligence by exercising their capacity to describe (D1), explain (D2), and predict (D3). It also helps students understand the process of transforming raw data to intelligence that answers a "need to know." The focus is on migration as one of the important security issues, where the effects of globalization in framing security relations can be clearly seen.

As a first step, students are provided with a large amount of data and also with criteria for assessing sources and data. These criteria help select relevant valuable information. Second, by relying on already selected information, students are asked to apply an "intelligence analysis toolkit" consisting of two analysis methods (the "What if?" and the "Competing Hypothesis Analysis"). By applying these analysis methods and then presenting the results of their analyses in front of their classmates, students improve their skills in identifying possible explanations and alternative scenarios.

The simulation also allows the instructor to discuss psychological implications, challenging students to identify potential vulnerabilities and limits in intelligence analysis, such as subjectivity, mental schemata, inexact memories, and cognitive biases.

KEYWORDS

Intelligence analysis; migration; descriptive analysis; explicative analysis; predictive analysis; teaching intelligence analysis; subjectivity; bias

This simulation is aimed at replicating, in conditions as close to reality as possible, the analytic process used by intelligence agencies to process raw data into intelligence products. What it attempts to facilitate with students—and future analysts—is the need for a better, more accurate understanding of the analytic process: its stages, limits, and traps.

Beyond the never-resolved dilemma whether or not analysis is science—recurrently addressed by various approaches to the formation of an intelligence analyst—when teaching it in the classroom, instructors use practical exercises, serious games, and simulations, which have been empirically proven to be successful in helping students to develop and sharpen their analytical skills. One of the promoters of this approach is Kristan J. Wheaton (2011), who embraces what is called "game-based learning" or "gamification, and what it means for intelligence," a neologism that highlights the increasing tendency to integrate games into serious tasks in order to increase participation or, in the context of education, learning. From Wheaton's own experience, "gamification" makes the intelligence course more fun but, at the same time, it obviously increases the quality of students' work. Therefore, our approach stemmed from the hypothesis that a game-based perspective on teaching can be successful in intelligence analysis, with obvious benefits to learning, improving performance, and increasing student satisfaction with the course.

For a better understanding of the elements included in the didactic process, we have opted for a model metaphorically titled "tridimensional analysis." Tridimensionality is in fact the result of juxtaposing the successive and interdependent stages specific to the analytic process. As a side note, it must be said that dividing the analytic process into stages has been done in order to facilitate pedagogical requirements. With all of the above in mind, we must also mention that this model was not designed to accurately render the various types of analysis performed by intelligence agencies (e.g., operational, tactical or predictive, to name just a few), but rather to "break down" the analytic process and thus illustrate it and explain it as a mental course that starts by describing, goes on to explain, and finally is completed with a prediction. Therefore, the simulation maps the analytic process in three distinct dimensions:

1. Descriptive: Allowing identification and acknowledgment of the general outline of a specific issue;
2. Explanatory: Facilitating identification of root causes and inner mechanisms; and
3. Predictive: Leading to mapping potential evolutions and forecasting future trends of development.

In using this staged representation of the analytic process, we do not in any way wish to suggest that it may bring significant added value in conceptualizing the analytic process in general. Its significance and utility is, nevertheless, of relevance most of all to students' education, as it can help them improve their ability to understand the analytic process as used by intelligence analysts in real-life conditions.

It is also important to mention that the simulation can integrate data and be performed with regard to any potential subject relevant to national security. In the current study, the simulation will focus on migration and its implications as a threat to national security. Our choice of migration as a preferred theme was motivated by its relevance to the current security environment, in which it can be perceived both as an opportunity and a challenge to internal and external security.

PREPARATIONS (15 MINUTES)

The exercise is accomplished simultaneously by three competing groups, each made up of five students: group A, group B, and group C, which are to perform similar tasks. We assess this method to be more efficient as it allows participants, once the exercise is over, to make comparisons and learn both from their own accomplishments and errors of judgment as well as from those of their fellow colleagues.

Before starting the actual exercise, prepare the material resources that are to be used: the documents, a flip chart, a sufficiently large classroom to allow working in three autonomous groups at an adequate distance from one another to minimize mutual interference, colored markers, access to computers equipped with the Analysis of Competing Hypotheses software.[1]

PRESIMULATION BRIEFING

The instructor presents the objectives of the exercise, its stages, and allotted time for each stage. The instructor also provides the criteria for analyzing intermediate materials resulting from the process and describes a set of analytical methods to be used in interpreting data.

Participants are presented with the three dimensions of the analytic process and their associated questions:

- The *descriptive* dimension—which will be covered by providing answers to the following questions: WHO? WHAT? HOW? WHERE? WHEN?
- The *explanatory* dimension—which will be covered by offering answers to the question WHY?
- The *predictive* dimension—which will be covered by providing answers to questions such as: HOW CAN THE SITUATION CHANGE? WHAT CAN THE FUTURE BRING?

In this stage, the instructor should answer questions asked by students and provide clarifying details on how the exercise is going to be performed.

SIMULATION OVERVIEW AND OBJECTIVES

D1: The Descriptive Dimension

Evaluating and Selecting Data (1 hour)

First, participants perform a process that can be described as descriptive, analytic, factual, and relational, in which they focus on facts. Their activity is structured toward solving a puzzle by searching explicit pieces of information (data) and identifying the way in which these relate to one another. In this stage, the key process is that of searching for and collecting information.

Each group is provided a folder containing documents with data on a given topic, in various degrees of relevance in terms of both content and time frame. Students are asked to read the materials, perform a preliminary evaluation, and select those data that can be integrated into an intelligence product.

This preliminary activity, compulsory to the entire process of analysis, is performed with the help of an evaluation drill containing a series of items that allow evaluation of both the source and the information (Table 10.1).

Once the evaluation has been completed, each group hands in to the instructor a product containing selected data and their evaluation. This stage ends with a common working session in which each group tasks a speaker to represent the group's findings. He or she will present obtained results, explaining the choice of the group for including certain data and leaving out others. The instructor highlights common elements as well as diverging points of view and advances explanations that will allow understanding of differences and evaluation errors.

Descriptive Analysis (30 minutes)

Based on information selected during document evaluation, a brainstorming session is organized, in which participants debate, within groups, trying to discover compre-

Table 10.1. Evaluation Sheet

SOURCE	CREDIBILITY/ AUTHORITY	Does the source identify itself? Does it hold relevant expertise with respect to the provided data?
	OBJECTIVITY	Does the source use neutral words/words with emotional impact? Are the data based on facts/opinions? If they are based on opinions, are these "informed opinions" that belong to experts?
DATA	NOVELTY	Are the data recent?
	RELEVANCY	Are the data relevant for the matter under discussion? Do they explain the phenomenon? Pay attention to the following trap: information is interesting but irrelevant.
	ACCURACY	Is the information validated by other sources?

hensive answers to the questions: WHO? WHAT? HOW? WHERE? WHEN? After the session, each group elaborates and delivers a descriptive analysis.

D2: The Explanatory Stage and the Method of Competing Hypotheses (1 hour)

In order to be able to provide the most appropriate explanations, participants should devise and then evaluate as many hypotheses as possible. An accurate method to test them is the "Analysis of Competing Hypotheses" (ACH). ACH allows the user to evaluate hypotheses by taking into consideration all of the details of the obtained information. Opting for ACH is justified by the fact that it allows an objective evaluation of explanations for a given phenomenon, their placing in a hierarchical order, and, finally, their validation or invalidation based on pros and cons (namely, information selected as a result of evaluating both source and content). Implicitly, using ACH also facilitates an identification of potential cognitive biases (in their turn discussed during the debrief held following the simulation). In conclusion, by applying this method, one avoids a series of errors in the analytical process and, as a consequence, eliminates the probability of incorrect decisions.

The method requires the development of a matrix in which hypotheses are introduced (in our case explanations) as well as relevant data obtained during the collection stage. The analysis matrix facilitates evaluation of a number of mutually exclusive hypotheses, where columns represent hypothetical alternatives and rows represent discovered evidence. The latter can, when related to hypotheses, bear three values: of validation, invalidation, or neutrality. Once data are centralized, the hypothesis that is invalidated by the least amount of evidence is considered the most plausible.

The advantages of using this method come from the fact that developing the matrix also allows for a revision of analyses and identification of ideas on which agreement/ disagreement can be reached. Data can be evaluated systematically, and using this instrument has proven its usefulness in identifying correct versus incorrect information.

The method benefits from the free software solution mentioned above, ACH 2.0, developed by Palo Alto Research Center (PARC) in collaboration with Richards J. Heuer, Jr., which facilitates calculations on the degree of discrimination of each hypothesis. It also helps reason out and evaluate alternative explanations on what has happened, what is happening, and what is likely to happen in the future.

Participants follow the eight steps of ACH (according to the model proposed by Richards J. Heuer [1999]), as listed in Table 10.2. Alternatively, instructors can also use Julian Richards's ACH simulation in Chapter 2 to perform this analysis instead of ACH 2.0.

D3: The Predictive Stage and the "What if?" Method (1 hour)

In order to accomplish the predictive dimension and provide valid scenarios as to the evolution of the situation, we recommend applying the "What if?" method. This way, facts and situations with critical value in the evolution of a given issue can be identified. It also allows for assessing implications before facts take their said turn. At the same

Table 10.2.   The Steps of the Analysis of Competing Hypotheses (ACH)

1. Identify the possible hypotheses to be considered.
2. Make a list of significant evidence and arguments for and against each hypothesis.
3. Prepare a matrix with hypotheses across the top and evidence down the side. Analyze the "diagnosticity" of the evidence and arguments, that is, identify which items are most helpful in judging the relative likelihood of the hypotheses.
4. Refine the matrix. Reconsider the hypotheses and delete evidence and arguments that have no diagnostic value.
5. Draw tentative conclusions about the relative likelihood of each hypothesis. Proceed by trying to disprove the hypotheses rather than prove them.
6. Analyze how sensitive your conclusion is to a few critical items of evidence. Consider the consequences for your analysis if that evidence were wrong, misleading, or subject to a different interpretation.
7. Report conclusions. Discuss the relative likelihood of all the hypotheses, not just the most likely one.
8. Identify milestones for future observation that may indicate events are taking a different course than expected.

Heuer, 1999, p. 122.

time, mental simulation of a phenomenon's potential evolution allows for an easier identification of factors that can influence, either positively or negatively, the supposed trajectory and thus also question preexisting ideas. This method challenges the analyst to see existing data from a multiplicity of perspectives and to imagine all possible consequences before a certain decision is implemented.

Discussion of the Psychology of Intelligence Analysis (30 minutes)

After performing the above-mentioned stages, each group presents summary reports of its findings, which are both individually and comparatively discussed and analyzed. The instructor presents conclusions drawn as a result of monitoring the methodological path undertaken by each group: strengths and weak points, limits, errors.

Participants are required to perform self-evaluations of subjective choices made during the analytic process. The premise is that there will be differences among the variants presented by each group, mainly explained by the subjective interpretations that occurred during the analytic process. Among these will be cognitive categories, preexisting scenarios, prejudices, stereotypes, cultural differences and preexisting routine, limitations of memory, heuristics and cognitive errors, difficulties determined by the formation of decisions, processes characteristic to group dynamics, and the persuasive and self-persuasive specificity.

CONDUCTING THE SIMULATION

In order to test the previously described simulation, we have opted for a theme relevant to national security in a modern globalized context: migration. Tailoring the simulation accordingly, we have tested for the implications that legal or illegal migration has on the national security of Romania. With this purpose in mind, students are provided various data on migration (both emigration and immigration) that were exclusively collected from open sources.

This subject is by no means an easy one, especially when one considers the difficulty of defining the concepts within which we operate. Nevertheless, this theme was chosen because the complex relationship between security and migration generates a rich range of significant effects, thus allowing students to observe the way in which the analytic process is accomplished and helping them to grasp the advantages and inconveniences of suggested methods.

At the present time, Europe is witnessing the effects of globalization that blur or cast out completely barriers and obstacles that once blocked international flows of people, goods, services, capital, and information. In the European strategic arena, migration is both a result of and a source for insecurity. In many cases, migration is directly or indirectly linked to organized crime groups, and the fact that, most often, drug trafficking routes are similar to those of illegal migration gives credence to this view. In this very context, European officials share a growing concern for the increasing level of violence and risk derived from migration.

The migration phenomenon can have implications translated as a threat to national security, for example, due to the fact that certain immigrants can be recruited and used by terrorist organizations to commit attacks on our national territory. Factors of risk derive also from the increasingly growing connections between organized crime and terrorism worldwide. Risks to the national and European security environment are triggered not only by the direct consequences migration has in general, but also, more importantly, by the connections illegal migration develops either with terrorism (by facilitating terrorists' access) or with various forms of organized crime such as money laundering, drug trafficking, among others.

In Romania's case, migration is favored—with direct implications to national security—by its geographic location as well as the presence on its national territory of foreign citizens from regions of the world well known as sources of migration. Romania is a transit area for migrants heading toward the West.

Step 1: Preparing the Simulation (15 minutes)

In this stage students, divided in three groups of five individuals, receive documents related to migration (Table 10.3), as well as all other necessary materials (flip chart, computer, etc.).

Step 2: Evaluating and Selecting Data (1 hour)

Students evaluate the information from Table 10.3 using the evaluation sheet (Table 10.1) and reorganize data so as to provide answers to the following questions:

- Who emigrates/immigrates?
- From where/to where do they emigrate/immigrate?
- How do they emigrate/immigrate?
- What resources do they use to emigrate/immigrate?

Table 10.3.   Open Source Materials to Provide to Participants

Documents	Sources
EU Membership has been good for the two countries, but is testing Eurocrats' patience, Economist	www.economist.com/node/21550330
EU Organised Crime Threat Assessment—OCTA 2011	http://migrantsatsea.files.wordpress .com/2011/05/octa_2011-1.pdf
EU organized crime threat assessment, Europol Public Information	www.europol.europa.eu/content/press/europol -organised-crime-threat-assessment-2011-429
Europe's Immigrant Issues	http://weekspopulation.blogspot.ro/2011/04/ eastern-european-immigrants-boost-uk.html
Final Report: Romanian immigrants in Spain, Access to Rights and Civil Dialogue for All	www.accesstorights.net/citizenships/ files/2012/01/Final-Report-on-Romanian -immigrants-in-Spain.pdf
France declares war on illegal migrants: Riot police smash camps and hundreds rounded up for deportation as Socialists take on gypsies	www.dailymail.co.uk/news/article-2186067/ France-declares-war-illegal-migrants -Riot-police-smash-camps-round-gypsies -deportation.html#ixzz25FRZnzPO
Heroin trade and illegal immigration in Southeastern Europe	http://serbianna.com/analysis/archives/1311
Illegal immigration in Austria	www.google.ro/url?sa=t&rct=j&q=illegal+migra tion+romania+strategy+research+project& source=web&cd=18&cad=rja&ved=0CF8QFj AHOAo&url=http%3A%2F%2Femn.intrasoft- intl.com%2FDownloads%2Fdownload.do%3 Bjsessionid%3D9095428C286A6547A69AC0 916B68DF79%3FfileID%3D278&ei=jN9EUL neDdCP4gStoYDIBg&usg=AFQjCNECjrRhheS hJvZMh_hapyMBKzgUjw
Migration in Central and South-Eastern Europe	www.iom.hu/PDF/IOM%20Regional%20 Strategy%20for%20CEE%20&%20SEE.pdf
Migration initiatives	www.iom.int/jahia/webdav/site/myjahiasite/ shared/shared/mainsite/published_docs/books/ Migration-Initiatives-Appeal.pdf
Migration management in Central and Southeastern Europe, IOM Strategy and objectives 2006–2007	http://publications.iom.int/bookstore/index .php?main_page=product_info&products_ id=139
Migration trends and policies in the Black Sea region—cases of Moldova, Romania, Ukraine, International Centre for Policy Studies	www.viitorul.org/download.php?file=cHVibGljL 3B1YmxpY2F0aW9ucy8xNjc1L2VuL01pZ3Jh dGlvbl9lbmcucGRm
Migration Trends and Policies in the Black Sea Region: cases of Moldova, Romania and Ukraine	www.icps.com.ua/files/articles/50/33/Migration_ ENG.pdf
New Waves: Migration from Eastern to Southern Europe	www.flad.pt/documentos/1256642168A6dXX1y n5Uq83QL7.pdf
Romanian migration in Greece: a first appraisal after Romania's accession at the EU	www.eliamep.gr/wp-content/uploads/2009/10/ idea_lazarescu_romanian-migration-in -greece_june-09.pdf

Documents	Sources
Romanian migration to Spain: motivation, network and strategies, Romanian Academy	http://pdc.ceu.hu/archive/00003393/01/romanian_migration_to_spain.pdf
Smuggling of Migrants	www.unodc.org/documents/human-trafficking/Migrant-Smuggling/Issue-Papers/Issue_Paper_-_Smuggling_of_Migrants_by_Sea.pdf
The Dynamics of Population Emigration from Romania—Contemporary and Future Trends	www.waset.org/journals/waset/v42/v42-98.pdf

Step 3: Descriptive Analysis (30 minutes)

Given the fact that all working groups received the same documents, the results presented by speakers should be fairly similar. Differences in approach should be minimal, if not negligible. The result is not surprising: the descriptive stage of the simulation—and, by extrapolation, all analytic processes—is highly dependent on the choice of information and its evaluation. By providing a set of documents and a working sheet, accidental elements that would have otherwise generated differences in the descriptive process have been removed. The role of systematization and evaluation based on multiple criteria was thus highlighted, as well as the importance of focusing on facts rather than on opinions and beliefs.

Step 4: Explanatory Analysis (1 hour)

Students now have to identify "alternative explanations" hypotheses for the migration phenomenon and its implications toward national security of Romania. They also have to test hypotheses based on the given facts.

The data analysis provided by independently working groups of students will highlight a wide variety of explanatory hypotheses. Some examples of typical alternative hypotheses produced in this step include economic crisis, technological developments, the changing of traditional values of stability in favor of a growing availability to migrate, increased discrimination level in today's society, the lack of correlation between greater expertise and improved quality of life, and the lack of job opportunities.

Participants apply the ACH method and test each hypothesis based on evidence previously selected. Each group presents two hypotheses they consider to have the highest relevance in explaining migration.

Step 5: Making Predictions (1 hour)

Once students have briefed their preliminary evaluations in step 4, they now will attempt to make predictions on the future evolution of this issue. Using the suggested "What if?" method, they will draft scenarios set on identifying certain elements ("X" factors) that can influence the evolution of the phenomenon. These factors can produce a positive or negative impact on national security. Later, they will perform mental simulations of the phenomenon's trajectory under the influence of these factors. Because the chosen theme was extremely complex, each group ultimately will choose only one factor they consider most relevant and likely to produce changes. Some typical proposals drafted by the three groups in recent runs of the simulation were as follows:

- Group A: Romania adheres to Schengen.
- Group B: As immigration continues to grow, xenophobia against immigrants rises.
- Group C: In Romania, VAT (value added tax) for food and agricultural products is reduced to 5 percent.

Advanced pros and cons were highly influenced by the specificity of the factor considered as the source of changes: global politics, macrosocial or macroeconomic issues.

For example, one debate that focused on Romania's accession to the Schengen space led to a separation of factors concerning emigration from those concerning immigration. Emigration is encouraged by the accession, its most important effects being felt on the national labor force. Depending on the features of these emigrants, national security can be affected, in group A's opinion from at least two points of view: (1) Losing the added value that highly specialized emigrants would have brought if they had stayed in their country; (2) There are recorded difficulties in cooperating with other states affected by the criminal behavior of some Romanians who emigrated to the respective countries. On the other hand, illegal immigration is encouraged (as an alternative to higher demands applied in accepting legal immigrants) and, as a consequence, there can be a higher cross-border criminality rate and higher unemployment. At the same time, there can emerge changes in the ethnic structure of Romania, with direct effects on social policies, psychosocial climate, among others.

The scenario drafted by group B can be considered a logical continuation of the one drafted by group A, as it refers to a drastic upturn of xenophobic feelings against the growing number of immigrants arriving in the country. In this situation, it is less important whether the immigrants have arrived legally or illegally. Among the most important factors provided by students were lack of a specific legislation devoted to an efficient management of immigration, foreseen xenophobia, and growing unemployment rates. At the same time, in this particular scenario, Romania would become a highly multicultural society before its citizens were ready to embrace such values. This gap would cause a flow of negative feelings toward various minorities. At the same time, in the event that these minorities would polarize around representation structures, they would in turn have the opportunity to gain seats in the parliament and the implicit capacity to influence decisions.

The scenario drafted by group C focuses on the impact that economic measures—such as VAT reduction—potentially has on migration. In this group's point of view, a VAT reduction would lead to better life standards, therefore producing a decrease in emigration and an intensified immigration. Students produced examples in Western countries where host societies, confronted with an inflow of migrants and a stabilization of indigenous population, produced a growth in the GIP (gross internal product).

Accelerated food consumption would stimulate, in its turn, agriculture and, therefore, creation of new jobs for individuals who would otherwise have emigrated.

Therefore, we can conclude that applying the "What if?" method proved its usefulness from two different perspectives. First, by polarizing debates and ideas on the intended X factor, it facilitated a detailed analysis. Second, it stimulated students' debating abilities and imagination. Proof lies in the fact that students managed to identify numerous elements connected to the potential evolution of this phenomenon.

Stage 6: Debrief—Discussion of the Psychology of Intelligence Analysis

Starting from the observation that some of the differences in the analytic products typically exceed the framework set by the documents provided, the instructor pointed to human subjectivity as a potential explanation. In order to be able to illustrate and explain the impact of subjectivity on the analytic process, participants were required to evaluate their activity and identify those situations in which its impact was most obvious. Even though it may seem paradoxical, starting from the premise that people usually find it more difficult to identify their own biases rather than those of others, participants were not pointed solely toward self-evaluation.

The debrief showed that participants did identify the impact of subjectivity in selecting and evaluating data, in drafting explanatory hypotheses, and in tracing the evolution of the phenomenon. At the same time, this stage's results highlighted participants' tendency to rationalize and justify assumed errors.

In order to facilitate understanding of potential analytic errors, the instructor provided a connection between students' observations and already validated theories in the field of social sciences.

Therefore, participants felt the need to cover areas where they did not have sufficient information and thus enlarge their view, at times causing them to feel inadequately qualified to produce valid conclusions on the debated facts. As a consequence, blank spots were filled in with new information, while those areas where information was perceived as too dense and detailed were simplified. These aspects were explained via the thesis on the construction of social reality. This allowed for further explanations on the way that distinct individuals view a "personal" reality. At the same time, this observation allowed the instructor to emphasize a specific aspect of the analytic process, namely, to constantly integrate new data into the process.

An often-cited example is that of how stereotypes can influence the way an analyst thinks. In the particular case under discussion, the existence of a stereotype on the image of the emigrant/immigrant influenced the suggested hypotheses and scenarios. Participants attributed an important role in building such stereotypes to media reporting, which has the potential to create (distorted) images and shape behaviors.

Another element discussed was the impact of life experience, which was quantified as a result of actions plus knowledge. For example, some pointed to the cultural values analysts hold (and their implicit differences from those held by migrants). In participants' opinions, these can fuel approaches characterized as xenophobic, nationalist, tolerant, or with a strong identity focus.

Self-monitoring and introspection showed that data previously known, existing routines, and mental inertia were cited among the most influential factors. Subjects admitted a tendency to select data in accord with already formed opinion, with the rest of the information being considered as irrelevant (in conformity with the cognitive bias hypothesis confirmation).

During the simulation, when members expressed conflicting opinions, they tended to reach a consensus that inclined toward the opinion expressed or shared by the group leader/majority, due to his or her credibility (in this case, conformity being reached in the absence of a quality criterion).

At the same time, participants noticed that they showed a tendency to exaggerate the number of those who supported them as well as to overestimate their contribution to the final product. Often, the error of the retrospective was present—"I knew it!" (individuals' tendency to overestimate their prior knowledge on a phenomenon and the capacity to formulate predictions over its development), as well as the deliberate originality effect (an individual's wish to appear original in order to attract attention).

Data interpretation was also influenced by the way the set of documents was arranged, the first and last information having more impact than those in between. Sometimes participants identified correlations between two events not connected in real life—"illusive thinking"—for example, associating a growth in criminality rates with growing immigrant numbers. At the same time, in some situations, they evaluated the likelihood of an event according to whether it corresponded to a previously established mental scheme (for example, the existence of a problem occurring due to tensions between a minority and a majority can be read as pointing to the immigrants as the source of conflict).

LIMITS AND SUGGESTIONS TO IMPROVE THE EXERCISE

A first observation is that there are implications generated by the fact that the simulation is accomplished in lab conditions and not in real circumstances. Moreover, the process itself depends strictly on the data that the instructor chooses. As a result, the simulation has its limits generated by artificiality, lack of time pressure, as well as lack of responsibility in adopting a national security decision. In order to balance these effects, a possible solution would be to introduce a requirement that students produce analytical products in a portfolio to be handed in to a potential future employer, as this would add significance to the very act of producing them.

Choosing a broad theme such as migration presents the risk of producing very diverse, even though correct, solutions. A solution for improving didactic purpose would be to narrow the scope of analysis, choosing a specific theme that could be treated comprehensively to draw common and complete conclusions. As a result, one can conclude that the wider the theme set for analysis, the higher the number of variants generated by students and the less comprehensive the solution is.

Subsequently, in using the ACH method, it is important to be aware of its limits. The way in which the hypotheses are generated is affected, as previously shown, by a number of subjective factors such as culture, identity, and religion. Such elements can influence even the fact of considering certain hypothesis or not, as well as the way in which pros and cons that validate or invalidate the thesis are evaluated.

Given the stages they go through, from descriptive, to explanatory, and then to predictive, participants follow a general analytic trajectory, one that is shared by all analysts, regardless of the obvious differences of procedure adopted by security agencies. Furthermore, given the requirements of hypotheses, scenario identification, and other factors, the simulation encourages and stimulates divergent thinking, which can lead to a change in the traditional perspective of analysis and thus provide innovative solutions.

NOTE

1. Open source freeware available at www2.parc.com/istl/projects/ach/ach.html.

REFERENCES

Heuer, Richards, J. 1999. *Psychology of intelligence analysis.* Center for the Study of Intelligence. Available at: www.cia.gov/library/center-for-the-study-of-intelligence/csi-publications/books -and-monographs/psychology-of-intelligence-analysis/index.html.

Wheaton, Kristan J. 2011. Gamification, and what it means for intelligence. Available at http:// sourcesandmethods.blogspot.ro/2011/02/gamification-and-what-it-means-for.html.

11

TEST Simulation Model (Team-working and Experiential Scenario-based Training): "Secrets and Mysteries"

Chris Jagger and Julian Richards

The idea that children and adults alike can learn as much from their own experience and from the experience of others than from straight theory has a long history of analysis and incorporation into learning techniques. In the 1920s, Lindeman (1926, p. 7) noted that "experience is the adult learner's textbook." A decade later, John Dewey's (1938) influential book *Experience and Education* promoted the idea of learning by doing, which played a major role in influencing subsequent educational practice at all levels.

This article outlines a TEST (Team-working and Experiential Scenario-based Training) simulation model called "Secrets and Mysteries." This is a day-long intelligence scenario exercise, embedded within a 2-day workshop in which the first day allows students to explore issues of cognitive performance and analytical pitfalls. The framing for the workshop derives from the Butler Report in the United Kingdom, which resulted from an official inquiry into intelligence on weapons of mass destruction (WMD) in the wake of the 2003 military campaign against Iraq. In this report, in a section titled "The Limitations of Intelligence," Lord Butler discussed the difference between "secrets" and "mysteries" and the importance for the analyst of recognizing which was which. Butler noted that "intelligence can be expected to uncover secrets . . . but mysteries are essentially unknowable" (Lord Butler, 2004, p. 14).

It is vitally important, therefore, for intelligence analysts to use the best analytical techniques and skills in uncovering secrets of true value to policymakers, but they must also recognize their limitations and those of the intelligence machinery in not being able to answer every question definitively. This is the nature of intelligence. A heightened awareness of these issues and where the boundaries are situated can be developed through scenario-based training such as TEST. This article presents the "Secrets and Mysteries" simulation, aimed primarily for intelligence analysts at various stages in their careers, but the exercise has proved stimulating and effective for students of intelligence studies and would doubtlessly work in any number of other environments in which analysis is a key skill.

Experiential learning is not necessarily clearly understood as a concept, and a number of models have been developed over the years to try to explain its process. Kolb (1984, p. 38) suggested that "learning is the process whereby knowledge is created through the transformation of experience." To explain this process, he built a four-stage "experiential learning cycle," which links concrete experience through observation and reflection; forming abstract concepts; and testing in new situations in an iterative and constantly repeating cycle. Kolb and Fry (1975, pp. 35–36) further developed the model into a schema of "learning styles" that best suit different stages of the process. This connected with some important work in human resources and business organizations on learning styles and preferences, such as that of Edward De Bono's (2008) *Six Thinking Hats* and Honey and Mumford's (1992) "learning styles" system. The central principle of all of these studies and models concerns the importance—and the challenge—of working in teams on difficult problems and enabling teams composed of disparate individuals to work together effectively and learn from one another.

Clearly there is not uniformity in the concept of experiential learning, since it can mean any number of processes at several different levels. Experience suggests that adults in professional situations tend to learn best "on the job," where they can apply theory to practice most readily. Weil and McGill (1989, p. 3) noted, however, that there is a spectrum of experiential learning activities in the environment, which they characterized as four "villages." These range from more personal processes of betterment to experiential learning aimed at wider business or societal change. This range of experiences, learning processes, and impacts is an issue to which we return later.

As Walter Laqueur (1983) noted, intelligence analysis bears similarities to other disciplines in which judgment must be exercised in the face of uncertain information, perhaps particularly to medical diagnosis. Both the doctor and the intelligence analyst have to "collect and evaluate the evidence about phenomena frequently not amenable to direct observation" (Laqueur, 1983, pp. 534–535). The same comparisons could probably also be made to meteorologists, economists, financial market traders, and any number of other challenging and uncertain analytical activities. As observed elsewhere in this volume, intelligence analysis also has to deal with the question of denial and deception. Indeed, Heuer (2005, p. 86) noted that the likelihood of success in intelligence analysis has a number of challenges placed in its way, including "cognitive limitations" among the analysts; a set of information on which to base judgments that is invariably "sparse, incomplete and ambiguous"; and a frequently (although not always) justified expectation of deception by the enemy or target. Add to this institutional pitfalls such as prevailing wisdom or "groupthink"; failures to share information appropriately among agencies; and bias and politicization of the judgment and decision-making process, and it is no wonder that a great deal of careful training must be undertaken to ensure that analysts deliver reliable assessments and judgments, at least some of the time.

The 2creatEffects TEST model aims to tackle these challenges head-on and provides a learning environment in which students can experience these challenges in relevant scenarios. They can then reflect on their experience and consider how it enhances their understanding and future performance in analysis. Significantly, however, the experience is not just about heightening awareness and becoming better at analysis in a passive sense. The "effects" part of 2creatEffects seeks to emphasize that intelligence, particularly in the modern world, is not just about analyzing but about making operational decisions on courses of action to be taken in the real world. It is also about considering the consequences of such actions on the environment, some of which may be unexpected and unwelcome. Modern intelligence analysis does not end with an assessment of the available information, but more often than not with a recommendation for which further actions should be taken and what the expected results may be. This may be ever more the case in the information and "cyber" age, where intelligence is becoming as much "active" as "passive" in its interaction with the Internet and its users.

The simulation model works by testing a set of core skills needed by intelligence analysts, which they can deploy in mitigation of analytical challenges and pitfalls. There are two core skills that form the central focus for the 2creatEffects simulation model: critical thinking and creativity. A third "C"—challenge—provides the framework for the simulation model in terms of how issues are introduced, and reflected upon by the students, throughout the course.

In addition to personal reflection on how biases and cognitive weaknesses can manifest themselves in all of us, one of the aims of the simulation exercise is to allow the students to reflect on the institutional dimension of these issues. This applies on several different levels: within small local teams; up to wider teams and divisions; and further up to the whole organizational culture. Significantly, some of the students may themselves already be managers and team leaders, or may become so at a future stage in their career, and it is important and beneficial to encourage such students to reflect on how they might be able to influence institutional cultures using their own power and influence in the organization. The question is asked: Does your own team allow for critical thinking and challenge at all times? If not, how could you change it?

TEST can easily be tailored to the participant's specific competency and learning requirements. A range of games, puzzles, case studies, group discussion, interviews, group and individual briefings, role play, and video, audio, among others, are introduced throughout the exercise depending on the particular requirements of the group.

Why team-working? Teamwork and cross-sector collaboration have become core components of most professional environments. This is particularly true of the intelligence community, where cross-departmental and interagency partnerships and joint operations are essential and commonplace. Teamwork also plays an important role in the individual's ability to learn. Furthermore, one of the most common learning barriers for adults is the fear of being judged by their subordinates, peers, and supervisors. Many adult learners therefore fail to put new knowledge to use outside the training environment since they are concerned about the risk of failure. This is in part due to how the adult learning is often delivered—as distance learning and conventional chalk-and-talk method whereby the individual learner does not have the opportunity to put the knowledge to use together with their colleagues in a neutral learning environment. By placing an emphasis on teamwork through interactive simulation exercises, TEST quickly creates a level playing field between group hierarchies for collaborative and developmental learning.

As discussed above, the genesis of this particular exercise is embedded in the study of human's and institutional failure in assessment and in doing so aims to address the core analytical skills of critical thinking and creativity. The program draws on examples from within the intelligence and security community where human and institutional failures have had serious consequences and from which valuable lessons have been learned, showing participants how progress can be built on the foundations of failure.

After an initial introduction to certain principles, theory, tools, and techniques, we focus on case studies and scenario-based exercises. During and after each exercise, we help participants reflect on what they have done and why they have done it, consequently highlighting dependence on previous norms rather than fresh thought and initiative. This is learning through experience; no prior knowledge of the scenario is necessary, and most find the experience both fun and, importantly, mentally liberating. Throughout the program the core principles of critical and creative thinking are highlighted, engendering new ways of both seeing and dealing with problems. This provides for a depth of understanding that will prove invaluable to both the individual and his or her organization in future.

On day one of the "Secrets and Mysteries" workshop, after an initial introduction to the principles and theory of critical thinking and creativity, studies of intelligence failure are examined, placing particular emphasis on the key findings of the Butler Report and the 9/11 Commission Report (2004), observing fundamental cognitive issues such as memory, perception, bias and prejudice, mirror imaging, self-deception and confirmation bias, groupthink, cognitive dissonance, functional fixedness, lack of imagination, risk aversion, and so on. Participants are challenged through short scenario and discussion exercises in which their perceptions and the theory will be questioned; the lessons drawn can then be discussed in the context of the participants' own employment and organization. Participants are then introduced to a wide range of tools and techniques for idea generating and problem solving, which are immediately put to the test in a series of small group exercises.

One of the critical elements of the exercise is that the tools and techniques are introduced very much in general principle, rather than as fully formed and complex set-piece techniques. Our experience is that the students can and will learn the nuts and bolts of such techniques elsewhere, either in training courses or by consulting manuals and training materials. The work of Pherson and Heuer, to name but two, provide what are probably the definitive guides to analytical techniques of relevance to the intelligence analyst at the present time (see in particular Heuer & Pherson, 2010). In "Secrets and Mysteries," therefore, we will spend less time on the mechanics of such exercises, but ensure that the students understand the basic essence of such concepts as brainstorming, lateral thinking, red teaming, and "What if?" analysis. We suggest that most analytic techniques are essentially variations on these core principles. As Coleman (1976, p. 52) noted in the context of experiential learning, the point here is that the learners establish some general principles of understanding and "see a connection between the actions and effects over a range of circumstances," rather than necessarily taking these models too literally and seeing them as prescriptive rule books for how to do analysis. It will often also be important for analysts to have the confidence to adapt basic techniques to their particular operational environments and to the type of analysis they are doing (such as whether it is strategic or more tactical or operational).

THE EXERCISE: OPERATION SMITHFIELD

The second day of the workshop comprises the main intelligence scenario exercise, called Operation SMITHFIELD. Participants are divided into groups, usually comprising around five students each. The groups are housed in separate rooms and provided with an initial situation briefing. This informs them that they are members of a newly established multiagency security team responsible for protecting their country's national security from imminent threats. The students are informed that, while they may come across any number and type of threats and will have to coordinate with colleagues accordingly, their particular section is the Serious Crime Intelligence Team. This provides the first piece of anchoring in the students' minds, which could affect their subsequent analytical judgments!

As is standard with scenario exercises of this nature, the groups are slowly fed batches of intelligence updates throughout the day up to a total of seven separate batches. These take the form of various intelligence reports, "secret" and open source, from a range of agencies both domestic and overseas. The intelligence feeds move the operation through a period of time comprising a few weeks, and students are instructed to treat each time stamp as the current time.

To keep the pressure up on the students and force rapid decision making, the batches of information are comprehensive and arrive at a fairly challenging rate. On two or three occasions throughout the day, the groups are instructed to prepare intelligence update briefings to senior policymakers with relatively little preparation time. At least one of these briefings is for an action-oriented policy customer such as the police, who press the students to make definitive judgments affecting operational decisions such as whether to make arrests. This part of the exercise tests the ability of the students to recognize uncertainty in the information they are processing and to communicate it effectively to policymakers, even when under pressure.

Depending on the facilities and the time available, some interactive elements are introduced to the program at various stages. These include the ability to interact with and task a "live military intelligence cell" based in Kosovo (where much of this particular scenario takes place). Artifacts are made available for the students to consider, such as a wallet recovered from the scene of a surveillance operation, which belongs to one of the main characters and contains within it a train ticket, a newspaper clipping, a photograph of a woman, and various pieces of information whose significance to the operation is not immediately obvious. A voice intercept of an ambiguous phone conversation is played to the students and, where time allows, the students themselves are invited to take part in a mini-HUMINT (human intelligence) operation in which information must be extracted quickly from a passing stranger.

For those designing similar exercises, any number of audio-visual aids, interactive elements, or flexibility to the story line can be introduced, such as the facility for "live" inserts of information written during the exercise and tailored to the way the students' analysis is unfolding on that day. All of these factors make the exercise more interesting and potentially more "real," although many of them have an impact on the time available to complete the exercise.

The particular scenario in "Secrets and Mysteries" is a complex story of several interwoven groups and individuals, each of whom appear to be pursuing different objectives but who may be cooperating with one another on a particular operation. All of these groups, and most of the agencies supplying the intelligence, are fictional to ensure "clean" thinking, but they do not necessarily need to be.

Throughout the exercise, there are operational factors that the students must consider, in addition to purely analytical factors. If a set of goods being moved clandestinely might be explosives rather than drugs, for example, this places a different set of considerations around when and how to conduct surveillance or interdiction of key individuals. Liaison possibilities can be far and wide, pushing students to think beyond traditional linkages between agencies and be creative about other possibilities, whether domestic or international, for gathering intelligence or achieving real-world operational outcomes.

Inevitably, all of the information that the students receive is completely ambiguous and supports any number of different hypotheses. At the end of the exercise, the groups are asked to brief on which hypotheses they considered and how they would rank them. Usually, the groups will suggest two or three possible hypotheses, centered around drug trafficking, terrorism, or illegal immigration. We then reveal to the perplexed students that we have so far identified 14 possible hypotheses, including all of the above and a set of variations on them, plus espionage, identity fraud, smuggling of other goods, and the "nothing at all" hypothesis, which must always be considered! Sometimes the students will come up with a new hypothesis that we have not previously considered, and we add it to the list for the next time.

The exercise is designed in such a way that the intelligence information maps on to, and demonstrates, the various types of cognitive issues that have been discussed in day one of the workshop. Anchoring and priming of the students is rife in the information. Statements are made as to the reliability of the information from various sources, and to how things have happened in the past, in such a way that inadequate challenge of such statements will lead the analysts down the wrong path. Connections are implied between various pieces of information, which, for those analysts well versed in intelligence and thus carrying some "mental baggage," could easily cause them to bite and jump to conclusions inappropriately. Similarly, connections are implied between pieces of information, which, if not analyzed very carefully for their precise details, could cause assumptions to be made, such as different vehicles of the same type, make, and color; partially viewed license plates; and so on. For those of us designing such exercises, it can be enormous fun to take each cognitive bias in turn and think about how it could manifest itself in some information supplied as part of an exercise of this nature. The number of scenarios and story lines that can result from such mapping is potentially endless.

KEY MESSAGES AND LEARNING OUTCOMES

The key messages this exercise aims to promote are:

- Critical and creative thinking is not the norm; most people are overly dependent on past experience and are constrained by established processes and structures. But it can become the norm in the right environment.
- Failures are all too frequently the product of a course of action, but they should be learning points.
- Change is not necessarily difficult if collectively embraced.
- Encouraging critical and creative thinking can help build a team and better ensure success.
- Collective critical yet creative analysis ensures better understanding between employees and management and enables better team work.

The key learning outcomes are that, among a plethora of valuable interpersonal skills, the exercise aims to:

- Break away from conventional thinking, and encourage delegates to challenge norms and old ways of doing business using constructive positive techniques.
- Arm participants with a range of practical tools and techniques for critical thinking, creativity and problem solving, and dynamic thinking.
- Help individuals to change thinking and bad business cultures and identify procedures and processes that lead to business failure.
- Instill confidence in uncertainty, complexity, and decision making under pressure.
- Develop effective communication and team-building skills.
- Prepare delegates mentally and emotionally for business change.

CONCLUSION

The challenge of successful intelligence analysis—or indeed any complex analysis for that matter—is to be able to take a fiercely objective view of information and evaluate its reliability and effectiveness in helping to form judgments, while recognizing and mitigating issues of deception, incompleteness of the information set, and the variable relevance of information. In this modern age, with a shift toward more "active" intelligence analysis, there are new challenges in being able to scope appropriate courses of action; to anticipate their consequences and "effects" in the real world; and to learn from those consequences and, in some cases, failures, when they occur.

Unfortunately, life is such that there are a host of individual and institutional barriers and pitfalls that often make the successful achievement of all of these tasks very difficult. At the individual level, barriers to free and unfettered critical thinking, coupled with a generally suppressed level of imagination and creativity in the workplace, can hinder the process. Added to this, natural limitations in perception, memory, and decision making can further compound analytical weaknesses, especially if such limitations are not recognized and understood. At the institutional level, government bureaucracies are often inherently bad at ensuring the right sort of work environment in which a more positive experience of the above challenges and environments can be allowed to flourish. Very often (with some honorable exceptions) the intelligence analysis environment is one in which firmly entrenched norms have been established over years, and these are compounded by a cultural environment in which free-flowing critical analysis and creative generation of alternative hypotheses can be difficult other than for the bravest of intelligence officers. It should be said that such issues are not the exclusive preserve of intelligence organizations: many of them will be recognized in a very wide range of business environments.

When considering how to train and exercise tomorrow's intelligence analysts in ways that will make a material difference to this state of affairs, the basic principles of experiential learning offer a great deal of scope. At the same time, training exercises that are fun and stimulating, but do not link adequately to the question of real business change in the work environment, can be exercises of nugatory benefit in the long term. The risks of such poorly targeted exercises can be magnified by a natural intolerance in the intelligence analysis community of training exercises that are perceived to be a waste of valuable time that could otherwise be spent on the serious and important business of national security. Such considerations need to be taken carefully into account by the designers of each TEST-type exercise.

REFERENCES

Coleman, J. S. 1976. Differences between experiential learning and classroom learning. In M. T. Keeton et al. (Eds.), *Experiential learning*. Washington, DC: Jossey-Bass, 49–61.

De Bono, E. 2008. *Six thinking hats*. London: Penguin.

Dewey, J. 1938. *Experience and education*. New York: Collier Books.

Heuer, R. J. Jr. 2005. Limits of intelligence. Analysis. *Orbis*, 75–94.

Heuer, R. J. Jr., and Pherson, R. H. 2010. *Structured analytic techniques for intelligence analysis*. Washington, DC: CQ Press.

Honey, P., & Mumford, A. 1992. *Manual of learning styles*. Maidenhead: Honey Publications.

Kolb, D. A. 1984. *Experiential Learning*. Englewood Cliffs, NJ: Prentice-Hall.

Kolb, D. A., & Fry, R. 1975. Toward an applied theory of experiential learning. In C. Cooper (Ed.), *Theories of group process*. London: Wiley, 33–58.

Laqueur, W. 1983. The question of judgment: Intelligence and medicine. *Journal of Contemporary History, 18*(4), 533–548.

Lindeman, E. C. L. 1926. *The meaning of adult education*. New York: New Republic.

Lord Butler of Brockwell. 2004. *Review of intelligence on weapons of mass destruction. Report of a committee of privy councillors*. London: TSO, HC898.

The 9/11 Commission Report: Final Report of the National Commission on Terrorist Attacks Upon the United States. 2004. New York: Norton.

Weil, S. W., & McGill, I. (Eds.). 1989. *Making sense of experiential learning*. Buckingham: Open University Press.

Part III

MULTIWEEK SIMULATIONS

12

Understanding Bayesian Thinking: Prior and Posterior Probabilities and Analysis of Competing Hypotheses in Intelligence Analysis

David Omand

ABSTRACT

In this exercise, students play the part of intelligence analysts supporting a UN arms inspection team seeking to locate a covert biological weapons research facility in the imaginary country of San Serriffe. The scenario involves probabilistic reasoning in identifying possible suspect sites for inspection and weighing new evidence to decide which suspect site of a number of alternatives is most likely using the logical structure provided by Bayes' theorem. The simulation demonstrates how different assumptions made by the analyst can affect the conclusion reached and the importance of making clear at the point of reaching a key judgment how far it rests on evidence that discriminates between possible explanations by using a Heuer table. The exercise has five parts, each designed to open up a class discussion about different key concepts in analysis: How do we know what we know? What degree of belief should we have in our analytic judgments? How do we avoid the inductive fallacy and apply an (nonmathematical) understanding of the logic behind Bayes' theorem as the most reliable way to use fresh evidence to alter prior judgments of probability? The scenario is written so it can be used by students for self-study or in a class with an instructor. The scenario can readily be amplified by maps based on the description in the text.

KEYWORDS

Intelligence analysis; intelligence simulation; collection plan; Bayes' theorem; Heuer table; analysis of competing hypotheses; teaching intelligence analysis

BACKGROUND TO BE READ BEFORE THE EXERCISE

San Serriffe is a rapidly developing coastal nation surrounded by hostile nations with eyes on its potential mineral wealth. The president of San Serriffe is a young military officer, the son of a military dictator who was in power for 40 years. San Serriffe has a large landmass (equivalent to France) but low population density, concentrated in towns along the coast and in the temperate highlands in the center of the country where there are a number of high mountains with ski resorts, much used by the San Serriffen officer class, and housing, education, training, and recreation facilities for the military, especially the elite Presidential Guard (PG) units. Much of the rest of San Serriffe is dense forest or semitropical scrub with only small settlements for logging along the main rivers.

To gain international support for economic development, and at the urging of the UN Security Council (UNSC), San Serriffe recently revealed that it had for many years for defensive purposes conducted chemical and biological warfare experiments in contravention to the Chemical Weapons (CW) Convention and the Biological Weapons and Toxins (BW) Weapons Convention and had a limited weaponized CW capability in the hands of its elite PG under direct control of the president. Its declared facilities have recently been dismantled under international UN supervision, and its small stock of chemical gravity bombs and biological agent (mostly based on botulism-type toxins) have been destroyed.

But suspicion lingers as a result of human intelligence (HUMINT) from a regular and reliable source inside the San Serriffen diplomatic corps that as a hedge for the future a small well-equipped biological laboratory with suitable containment was set up covertly in-country by the military authorities along with a small group of key medical researchers to continue BW research to develop a deterrent against any aggression by San Serriffe's neighbors. This intelligence has been presented in summary form to the UNSC. The president of San Serriffe has denied these reports and has invited the United Nations to send inspectors to confirm his statement. The UNSC has therefore authorized an arms control inspection team to visit San Serriffe. UNSC members have promised full intelligence support to the team.

You are intelligence analysts on loan to this arms control inspection team now in the final stages of preparation in the capital of San Serriffe with the task of ensuring that prohibited biological warfare activities have genuinely ceased. Your initial brief is to help them by providing intelligence support and to choose suspect sites to inspect.

Practical limitations on the availability of specialist detection equipment and protective clothing mean that the team can only inspect one site at a time, and San Serriffen patience at being under suspicion is assessed by the United Nations to be limited. Already there is considerable local obstruction to the setting up of the team. So there is pressure on you to come up quickly with a prioritized list of sites to inspect. This exercise will illuminate ways of thinking about that problem and involve use of probabilistic reasoning, Bayes' theorem, and use of a Heuer table and the "Analysis of Competing Hypotheses" (ACH). These terms will be explained during the exercise.

STEP 1 OF THE ANALYSIS

You consult your scientific adviser who says you should be focusing on buildings, probably new buildings, with air conditioning and air filtration. Windows are unlikely to open. There will almost certainly be physical security in the form of fences, closed-circuit TV, and armed patrols. Waste water will need filtration, and there may be special arrangements for taking away rubbish in sealed sacks. A compound for the scientists working there is likely, including VIP housing. Some military or paramilitary guarding is certain, so there will be troop accommodations and transport garaging, probably at company strength.

A first question to ask is whether it is likely any of the previously declared sites is still being used for prohibited activity. Advice from the past UN inspection team is that they did a thorough job and it is highly unlikely that San Serriffe would take the risk of trying to reuse any of their declared sites. They also judge it is unlikely that the facility will be in a major population center, where it would be harder to keep secret the fact that scientists are working on a covert program.

So your task is to look in a country the size of France for a very small hidden site!

You examine the data collated by the UN team that oversaw the dismantling of the previous program.

You note that they had logged 50 sites (see Table 12.1) as being definitely or very probably associated with prohibited programs (which the United Nations together termed suspect sites). You further note that no less than 40 of these sites have the characteristic that responsibility for their security was in the hands of the elite PG, whereas only 10 were guarded by regular army units. This could therefore be a useful discriminator.

Table 12.1. Suspect Sites

	With Presidential Guard	*Normal Army*	*Total*
Suspect sites	40	10	50

Discussion 1

Do you conclude, since these suspect sites were four times more likely to be guarded by PG units, that you need only think of inspecting sites similarly guarded? That would certainly make it easier to narrow down the search for a hidden BW facility. But is it that simple? What information would you need to analyze how far the PG connection helps the situation?

Now work through Appendix A and discuss again.

STEP 2 OF THE ANALYSIS

From the analysis in Appendix A, the sensible conclusion should be reached that the analysis of places to search should start with examining sites guarded by the PG that were not previously established as suspect sites. From the master orbat (military order of battle) declared to the United Nations last year, that amounts to 510 sites! (See Table 12.2 in Appendix A.)

Discussion 2

How might you go about constructing an outline collection plan at this point to gather intelligence relevant to filtering the large number of PG sites?

What ideas do you have for additional information and intelligence that might help? Look at Appendix B and critique it, adding your own ideas.

STEP 3 OF THE ANALYSIS

A few days later, in response to the requests in your collection plan, additional information starts to arrive:

1. A national SIGINT (signals intelligence) agency reports the continuing existence of a VPN (Virtual Private Network) associated with WMD (weapons of mass destruction) activity, including the army headquarters and at least one unlocated and unidentified PG unit as a member of the network. Some traffic on the network is strongly encrypted (and is not available).
2. Media monitoring picks up a Health Department advertisement in all the San Serriffen newspapers for lab technicians in biochemistry. Enhanced salaries are offered. Inquiries by a friendly embassy reveal that there is a shortage of technicians since a number unexpectedly left at the end of last year "to further their careers elsewhere."
3. A national HUMINT agency shares with you a report that a new source on trial who claims good connections to the senior military has reported that consideration was indeed given to having a covert BW unit, but after the UNSC challenged the president and he denied it, the president returned home to discover what was being done and ordered it stopped.
4. Open sources reveal in the house magazine of the National University photographs of Professor Em, an identified senior figure in the previous BW program and a renowned biochemist at a retirement party in his honor thrown at the university. UN records show that Professor Em is still several years away from the official retirement age.
5. A source in the Presidential Palace briefs the media that the professor is leaving with his wife to live on an isolated part of the coast, and that he intends to spend his time swimming and scuba diving.
6. Analysis of the Professor Em photograph shows several senior officers in PG uniform at the back of the room, one of whom is identified as probably the president's military chief of staff.
7. A major in the San Serriffen army's intelligence branch has just claimed asylum in a South American country on an official visit. Liaison with the intelligence

service of that country reveals that in an initial debrief the officer explained that he had a falling out with the president's chief of staff over the president's decision to abandon plans for a covert BW program and feared demotion. But the major is vague about the plans for the facility. The liaison service comments that they believe his wish to settle in their country is genuine and that he is currently cooperating on intelligence matters but have doubts about whether they are getting the real story from him on BW.

Discussion 3

Discuss what to make of the evidence above. What if anything would you say to the head of the inspection team or UN senior management about what the intelligence picture now reveals? Would you raise doubts about the basis of the mission? Do you see a counterintelligence dimension?

Use a Heuer table to try to weigh the evidence for the propositions that there is, or there is not, a covert BW research unit in San Serriffe. What does your judgment hinge on?

Study Appendix C for more information.

STEP 4 OF THE ANALYSIS

From the Heuer analysis you probably concluded that it is likely that the prohibited program continues, and the authorities are trying active measures to conceal this. But there is no definitive evidence at this stage, and it is possible that the BW program was indeed stopped. Your UN mission reports this. The message back from UNSC capitals is clear: press on with inspections as quickly as possible since the situation must be resolved quickly. You sense that there is a danger of politicization in some of the national briefing of policymakers.

A further intelligence report arrives: From a national SIGINT agency, an intercepted e-mail on a low security PG administrative computer network from a Major Jose to Col Pico at army headquarters says:

> My Colonel, I have done exactly as you asked and transported the wife of our old scorpion to her new quarters with her furniture. She insists that the cooker in the kitchen is too small and old and wants me to order a new one for which I do not have funds enough. She threatens to tell her husband that we are going back on our agreement. Otherwise all is well. May I order a cooker on the regimental account and have it delivered to your successor from whose quarters I can collect it without attracting attention?

The reply from army headquarters is: "Major, request agreed, but all future messages on this subject must come on the proper channel."

A comment is added to the report by an analyst that Major Jose is not identified but there is a Colonel Pico, G4 Logistics, at army headquarters who was previously a senior army representative at the San Serriffen National Army Staff College in the Central Highlands, and before that commander of a San Serriffen Special Forces unit.

Discussion 4

Discuss what this additional piece of information might reveal about the general location of the suspect facility. Would you suggest altering the Heuer table and the collection plan to focus on a particular region?

Now study Appendix D and discuss further.

STEP 5 OF THE ANALYSIS

Another intelligence report arrives. The contents of computer disks seized by the United Nations at the time of the first inspections (and that were validated as containing accurate information on the prohibited programs) have been reexamined. Among a mass of nonrelevant scientific data on the previous programs are copies of detailed internal layout and engineering schematics dating back several years for fitting out a small modern bioresearch secure facility. The designs show small containment labs with scrubbers for air conditioning. The plans are assessed as feasible and sensible by BW experts in capitals. In an accompanying comment a British defense intelligence analyst points out that the buildings that are being converted have provision for significant central heating in addition to the air conditioning for the labs. The layout would be consistent with a chalet-style building on a slope with labs on the upper floors and machinery on the ground floor. There is an annotation "old live firing area" on a corner of the site that is shown on the plan.

Discuss this evidence. Do you agree:

- Since the computer disks have been validated and were in UN possession before the doubts about the covert facility emerged, it is very likely that these plans are what they seem.
- The plans are copies so the originals are still in San Serriffen hands.
- Although there is nothing on the disks to indicate the facility has been built, it is likely that if San Serriffe wanted such a facility they would have used these plans.
- The plans are most likely to be for a location in part of a military reservation in the hilly Central Highlands.
- This intelligence, together with that in stage 4, is good enough to use to focus an initial search.

You identify from the master orbat of the PG which of their units is located in the Central Highlands and task the imagery community to examine them and the SIGINT community to look for unusual communications.

The imagery analysts identify three PG-associated sites in the Central Highlands that are consistent with the description in the plans. SIGINT shows that all three of them belong to the active secure VPN network. At last the problem appears to be reduced to manageable proportions.

The imagery analysts provide a before and after three-dimensional, multispectral analysis of the areas around these three PG sites.

- Site A. New security barriers and a guard post have been built at the entrance to a long forest road that leads to a remote ski station with several chalet-style buildings believed to have been used in the past only by the PG military and their families. There has been recent construction work including a new perimeter fence. Infrared imagery shows there is no evidence of the ski lift being used. An attempt by a friendly defense attaché to drive up the road was recently abruptly refused by an armed guard.
- Site B. There is construction of new housing behind a perimeter fence that also has administrative buildings and workshops inside the fence. The site is close to a barracks and sophisticated training facilities including a mock-up village used by the San Serriffen PG for VIP protection training. This area is known to be heavily out of bounds to visitors.
- Site C. Heavy cloud cover has obstructed direct photo reconnaissance, but radar imagery shows several buildings that could fit the plans inside a training area that includes close-quarter combat ranges a few miles from the Army Staff College. Analysis of infrared imagery shows the area has been fenced off with a substantial barrier (whose differential heat signature shows up at dusk) as well as areas of disturbed earth close to the entrance to an old mine. So the imagery analysts speculate that there are also underground facilities there.

Call them sites A, B, C. There is some evidence to support each of them as being the best bet to visit first.

If there were no further intelligence available to discriminate among them, then each of the three sites is a realistic possibility, so the probability that it is at any one of these sites is one-third, written as $P(X) = 1/3$, where X could be A, B or C, and you could pick one at random.

After careful consideration and study of the imagery, however, you decide you can rank the sites for inspection in terms of the probability of being suspect:

$$\text{Site A: } P(A) = 5/12$$
$$\text{Site B: } P(B) = 4/12$$
$$\text{Site C: } P(C) = 3/12$$

So you pick site A and prepare an intelligence package on the site for the inspectors, pulling together the computer disks' information with all the relevant imagery. You have now had good photos of all the sites as well as open source material on the area and information on scientists and military figures known to have associations with the previous programs (and not forgetting to ask for checks on whether there is a Major Jose there!). You brief the inspectors; you assume that from this point the San Serriffens will get wind of where you intend to start inspecting.

That evening at a reception you are chatting with the U.S. defense attaché who reveals that the next day there will be an announcement of a new confidence building measure with San Serriffe. The U.S. Department of Defense (DoD) has accepted an invitation from the San Serriffen chief of defense to send a U.S. Special Forces training team to help raise the standards of the San Serriffen VIP protection team. The training will last several months and take place at a San Serriffen PG training grounds in the Central Highlands. The United States is waiting for a decision on which site it will be.

The next day you hear from the U.S. attaché that the U.S. forces have been told they will conduct the training at either site B or site C, with the choice to be made by the PG shortly.

Discussion 5

Discuss how this new information might affect your view of the likelihood that sites B and C are a possible location for the covert facility.

- Prima facie, it is surprising that San Serriffe should be thinking of inviting, of all troops, U.S. Special Forces to an area you think might house a covert facility.
- Is it likely to be a deceptive bluff? Hiding in plain sight can be a good tactic in some circumstances.
- Could this invitation have been issued by part of the system that did not know of the covert facility? "Cock-up rather than conspiracy"?
- Is this partial evidence that there is in fact no covert facility at all?

If you concluded that the chances of a site that is opened to the United States being the covert site are now very small, and can be ignored, so that just two sites, site A and either B or C, will shortly remain in the frame, how would you then recalculate the probabilities? Do you think you will want to continue with site A as the first site to ask the inspectors to visit once you know where the U.S. training will take place?

Did you argue that site A was judged more probable than either site B or C in the ratio 5/12 to 4/12 and to 3/12, respectively? So on that basis would you want to continue with site A as the top priority, whichever of sites B or C were used by the U.S. Special Forces?

If so, you may be about to make a mistake!

Now study Appendix E.

STEP 6 OF THE ANALYSIS: FINAL DISCUSSION

Have a final discussion to end the exercise and list the learning points that have emerged.

APPENDIX A: APPLYING BAYES' THEOREM AND BAYESIAN THINKING

Care is needed not to fall into a common probability trap, often called the barristers' fallacy (since it can turn up when lawyers argue over the relevance of forensic evidence to the guilt of a suspect). In this case, the evidence that suspect sites are four times more likely to be guarded by the PG units than other army units does *not* imply that being guarded by the PG rather than regular units makes a site four times more likely to be suspect than not. The probability that a unit guarded by the PG is suspect does not necessarily equal the probability that a suspect unit will be guarded by the PG.

We can express the position more clearly using symbols:

Let S be the proposition that a site is suspect and $P(S)$ be the *probability* that the proposition is true, that is, that a site is suspect (recall that probabilities have to lie between 0, impossible, and 1, certain).

For example, if the inspectors judged 50 sites to be suspect out of a potential master orbat (order of battle) list of 750 army or other guarded government locations, then $P(S) = 50/750 = 1/15$, which equals the chance of picking a site at random from the 750 and finding that it is one of the suspect ones.

Similarly, let PG be the proposition that a site is guarded by the PG and $P(PG)$ be the *probability* that the proposition is true, that is, that a site is guarded by the PG.

For example, of the 750 sites on the inspectors' potential sites list, suppose you are told 240 are associated with the PG, then $P(PG) = 240/750 = 8/25$, the probability that a site picked at random will be PG associated.

These are examples of *prior probabilities* where no conditions are imposed on picking at random from the total. We could, however, have additional information to bring to bear that will constrain the choice and thus affect the probability of picking a suspect site.

To take the example above, we have shown that the prior probability is $P(PG) = 8/25$. But what is the probability that a site is guarded by the PG *if* we already knew that it is one of the suspect sites?

This is an example of a *conditional probability*. That is conventionally written by placing a vertical bar (|) in the probability statement to separate the proposition concerned from the information we are bringing to bear: $(PG|S)$, which is read as "the probability of finding a site guarded by the PG given that it is a suspect site."

The numbers in our example can be written as shown in Table 12.2.

Table 12.2. Responsibility for Suspect Site Security

	With Presidential Guards	*With Normal Army*	*Totals*
Suspect sites	40	10	50
Nonsuspect sites	200	500	700
Totals	240	510	750

Thus, if we already knew from analysis that the site we are picking is a suspect one, then the probability that it is guarded by the PG is $P(PG|S) = 40/50 = 4/5 = 0.8$, as before. But if we start, as we will as inspectors, only with knowledge that the site is guarded by the PG, then the probability of it being suspect is $P(S|PG) = 40/240 = 1/6 = 0.17$.

So we can conclude that if we were just to pick one of the 750 sites on the list at random, the chances of success (i.e., the site being suspect) is only $P(S) = 50/750 = 1/15 =$

0.07, but if we could work out which were PG-associated sites and pick from that group, our chances would go up to P(S|PG) = 0.17, more than double the odds, thus still worth using as a selection filter to try to narrow down the search. (Note, however, how much smaller this is than the 4/5 figure you get if you fall into the barristers' fallacy!)

Caveat: Now, there is a big assumption built in if we apply this finding to the current inspection task. We are assuming that the statistics from the original inspections and declarations are still relevant to the chances of finding the covert BW site. Is that legitimate? The San Serriffens might have suspected that the UN inspectors had worked out the PG connection and would therefore not use the PG for the new covert site.

The best that can be said is that in intelligence analysis, assumptions do have to be made; the important thing is not to forget what they are, and we thus must be prepared, in the light of new evidence, to rethink the approach. The exact values of the probabilities in numerical terms are unlikely to be relevant, but the finding that having the PG at a site roughly doubles its chance of being found to be suspect looks worth hanging on to as a discriminator.

Bayes' Theorem Itself

Without saying so, we have just applied Bayes' theorem. We drew the required probability P(PG|S) from Table 12.2. We could equivalently have applied a formula that was first found after his death in 1761 in the papers of the Rev. Thomas Bayes, a nonconformist clergyman in Tunbridge Wells, England:

In our example, Bayes' theorem is written

$$P(S|PG) = P(S)*[P(PG|S)/P(PG)]$$

The Bayesian approach forms the basis for all scientific assessment of conditional probability. It is the only scientific way of altering your prior degree of belief in a proposition or hypothesis, say P(S), when new evidence arrives, say PG. Your original *prior probability* estimate P(S) becomes the *posterior probability* P(S|PG) by multiplying P(S) by the factor P(PG|S)/P(PG), which measures how likely it is that you would have found this evidence if the original proposition S was in fact the case.

A Further Example of Applying Bayes' Theorem

HUMINT reported that in the previous year San Serriffe had imported a number of small stainless steel fermentation chambers. San Serriffe said it was for civil purposes as part of an agricultural program.

You assess that is very likely true, based on other evidence of an active bioscience research program to prevent animal diseases in the agriculture sector; but you leave a one in five (20 percent) chance that it might after all have been part of a military BW development, leaving a four in five (80 percent) chance it is a civil program.

SIGINT then reports that the overseas invoicing was handled by a San Serriffe finance officer associated with past military programs.

What information would you look for to help you reassess the probabilities? You investigate past data and might discover:

All relevant civil imports to the agriculture program also were passed by the same military finance officer. So the SIGINT information adds nothing, and you keep your estimate at 80 percent likelihood of civil test.

Or you might discover:

No relevant civil imports have ever before been handled by this finance officer. So you might reassess the chances of the end use being civil sharply downward or even say they are zero.

But what if research shows 8 of 10 past imports used military invoicing, and 5 of 10 imports known to be civil did? We need to apply Bayesian reasoning. Let A be the hypothesis that the import was for civil purposes. Let B be the evidence that the invoicing was military. Our prior estimate for prob(A) was 80% = 4/5:

$$\text{Posterior prob}(A|B) = 4/5 * \text{prob}(B|A)/\text{prob}(B)$$

We know 8 of 10 past imports used military invoicing, and 6 of 10 imports known to be civil did. So

$$\text{prob}(B) = 8/10 = 4/5 \text{ and prob}(B|A) = 6/10 = 3/5$$
$$\text{i.e., prob}(B|A)/\text{prob}(B) = 3/4$$

We can then apply Bayes' theorem to give our new estimate for the chances that the import is for civil agriculture: prob(A|B) = (4/5)*(3/4) = 3/5 = 60%, reduced from the 80 percent you started with.

It has now become only probable that the import is civil, as opposed to your initial assessment that it was highly probable (see Table 12.3 in Appendix C for probability ranges and other terms).

APPENDIX B: THINKING ABOUT A COLLECTION PLAN TO DISCUSS WITH THE AGENCIES

There is no limit to the imagination that can be brought to bear. But examples might include the following:

- You examine the records of the previous UN work to establish the names and institutions of all the scientists and doctors previously associated with the prohibited programs. You conduct an open source search for references to them through university and hospital staff lists, their published work, teaching courses, and general media references to establish for as many of them as possible where they are now and what they are engaged in. You are particularly interested in anyone who seems to have fallen off the radar who was previously known to be working in relevant fields.

- You task national intelligence agencies for any HUMINT from within PG circles of talk of a new unit being formed or a new secret enclave in an existing establishment or compound. Have any officers of major or colonel rank who were clearly trusted and rising stars not been seen around recently?
- You put together as complete a list as you can (from SIGINT-derived address lists and call signs and past imagery and geographic intelligence data) of the locations of PG order of battle down to the company level. (Intelligence analysis involves hard work!)
- You task national geospatial and imagery organizations for any evidence of new construction or unusual movement at these PG sites.
- You ask the SIGINT community to look for any anomalies in recent San Serriffen traffic.

APPENDIX C: ANALYSING COMPETING HYPOTHESES: HEUER TABLES

Richards Heuer was a long-term CIA analyst who taught intelligence analysis for many years. He adapted modern scientific method to intelligence work by insisting upon the formulation by the ACH to explain what is going on, bring to bear the available information of all kinds to discriminate between the hypotheses.

When working on difficult intelligence issues, analysts are, in effect, choosing among several alternative hypotheses. Which of several possible explanations is the correct one? Which of several possible outcomes is the most likely one? ("Hypothesis," in its broadest sense, is used as a potential explanation or conclusion that is to be tested by collecting and presenting evidence.) If analysts focus mainly on trying to confirm one hypothesis they think is probably true, they can easily be led astray by the fact that there is so much evidence to support their point of view. They fail to recognize that most of this evidence is also consistent with other explanations or conclusions, and that these other alternatives have not been refuted.

The aim is to find the hypothesis that best explains the situation consistent with the known information and introduces the least number of extraneous assumptions as possible. ACH requires an analyst to identify explicitly all the reasonable alternatives and have them compete against one another for the analyst's favor, rather than evaluating their plausibility one at a time. To this end, Heuer recommends laying out the hypotheses and the evidence in the form of a Heuer table (Heuer, 1999).

A worked example is presented here, based on the intelligence so far in this exercise. You can probably improve it. But note that some intelligence reports are compatible with either hypothesis and should be put to one side. And which hypothesis you choose depends on whether you believe you may be at the receiving end of a deception by the PG.

The Heuer (ACH) approach helps analysts avoid a number of traps:

Too much attention can be given to intelligence that in its own terms is fascinating and a triumph of tradecraft (and usually very highly classified) but does not actually help discriminate among the hypotheses. This important concept is known in the literature as the *diagnosticity of evidence.*

It forces the analyst to write down for each piece of intelligence how far it is believed to be reliable and what assumptions may underlie it.

Analytic conclusions that rest upon inference, historical data, or assumed behavior have to be made explicit.

In the current example, we could examine two simple alternative hypotheses: H1—covert BW program continues; H2—a covert BW program does not continue (for example, because the new president stopped it). These hypotheses form the columns of the matrix in Table 12.4 to Appendix C.

We list in the first column each piece of information (whether secret source intelligence, open source, or simply assumption) that we think is relevant to the problem. In the second column, we classify each piece by type, reliability (including flagging doubts we may have about the reporting), and *diagnosticity.* We then note for each piece of intelligence whether or not it confirms each of the hypotheses. We are working horizontally across the table. Resist the temptation until you have finished the matrix to work down vertically each hypothesis to see which one looks strongest against this evidence.

We then apply a mental process of totaling up each hypothesis column to see how the sum of the intelligence helps us choose between them. If we cannot make a choice, then we have to be honest and say that we are unable to confirm on the basis of the evidence available.

We can also conduct a *sensitivity analysis* on our conclusion: Is it heavily dependent on any single piece of intelligence? (In which case, let's rescrutinize that report.)

As Heuer concludes:

You certainly would not want to do this type of analysis for all your everyday personal decisions or for every intelligence judgment. You may wish to do it, however, for an especially important, difficult, or controversial judgment, or when you need to leave an audit trail showing how you arrived at a judgment. (Heuer, 1999, p. 94)

Table 12.3 is a useful table showing the conventional association of probabilities with descriptions in intelligence reports.

Table 12.3. Qualitative Statements and Associated Probability Ranges

Qualitative Statement	Associated Probability Range
Remote/Highly Unlikely	<10%
Improbable/Unlikely	15–20%
Realistic Possibility	25–50%
Probable/Likely	55–70%
Highly/Very Probable/Likely	75–85%
Almost Certain	>90%

Table 12.4 is an example of a simple Heuer table, where:

> H1: there is a continuing BW program
> H2: the BW program was stopped

Table 12.4. Example of a Simple Heuer Table

Evidence	Validation	H1	H2
Past behavior and obstruction of inspectors	Inference	+	–
Diplomatic source says covert BW program continues	HUMINT Regular and reliable	++	—
Secure VPN continues, associated with past WMD PG activity	SIGINT Reliable	+	+
Shortage of lab technicians due to unexpected departures	Open source Reliable	+	
President has ordered covert program stopped	HUMINT New source on trial ?? if part of a deception plan	—	++
Professor Em previously a senior figure in the BW program "retires"	Open source Documentary, ?? if part of deception plan	– ++	+ —
Professor Em associated with PG	Open source Reliable	++	+
Professor Em and family to live on remote coast	Open source media ?? if part of deception plan	– ++	+ —
Defecting major says program has ceased	Defector If believed If part of deception plan?	? — ++	? ++ —

Key: ++ strongly confirms; + confirms; — strongly denies; – denies; n/a not applicable

APPENDIX D: AVOIDING INDUCTIVE FALLACIES

Interpretation of the report should be straightforward. The risk is of jumping to over-definite conclusions.

If we assume that "the old scorpion" is Professor Em, or at least another scientist working on a covert BW program, then the inference is clear: we should be looking in the Central Highlands, within easy driving distance of the Army Staff College where Colonel Pico was previously stationed. That he has a special forces background, and that the topic was judged sensitive, adds credence to this interpretation. But even if the professor is the subject of the e-mail, that does not necessarily mean there is a covert program. The authorities might be helping him on retirement or getting him out of the limelight so as not attract journalistic attention in present circumstances.

There could also be other interpretations. The reference in stage 2 to the professor looking forward to scuba diving in retirement might be coincidence, or even deliberate deception. Or the "old scorpion" mentioned could have nothing to do with the case, and is perhaps a case of a senior officer caught in corruption and going quietly into forced retirement (hence the security) or an opponent of the president being sent into house arrest.

The search for evidence is naturally going to be geared toward trying to establish as quickly as possible where the covert site might be hidden so as to guide the inspectors, rather than trying to test the more basic negative hypothesis that the site does not exist. There is a risk, therefore, of falling into the *inductive fallacy*, sometimes known as the Black Swan problem. That is, you look hard for evidence to confirm a proposition, find it (no surprise there), and imagine that this should greatly strengthen your belief in the proposition. At that point, *groupthink* can kick in, and it becomes harder in the analytic group to be the odd one out who retains rational skepticism about the prevailing answer. Keep asking: What would I expect to see if the proposition were true and do I see this? And what sort of evidence would cast doubt on the proposition and have we checked for that? The more pressure there is to come to a quick conclusion and the more you all know what answer the policymakers want to hear, the more likely it is that these errors will occur.

So this report needs to be looked at with care and should not be used in isolation to focus the search. Luckily, another rather firm report arrives that points to a different region. Move on to step 5.

APPENDIX E: THINKING ABOUT PROBABILITIES

Table 12.5 illustrates the analysis. You have chosen site A to inspect but cannot be certain that is the suspect site, but you assume the PG knows the truth.

Table 12.5.   Probabilities of Different Outcomes

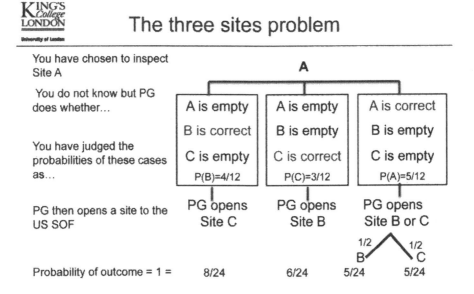

There are three cases to consider, as shown, dependent on whether A, B, or C is in reality the suspect site being looked for. You have judged the probabilities of these outcomes as 5/12, 4/12, and 3/12, respectively.

Now the PG says they are inviting the U.S. Special Forces into either site B or site C.

We can assume if the PG knows site A is the suspect site, then they can invite the U.S. Special Forces into either site B or site C. We have no further information about their choice, so assign half probability to each. The probability of the outcome (we chose A and PG opened B) = 5/12*½ = 5/24, and similarly for outcome (we chose A and PG opened C) = 5/24.

If, on the other hand, the PG knows that site B is the suspect site, then they will have to invite the U.S. Special Forces into site C, with a probability as you assess it of 4/12 (= 8/24), and similarly if site C is the real suspect, then the PG will open site B with a probability 3/12 (= 6/24). To check the reasoning, we see that these outcomes exhaust the probabilities: 5/24 + 5/24 + 8/24 + 6/24 = 1.

If we stick with the original choice of site A, the chance of a favorable outcome of finding the right site is 5/24 + 5/24 = 5/12.

But if we switch to the site not being opened by the PG (B if he opens C and C if he opens B), then the chances of success rise to 8/24 + 6/24 = 7/12.

So our order of priority for inspection should switch from site A to either B or C (whichever has not been chosen by the San Serriffens to host the U.S. Special Forces) due to the new information that the PG is inadvertently giving us.

Some students will have noticed that this last stage is a disguised version of the famous Monty Hall problem in statistics. This name was derived from Monty Hall, who was a U.S. game show host where the competitor was faced with three doors, behind one of which was a prize. After the competitor has chosen a door at random, the quizmaster opens one of the other doors to reveal nothing behind it and then invites the contestant to stick with the original choice or switch to the remaining door. There is an extensive Wikipedia article on the subject.

Most people reason that there are now two doors. You do not know which is the right one, so the chances cannot be better than 50:50. But this ignores that you are dealing with a Bayesian posterior probability, given you have the information that the quizmaster opened an empty door. This puzzle even merited an article in the *Economist* since it is so counterintuitive.

Lessons from this (admittedly very artificial) scenario include the need to recognize that intuition can sometimes be a guide, but there is also a risk that analysts will go for the solution that is most obvious and thus emotionally comfortable. There is no substitute for getting the problem down on paper and analyzing it logically. It helps to draw diagrams. If there has not been time for a full analysis (as there often isn't), then the customer should be warned.

Another lesson is to recognize the importance of the assumptions you have made. It would only take a few changes in the scenario to change the Bayesian analysis. There might, for example, have been quite different reasons why the San Serriffens decided on site B or site C for the U.S. training. Or the person making that choice might not have been in the know about the secret facility on the site.

Finally, your analysis may well have helped increase the chances of the inspection finding the suspect site quickly. But the scenario does not reveal whether or not that happened!

REFERENCE

Heuer, Richards. 1999. *The psychology of intelligence analysis*. Langley: CIA. Chapter 8 available to download at www.cia.gov/library/center-for-the-study-of-intelligence/csi-publications/books-and-monographs/psychology-of-intelligence-analysis/PsychofIntelNew.pdf.

13

Jointery versus Tradecraft: The Brunel Analytical Simulation and Alternative Approaches to Intelligence Analysis and Analytical Professionalization in Postgraduate Academic Teaching

Philip H. J. Davies

The Brunel Analytical Simulation Exercise (BASE) is an annual practical that is run each year as part of Brunel University's MA in Intelligence and Security Studies (ISS). The usual thumbnail description that I give of BASE is a term-long annual practicum in intelligence analysis in which students, divided into syndicates, produce open source intelligence appreciation of a real-world topic loosely following aspects of the UK's Joint Intelligence Organisation and U.S. analytical conventions and methods. I say "aspects of" because in practice BASE involves cherry picking from across the history and development of intelligence assessment in the United Kingdom. And so, as will be elaborated shortly, the students work in syndicates or "drafting teams" that approximate the functions of the Joint Intelligence Office's (JIO) Joint Intelligence Staff (JIS) during the mid-1960s, but they produce papers that conform to JIO length and formatting conventions from circa 2006–2010 and in the process employ "analytical tradecraft" and structured analytical techniques (SATs) that originated largely with the Central Intelligence Agency (CIA) during the 1990s and early 2000s. It has been running since winter/spring of 2005.

In 2006 I published an article in the *International Journal of Intelligence and Counterintelligence* describing its basic operation (Davies, 2006), the basics of which have continued fairly consistently. In summary, under BASE the MA/ISS cohort is divided into four- or five-person "drafting teams" who are internally stovepiped by social science collection disciplines (interviews, documents, and various types of secondary sources). In those teams they draft open source intelligence appreciations of one or more real-world issues using processes loosely modeled on the UK Joint Intelligence Committee (JIC) model. This chapter discusses how BASE has changed over slightly less than a decade and how those changes have been driven partly by the underlying design logic of the exercise and partly by rapid and sometimes radical changes in the intelligence environment.

BASE is run in the second term of each teaching year and is delivered in three stages. Phase I is a lecture program on the essentials of social science research methodology, which occupies the first month. At the same time, students are assigned to their drafting teams and the intelligence requirement (IR) and terms of reference (ToRs) are issued for that year's topic or topics and they commence research on the topic. Phase II is a second lecture program also running around a month on "analytical tradecraft." In the final month, phase III, the students meet in their teams and have one meeting once per week to draft their assessment. On the last class day of the second term—the last teaching day of the year—the entire afternoon is given to the BASE Final Review Event in which syndicates brief their appreciations to a BASE Final Review Panel of academics and current and former intelligence practitioners who provide a final challenge and review session. This BASE Finale provides a crescendo that ends the taught part of the MA with the proverbial bang, and students go forward into their summer to write their dissertations on an intellectual and emotional high point.[1]

AIMS AND OBJECTIVES

BASE was designed with four priorities that were not entirely mutually consistent. The evolution of the exercise has, therefore, been characterized not only by balancing these four priorities but also by ongoing change in the state of the art in these four very different spheres.

The first motivation for providing such an extended and intricate practical was to provide a counterbalance to the potentially sterile "book learning" represented by the academic study of intelligence assessment. Academic examinations and official inquiries have a number of problems, but perhaps one of the most significant is that they underrepresent the difficulties, complexities, and uncertainties affecting real-world assessments in real time. The hindsight bias that affects many after-action studies of failures of warning or strategic forecasting makes elements omitted, under- or overvalued, and cognitive slipups appear to verge on the obvious and the putative intelligence failures akin to incompetence. This runs the risk of prompting a certain complacence and judgmentalism among observers and commentators. Scholarly and official treatments of this or that failure can all too readily slip into, or simply feed, a certain condescension and cynicism toward the intelligence assessment process. Much of such commentary runs the danger of being akin to fans criticizing the skills and performance of team sports players when, in fact, confronted with the worm's-eye view whirlwind of events and information actually experienced by players on the field the fan would perform radically worse. When considering the prospect of teaching a program that would discuss the literature of such postmortems, my sense was that the temptations of complacence and arrogance could only be checked by something akin to a firsthand experience of doing intelligence assessment—and, like so many practitioners, having to produce that assessment is one of a number of parallel responsibilities and tasks that compete for analysts' time, attention, and energy.

The second motivation was to capture, and if possible inculcate, aspects of intelligence assessment practice that were poorly addressed by the then-rapidly developing (and otherwise often impressive and thought-provoking) U.S. literature on analyst training and competencies. The original inspiration came from Douglas MacEachin's (1995) writings on "analytical tradecraft," analytical drivers and linchpins, and, shortly thereafter, Frank Watanabe's (1997) pithy 15 axioms for intelligence analysts, David Moore's (2006) ruminations of critical thinking, and an earlier collaboration with Lisa Krizan on analyst competencies (Moore & Krizan, 2002). These texts contributed to a growing impression that U.S. thinking on "analytical tradecraft" focused almost exclusively on attributes and development of *individual* analysts. Collaborative assessment, especially in a joint, interagency context, feature in very few such discussions. And while joint assessment in the United Kingdom is largely considered a success story, the U.S. history of frequently vituperative interagency disputes, formal dissent notes, and the ultimate failure and collapse of the original CIA Office of Reports and Estimates *and* its replacement by the Board of National Estimates (replaced with the National Intelligence Officer system in 1976 and National Intelligence Council in 1979)[2] suggested that while the United States clearly had sound ideas on professionalizing the individual analyst, its approach to, and skill-set for, joint assessment was clearly less robust. Might it be possible to try and, at least partially, capture and inculcate the challenges and skills of joint assessment as well as individual tradecraft competency for students? Could something of the skills and practices of the British Joint Intelligence Organisation be articulated and turned into something students could try their hands at?

This presented considerable difficulties, chiefly because there was so little information in the public domain about how the JIO operated in terms of daily routine, and there was absolutely no existing volume of prescriptive documentation of methods and professional practice in the United Kingdom's analytic community. Indeed, this was almost an oxymoron for a UK intelligence ethos where the CIA has often been viewed in Sir Burke Trend's words as "a very large collection of 'experts' on almost every subject under the sun, who will produce at a moment's notice an intelligence appreciation . . . which is 'technically' impeccable but may be politically irrelevant or misleading" (Trend, 1967; Young, 1967). Assertive to the point of arrogance at times in its passion for intelligence amateurism, the prevailing UK approach to recruiting individuals to work as "drafters" (the implicitly professional term "analyst" remained all but anathema to British intelligence parlance at least until the late 1980s) treated good drafters as born but not made. Deliberating on a thoroughgoing reform of the JIO in 1967, one official argued that to produce good assessments one required "First class men with a variety of backgrounds" who "must be skilled drafters and active in seeking the necessary information within Whitehall and, if necessary, beyond it" to produce "literate, relevant, comprehensive and timely reports capable of commanding the attention of those responsible for the formulation of policy" (Richards, 1967). Methodology was at best optional; what was necessary was to be articulate and gifted with innate good judgment. Good drafting could be learned on the job, apprenticed to practiced elder officials who would share their experience and wisdom before rotating back to their home departments' equivalent of the real world. As it would transpire, the evolution of BASE ran in parallel and eventually drew increasingly on my own research into the JIO as part of my comparative study of national intelligence in Britain and the United States (Davies, 2012) and also later on my work for the Ministry of Defence on the third edition of the UK's military Joint Intelligence Doctrine (Developments, Concepts and Doctrine Centre, 2011).

There was, however, also a desire at the outset to give students some exposure to alternative approaches to intelligence beyond the United Kingdom's collaborative and consensual approach. Consequently, I decided to also draw on U.S. thinking on alternative and competitive analysis. Thus each year's BASE would also replay the notorious but formative U.S. "Team A/Team B" experiment (albeit without the putative entrenched ideological convictions) (Rovner, 2010) by having multiple teams assess a common requirement independently of one another and then compare and contrast their findings. In the first three iterations the idea was to sharpen students' competitive motivations by making the event competitive and declaring a winning team and paper at the end of each BASE iteration. However, this worked too well, with teams adopting strict counterintelligence protocols that resulted in an icy, chilly wind among teams in the corridor between classes, limited covert collection efforts against one another's members, raw data, and draft papers, and such a profound and lasting sense of having been unjustly treated among the losing teams (who had poured heart and soul into the effort) that it was eventually judged wiser to shift the emphasis from *competitive* assessment to *alternative* assessment and do away with the *frisson* of explicit adversarial competition. The academic team also noted a problem in assessing papers on the basis of both analysis and drafting: the best-reasoned papers were not always the best written and vice versa. It became, therefore, simpler as well as more humane to encourage comparison, contrast, and reflection by participants as the goals of the parallel team efforts.

The third goal was to give students a detailed grounding in social science methods. This was driven in the first instance by what I saw as resemblances between all-source intelligence assessment and contemporary social science methodology. Articulated in the first iteration of BASE shortly before the republication of a 1970s handbook of social science research and analysis for intelligence practitioners (Clauser, 2008), during my doctoral work I had been struck by logical and epistemological parallels between all-source analysis and social science multimethodological strategies of "triangulation" (Webb et al., 1986), that is, examining a topic through two or more collection methods to cross-reference, test, and (ideally) confirm findings. Indeed, having published at the turn of the previous decade on the use of triangulation in the oral history of intelligence services (Davies, 2001), I was also struck by analogies between human intelligence and qualitative elite interviewing (and also, in particular, working with archival documents and the exploitation of communications intercepts). This, I reasoned, would also assist intelligence practitioners by encouraging them to deliberate explicitly on epistemological and methodological concerns relevant to, and sometimes even implicitly underpinning, intelligence practice. Thus it seemed to me one could profitably examine and draw on the commonalities between social research and intelligence assessment. At the same time, one could also reinforce students' methodological skills in preparation for their MA dissertation (and, potentially, PhD study should they wish to return to Brunel to pursue intelligence scholarship still further).

Another goal was to get students to reflect and, in their after-action paper, comment on the strengths and limitations of open source information and its value in intelligence production. Open source intelligence advocates tend to talk about open sources as something akin to a panacea (e.g., Mercado, 2004), while traditional practitioners and commentators tend to view them with some distrust, largely because of a widely held view that the essential concern of intelligence is the penetration of denial and deception (D&D).[3] BASE scenarios generally deal with topics where some D&D is likely to occur (see Appendix A) but also where much can be gleaned about the *intentions*, and sometimes also capabilities, from the open domain.

The final consideration was explicitly directed toward the postgraduation employability of MA/ISS students. I was keen to offer students a program that would allow them to go to potential employers and say that not only had they studied intelligence in the abstract but they had also had the chance to develop hands-on practical skills in intelligence analysis and professional drafting. They could reasonably say that not only had they scrutinized intelligence, they had learned, at least in part, to *do* intelligence as well. Consequently, giving students as much access to U.S. work and training materials on analytical methodology as possible was also viewed as being essential to the delivery of the exercise. This created the most significant divergence from British practice, more so than the alternative analysis aspect because that could be viewed as an add-on to a task otherwise undertaken along JIO lines. Instead of being untrained but, hopefully, talented amateurs trying their hand at writing compelling, literate papers, BASE participants would come to the task with a lexicon of individually oriented ideas and techniques drawn from the U.S. "analytic tradecraft." MacEachin, Watanabe, and Moore were chosen as principal sources. Students were required to formally identify drivers and linchpins during analytic discussions, refer to Watanabe's guidelines when drafting and preparing their "Ministerial Briefs," and look to Moore for underlying principles and awareness.

Analytical tradecraft, however, proved to be somewhat of a moving target. In the post-Iraq environment of intelligence reform and frantic efforts to restore analysts' credibility and perceived professionalism among governmental consumers, the media, and the electorate alike, analytic tradecraft became a fast-growing industry, generating a succession of shiny new "innovative" analytical techniques and tools. SATs entered the outsider's as well as the practitioner's vocabulary, capturing some existing methods (such as various forms of alternative analysis that had been in circulation at least since the 1970s such as red teaming and devil's advocacy) while adding or at least formalizing others (most notably "Analysis of Competing Hypotheses," to which I will return later). As a result, there was ever more practical, hands-on training material upon which to draw. Incorporating that elaborate new material steadily moved BASE further from the vague, amiable amateurism and "intuitive" assessment practice of the traditional Joint Intelligence model.

In fact, BASE and the MA/ISS team delivering it had to work to stay abreast of two very different moving targets in terms of the state of the art in intelligence studies. The first may have been the evolution of analytical tradecraft and SATs, but another was a steadily increasing awareness of the evolution and operation of the JIO, an awareness that reached further back into history as it became apparent that the JIO had gone through a succession of reforms and transformations, some of which were found to be more pedagogically useful than others. Indeed, between BASE 2008 and BASE 2010 the JIO underwent a succession of fairly radical changes that culminated in a profound change in the status and role of the JIC under the current government's UK National Security Council formula. Both of these shifting boundaries also converged with regard to the reception of SATs in British intelligence practice in the aftermath of the intelligence surrounding the invasion of Iraq. Formal techniques were increasingly taken up by a branch of the JIO concerned with analytical professionalization, the Professional Head of Intelligence Analysis (PHIA), and its counterparts in the Ministry of Defence.[4]

This latter development would prove something of an unexpected boon to BASE by simultaneously resolving some of the tensions between the intelligence aims and career development goals while also making the Brunel intelligence masters more marketable and successful than I had ever expected.

APPROXIMATING JOINTERY AND ADOPTING THE 1964 FORMULA

The machinery and process for the production of national assessments in the United Kingdom is, overall, far more similar to the U.S. national estimates process than is often appreciated. In the United Kingdom, such assessments are produced by the JIO, which is composed, most famously, of a heads of an agency-level committee that sets annual requirements and is the final forum for review and, in the U.S. sense, "coordination" of departmental views called the Joint Intelligence Committee. In this sense it is a direct counterpart in the U.S. National Intelligence Board (NIB; and its numerous precursors). A great deal is often made of the presence of supposed "policymakers" on the JIC, but this is largely a linguistic confusion. Representatives of policy departments who are career civil servants sit on the JIC but act chiefly as conduits for departmental open and confidential sources of information and to represent their departments' analytical views on the JIC (Davies, 2012, pp. 36–37). As top level review and approval, therefore, the JIC subsumes the roles of both the NIB *and* the National Intelligence Council (NIC). The actual drafting of papers is performed by the Assessments Staff, a body that replaced the JIS (which had its roots during World War II), through the 1967–1968 reorganization of the JIO by Cabinet Secretary Sir Burke Trend. The Assessments Staff (and JIS) are, therefore, the direct counterparts of the NIC staff. Draft papers are subject to senior working-level challenge and review at meetings of geographic and functional subcommittees of the JIC called Current Intelligence Groups (CIG; which replaced the earlier Heads of Sections committees in the mid-1960s). The CIGs (and previously Heads of Sections) would have been loosely analogous to the analytically oriented director of central intelligence (DCI) "substantive" interagency committees prior to the establishment of the office of the director of national intelligence (DNI).[5] Significantly, until the late 1980s or 1990s, one almost never saw the term "analyst" used in the UK intelligence community.

As I have shown elsewhere (Davies, 2012, pp. 39–41, 189–190), the main drafting component of the JIO can be seen to have passed through three stages after World War II. Between the late 1940s and 1964, drafting the JIS was composed of, at various times, between two and five teams of senior working-level officials appointed on a departmental basis. Thus a JIS team prior to the 1964 Mountbatten reforms of the Ministry of Defence would typically consist of representatives from the Foreign Office, Colonial Office, and Commonwealth Relations Office; the three armed services; and the largely civilian-staffed Joint Intelligence Bureau, which housed the national hubs for economic and scientific intelligence (Davies, 2012, pp. 154–155). It is important to note that all of these were civil service departments responsible for conducting *assessment*. At this point the three national agencies and other collection elements were kept strictly sequestered from the analytical process and, indeed, had no signing authority on JIC assessments alongside the representatives of the services and the policy departments. Much of this had to change, however, after the subsidation of the armed services and their intelligence branches to the Ministry of Defence. With the three service intelligence branches amalgamated with a post-war analytic organization called the Joint Intelligence Bureau into a single Defence Intelligence Staff (DIS), there was now only one defense intelligence voice on the JIC instead of four. During the same time the Colonial Office was wound up and its affairs subsumed by the Foreign Office, followed in short order by the Commonwealth Relations office also being absorbed to create today's Foreign and Commonwealth Office (FCO). In response to the dwindling number of Whitehall assessment voices in the intelligence community, the Cabinet Office looked for the first time for the national agencies to provide drafters for the JIS teams. While this developed in fits and starts, the result was a JIS model that consisted, in principle, of a representative of each of the national agencies plus several officials from the FCO and the DIS (Davies, 2012, pp. 189–190). This arrangement continued for about four years until the full momentum of the Trend reforms developed.

Under the 1967–1968 reorganization, the JIS was officially wound up and replaced by an Assessments Staff that was constituted very differently from its predecessor. Where the JIS had been based, like the JIC and Current Intelligence Groups, on departmental representation, appointments to the Assessments Staff were to be ad hominem. That is, drafters would be selected on the basis of individual ability rather than a departmental balance of power. In practice, informal norms of equitable department representation took shape (with, for example, MoD providing the head of one drafting team, the FCO head of another, and the national agencies head of the third) (Davies, 2012, pp. 39–40; Trend, 1968). But the teams were no longer to be explicitly about joining stovepipes and, in some respects, turned the Assessments Staff into a stovepipe in its own right, albeit one drawing on other government departments for the raw material for its analytical work.

From a pedagogical point of view, the main priorities in designing BASE were to create fairly robust stovepiped processes that might emulate some of the critical features of sharing qualitatively different information across agencies, on the one hand, and to force students to explicitly address questions of source evaluation and interpretation in making analytical judgments, on the other hand. With this perspective in mind, the transitional form of the JIS between 1964 and 1968 appeared the most useful, with JIS membership drawn from the three national collection agencies plus the analytical voices of the FCO and DIS (although it has to be acknowledged that DIS also controlled a range of service collection elements such as the Joint Air Reconnaissance Intelligence Centre). The next trick was finding a comparable open source, academic division of disciplines analogous to the collection disciplines that the national agencies specialized in (i.e., mainly HUMINT [human intelligence] plus a minority of technical methods in Secret Intelligence Service [SIS] and MI-5 and SIGINT [signal intelligence] in Government Communications Headquarters).

I have noted the parallels between qualitative elite interviewing in social science practice and the handling of human sources in intelligence, noted elsewhere (Davies, 2001), suggested an almost natural solution to creating collection and analytical stovepipes. BASE drafting teams were to be divided according to the standard research methods of the social sciences, specifically semistructured elite interviews; documentary sources (in some respects analogous to SIGINT but directly paralleling intelligence document exploitation [DOCEX]); secondary sources from academic and professional literature; secondary materials from the news media; and finally secondary materials from the Internet where a 4-person team (instead of 5) was necessary because of this as the cohort, the media, and Internet roles were combined.

There is also the question of managing the collaborative work of a drafting team. To this end, besides each student acting as collector and single-source assessor, each also takes on an administrative role in the team. The key figure is, of course, the chair who is responsible for keeping the entire collective effort on track. It is somewhat conventional wisdom about the United Kingdom's joint intelligence process that the JIC's effectiveness hinges on a strong, authoritative figure as the chair. There is a recording secretary responsible not only for producing minutes of syndicate sessions but also for managing the workflow of draft assessments and other incidental papers over the team's space in Brunel's Blackboard virtual learning environment. A first drafter receives direction for format and content from the team as a whole and tries to capture that in the team's Preliminary ("P") paper. A second drafter is responsible for both revising the "P" version of the paper on the basis of syndicate internal challenge and review and preparing and delivering the team's 5-minute briefing at the BASE Final Review Event. Finally, since 2008, a structured analytics officer is responsible for data entry into a hypothesis matrix, usually employing Palo Alto Research Center (PARC) "Analysis of Competing Hypotheses" (ACH) software, and managing that matrix when the teams compare their intuitive judgments in the first draft with results generated by the software.

In basic terms, the production of national assessments in the United Kingdom passes through roughly 10 steps:

1. Formulation and issuance of analytical requirement by consumers or often the JIC itself where a need is perceived;
2. Articulation of the Terms of Reference for the paper covering, broadly, the aspects of the required topic that need to be covered and in what expected depth by the JIC;
3. Call for contributing papers from departments and the national agencies;
4. Assessments Staff (or, pre-1969 the Joint Intelligence Staff) Team apportion drafting parts of the paper among themselves;
5. Drafting team leader assembles and edits together the complete paper, and the drafting team then meets to challenge and review those inclusions and make revisions;
6. Circulation of a draft or Preliminary ("P") version to departments for comment;
7. Challenge, review, and in the U.S. sense "coordination" of departmental views of the topic and draft at a meeting of the relevant Current Intelligence Group chaired by the head of the drafting team that prepared the paper;
8. Revision of the Preliminary paper by the Assessments Staff (or JIS) and recirculation for comment (possibly followed by a return to step 6 if significant disputes or differences remain);
9. Presentation of the paper to the JIC main committee by the Assessments Staff (or JIS) including identification and resolution at the executive level of any remaining differences;
10. Production of the final paper and its publication by the JIC Secretariat.[6]

In the BASE process, the teaching team formulates the IR and issues ToRs. Staff also assign students to their drafting teams, engaging in a measure of "social engineering" to distribute skills and talents roughly even across the teams. Staff also assign the collection roles based chiefly on considerations such as known student aptitudes or professional constraints (for example, students who work for the government in secure roles face difficulties if expected to conduct interviews with foreign nationals). The students, however, negotiate and agree to their own administrative roles within their teams. There are also no equivalents to the Current Intelligence Groups. So essentially BASE consists of steps 1 and 2—prepared by staff—steps 4 and 5 are undertaken by the students, and then BASE skips ahead to step 9 in the form of the Final Review Event.

TECHNIQUES, TECHNOLOGY, AND TOOLS

On the one hand, the BASE drafting process has become lodged ever more firmly in the past, emulating methods that had been abandoned as both rigid and labor intensive at the cusp of the 1970s. On the other hand, the desire to give students formally articulated, technical skills in intelligence analysis meant that the practical training leg of BASE was becoming ever more elaborate, ever more formally articulated, and ever more sophisticated. The eternal verities of the research methodology leg of the module were pretty stable, but analytic methodology was becoming an increasingly demanding, fast-changing affair. U.S. discussion of analytical professionalization and technical skill gained considerable momentum with a push toward reforming intelligence analysis after the Iraq incident. One of the issues that attracted a great deal of practitioner interest was the use of hypothesis matrices, a concept that seemed like something that might readily be applied in an academic context, at least in a rough and ready context.

In the summer of 2007 I prototyped this use of a "rough and ready" hypothesis matrix in a "mini-BASE" exercise run for the Malaysian National Security Council (Majlis Keselematan Negara) staff. Sundri Khalsa's conceptual framework for hypothesis matrices (as opposed to her elaborate procedural and software architecture) provided further refinement. In particular, her notion of a "utility matrix," in which a combined value for the reliability and *relevance* (in sociological terms *validity* or what market research calls *fit*) was used to provide the weightings in a hypothesis matrix, was both elegant and powerful (Khalsa, 2004, pp. 24–25). Therefore, in BASE 2008 students were required to use a simplified hypothesis matrix using Excel to sort and reflect on the weight of evidence underpinning analytic judgments they had reached by "traditional," "intuitive" means. At around that time, the PARC ACH[7] became available publicly and free to use for educational purposes and so, from BASE 2009, BASE has employed PARC ACH.

Opting for PARC ACH "off the shelf" was not, however, a straightforward decision. Using the PARC software meant abandoning the classroom task of formulating Khalsa-style net utility values to produce a utility matrix, a very important intellectual exercise in reflecting on the relative value of the reliability versus relevance of sources in gauging their usefulness. Indeed, after the exercise, a cohort of MA/ISS students led by Mohammed Gaballa (currently undertaking a PhD on structured analytics at University College, London)[8] re-ran the assessment stage of the 2008 exercise using the PARC ACH software in comparison with the use of intuitive techniques. Their conclusion, presented at a Brunel Centre for Intelligence and Security Studies (BCISS) internal seminar, was that the software prompted few if any significant alterations to their analytical judgments and, moreover, the team took *four times as long* to enter the data into the application as it had to process it intuitively and through conventional deliberation and discussion. In the last analysis, however, the PARC package represented the state of the art and a genuine, kite-marked intelligence community analytical tool that students could say to potential employers they had acquired hands-on experience with while on the Brunel MA. And that was taken to be the compelling consideration in choosing to use the software.

In 2005 I published an article on SIS HUMINT reporting on Iraq nonconventional weapons and its exploitation in JIO assessments (Davies, 2005) based largely on information about SIS reporting in Lord Butler's (2004) *Review of Intelligence on Weapons of Mass Destruction*. This provides a ready-made illustrative data set and flagged some of the issues surrounding hypothesis matrices very nicely. Students are, therefore, introduced to the use of hypothesis matrices initially using Excel and employing Butler's information about SIS's standard of half a dozen agents and subagents. Students are provided with copies of my article and the relevant pages from the Butler Report. A simple six-row/two column table is set up in Excel listing the agents down one axis and two very simple hypotheses—Iraq has/has not got weapons of mass destruction (WMD)—along the other. The beauty of the Butler-SIS information is that if one simply adds up sources reporting that Iraq did have WMD and sources reporting, as Butler put it, "less alarmingly," one would get a clear, two-to-one weight of evidence in favor of the presence of WMD. Students are then, however, asked to assign Admiralty Code ratings to the SIS reporting on Iraq. Under the traditional Admiralty Code, an intelligence report is assigned two values with one indicating the reliability of the source and the other the probable accuracy or truthfulness of the report.[9] They then add up the weight of reporting in terms of the Admiralty Code values assigned to the reports. Depending on the ratings assigned to the six sources, one can now get results varying between parity for the two hypotheses or a marginal lean toward Iraq not having WMD (Appendix B, Figures 13.1 and 13.2). Having run a "rough and ready" ACH exercise using a basic spreadsheet, students then map the exercise to PARC ACH (Appendix C) and experiment with how very subjective judgments about the diagnosticity values applied in the application can alter the outcomes of a simple exercise with a small number of sources quite dramatically.

Having been walked through the ACH process and the operation of the software tool, students then undertake classroom practicals including a formal key assumptions check and then generate hypotheses they will test in their own assessment and feed into their team's own PARC ACH matrix. The ACH matrix is submitted at the end of the exercise along with the team's final report, although it is a "formative" task; the students are not graded on it because the goal of the course is to produce a clear, robust written analysis. The use of formal SATs and software tools is, in the last analysis, no more than a means to an end and not the end itself.

REQUIREMENTS AND PRIORITIES

As noted above, the intelligence requirements are set at the beginning of the term by MA/ISS teaching staff. This actually consists of three elements. The requirement topic is supported by a hypothetical scenario that gives the requirement a context. A typical scenario will indicate the sponsoring department or body of the British government laying the requirement on the JIC and some backstory to why that requirement is being issued. For example, in BASE 2013 one of the topics was an appreciation of India's attempts to develop a completely sovereign nuclear triad, that is, a suite of land-, sea-, and air-based nuclear weapons systems. This was notionally being laid upon the JIC by the UK National Security Council as part of deliberations underpinning UK policy concerning an eventual replacement for the Trident ballistic missile system and for the impending 2014–2015 Strategic Defence and Security Review (SDSR). Another topic, forecasting prospects for power transition in Zimbabwe after the death of President Mugabe was presented as primarily a joint FCO-MoD requirement where the FCO was concerned with the risks of destabilization and the MoD with the possibility of planning an operation to extract UK nationals in the event of widespread violence and civic disorder.

In 2010 an additional set of procedures were added because of the topic. That year, students were required to assess the likelihood of unilateral Israeli military action against

Iranian ballistic missile and nuclear development programs in the next 24 months. Tensions surrounding Iran were high at the time, and so the basic BASE procedures were enhanced with an Intelligence Alert procedure based on procedures for indicators and warning alerts of Soviet aggression issued by the JIC during the 1960s that had been released recently into the National Archive. Largely this was a ploy to heighten the sense of urgency among team members (there was an admittedly remote possibility something might actually happen within the lifetime of the exercise), but also to get students thinking about the wolf-crying problem of intelligence warning because if a team issued an alert it would have been circulated to the entire class as well as the teaching staff.

One of the more demanding developments was the shift from a single annual BASE topic to three or more. As noted above, the original idea had been to get a range of alternative assessments of a common topic, chiefly to get students to reflect on the oft-noted tendency of parallel analytical teams working the same material to reach different conclusions. This eventually became untenable because of the growth of the MA/ISS intake. It has swollen from an initial cohort in 2004–2005 of four students in its first year to 24 in the next academic year and since 2010 an average intake of slightly over 30, making the MA/ISS the largest master's degree delivered by Brunel's School of Social Sciences. Consequently, by 2008 there were signs that that team were "overgrazing" their sources, especially where interviewing was concerned. On one occasion, three of four teams made separate approaches to the same foreign ambassador (thankfully from a friendly state), with said august personage eventually arranging to do a collective Q&A session with all four teams. It was clear, however, that others might not take "line-crossing" between the Brunel teams quite as good humoredly, and so from 2011 it was decided to assign multiple topics with no more than three teams working the same requirement. While this has increased the volume of preparation required, it has also resulted in a much more varied, interesting, and rewarding BASE Final Review Event.

It should be noted that, while most of the topics undertaken have proven both doable and pedagogically successful, one year we did attempt to take a conceptual bridge too far. In BASE 2009 the teaching team elected to try running a red team case, with the students taking the role of a thinly disguised Iranian national security apparatus assigned to assess and forecast UK long-term commitment in Afghanistan. In the event, the students—*including* practitioners—proved largely unable to distance themselves sufficiently from their day-to-day British frame of reference to generate convincing appreciations. Since then, BASE topics have stayed closer to home.

THE MOMENT OF TRUTH AND THE FINAL REVIEW EVENT

From the outset, one of the key features of BASE has been the BASE Final Review Event or "BASE Finale," which typically occupies the entire afternoon of the MA/ISS's last day of taught modules at the end of March. In the Final Review Event, the teams are required to brief their papers to a challenge and review panel of BCISS academics, former intelligence officers, and, increasingly, currently serving and often quite senior intelligence analysts from the JIO and DIS. Indeed, the weight of Whitehall participation in the Final Review Event can be seen as a strong indication of UK intelligence community awareness of the Brunel program and the value it offers through the hands-on practice as well as theory- and history-rich MA/ISS. Originally the Final Review Panel consisted of the main BCISS academics plus one or two retired UK practitioners who held visiting fellowships at the university and, occasionally, a former senior allied intelligence officer who had settled in London on retirement.

On BASE 2008, the Finale, on Russian use of its energy resources for strategic pressure on the United Kingdom and Western Europe, was attended by a DIS analyst working that same account in the Old War Office Building. The 2011 event likewise had participation from an official working in South Atlantic Affairs. In recent years, panel members have included a deputy chief of the Assessments Staff, a DIS division head, and a range of Assessments Staff and DIS analysts often working the same topics as the simulation. I have noted a definite and even increasing eagerness on the part of intelligence practitioners to participate, with the problem often being more than one of too many offers to take a role than too few. Notionally, the event is a ministerial briefing with the senior JIS analyst presenting his assessment to senior UK policymakers. However, with the increasing presence of serving Whitehall officials, the idiom has often shifted more toward the JIS or Assessments Staff briefing their final draft to the JIC main committee.

The goal of the Final Review Event is varied. In part, it is to focus teams' minds even more acutely on the need to generate a result that will go to supposed "consumers" who will have their own views on the matter at hand. This shifts the whole BASE task from being a purely detached one and also provides something of a foretaste of the dynamics of the producer–consumer relationship and the pressure to conform to readers' convictions and preconceptions (occasional panelists have intentionally role-played the unreceptive policymaker, thankfully stopping short of a John Bolton–style "hammering" of the analyst). In another part, it is to give the students any opportunity to receive feedback and advice on doing assessments from professionals who produce finished intelligence for a living.

Feedback on the quality of the papers has often been surprisingly positive given that they are often first-time trial runs for students without real-world experience, the papers are often described as comparable with pieces actually coming out of the intelligence community, varying from very supportive observations that the papers on one event differed in their principal content from a recent intelligence community appreciation very little apart from a single paragraph referring to secret sources. A more backhanded compliment took the form of "I've seen worse products come out of the Community" and more recently a panelist made the rather bleak observation that the papers read "rather better than some official JIC reports . . . probably because they haven't been through the JIC process," which can "smooth off" contentious "rough edges." Typically, officials participating in the BASE Finale explain their participation as being driven by a desire to encourage and support professional development in intelligence and especially intelligence analysis. Some participants have also noted a direct value to themselves from being "on the other side of the table" and seeing their task from the consumer's point of view.

The BASE Finale represents the zenith of the taught leg of the intelligence MA. The BASE experience is a very high-pressure environment with one of the highest performing early student participants describing it as having "the learning curve of a rocket launch." At the Finale, all of the teams come together in a shared experience, and then the class demobs to the preferred local public house with the Review Event panelists for informal discussion of the event and life in the analytical profession. Roughly a month later, students are required to produce an After-Action Paper in which they reflect on lessons learned from the BASE experience and situate that experience in the literature on intelligence analysis and intelligence theory. Unsurprisingly, the MA/ISS also has one of the largest and most active alumni organizations at the university, run through a professional social networking site and supervised by BCISS's Deputy Director Kristian Gustafson. BASE helps create an esprit de corps among MA/ISS students that many have since carried forward as a professional network in their work life after graduation.

THE FUTURE?

Despite the success of BASE and the MA/ISS, the program has not been without its issues. BASE has, as one member of the teaching term observed, "a lot of moving parts," and providing documentation and guidance to help students navigate even the basic design has proven challenging. A number of its features have been subject to continuous debate and reflection, occasionally being subject to experimental tweaks and tests such as the Iran Red Team exercise. One of the most controversial aspects of the simulation design is stovepiping the collection effort—admittedly artificially—between collection disciplines. In principle, this generates reasonably different evidence bases that need to be reconciled, and thereby forces students to explicitly articulate and address the evaluation and interpretation of those sources and how to weight conflicting sources with differing validation issues in forming a net judgment. In lectures, I frequently compare all-source analysis to doing a vector sum in mathematics. Items of reporting point toward or away from certain hypotheses to varying degrees; they can therefore be said to have *direction* and *magnitude*. Collection silos appear to provide the best setting to force students to identify those directions and magnitudes and their cumulative net value.

In the world of "Web 2.0," however, information is far less naturally placed in such silos. The "Internet" collection role in BASE has become an increasingly problematic function as the Internet has evolved even over less than a decade. It has to be kept in mind that the first iteration of BASE took place in 2005, nearly a decade ago when the Internet was a very different environment from that of today's Internet. Nowadays almost all published material is echoed in digital forms accessible online, from academic journals and the principal news media to government reports and even, increasingly, archival documents. So the "Internet" role has become increasingly narrowly defined, covering sources such as activist websites, the so-called blogosphere, and, now explicitly refered to as Social Media Intelligence (SOCMINT) where openly accessible (Omand, Bartlett, & Miller, 2012).

Therefore, there has been a running discussion among teaching staff and the students themselves of whether having students undertake individual all-source appreciations that need to be coordinated during syndicate drafting sessions might make the process less difficult to manage. Consequently, during BASE 2014, I will take the joint assessment model of an even earlier iteration of the JIS in which the drafters were appointed from the assessment elements of policy departments such as the Foreign Office, Colonial Office, Commonwealth Relations Office, the three armed service intelligence branches and from a precursor to the DIS called the Joint Intelligence Bureau. The drafting team members will assemble all-source appreciations but focus on the political, defense, domestic security, economic, and scientific/technological aspects of the task at hand, notionally representing the FCO and Home Office and from the Defence Intelligence Staff, what used to be the Directorate of Service Intelligence, Directorate of Economic Intelligence, and Directorate of Scientific and Technological Intelligence.[10] After this iteration, and once feedback in the students' After-Action Papers has been collated, we will decide whether to retain a "substantive" rather than "collection" division of labor in the BASE teams.

Another technology-driven concern is the fitness to purpose of the university's Blackboard virtual learning environment. In the original iterations of BASE, the teams conducted their internal correspondence through e-mail copied to the teaching team. Late in the past decade, this was migrated to Blackboard's internal group messaging application, referred to as the Brunel Intelligence Messaging System, a play on the early UK secure intelligence sharing system, the UK Intelligence Messaging System. In the past two years, however, students have increasingly bridled at the limitations of the Blackboard system, opting where possible for alternative arrangements set up via popular social networking sites. From a university point of view, this presents significant problems in terms of the conduct of internal, proprietary correspondence via an external system (with a history of security and data integrity issues) while at the same time making it difficult or impossible for staff to scrutinize and assess students' individual contributions to the collective process. Consequently, we have to look into either some sort of regulated use of external sites for virtual intelligence collaboration or look at an internal, stand-alone alternative.

Finally, PARC ACH is beginning to show its age. It is no longer maintained and updated, and consequently is becoming less and less compatible with each new Windows or Mac OS edition (the Linux environment has fewer such problems, but has almost no uptake among MA/ISS students). Absent a comparable and affordable tool, the likelihood is looming that we may have to return to the original rough-and-ready Excel approach and some variation on the Khalsa utility matrix model. We are, however, examining a range of alternatives, including possibly developing an in-house Excel macro that would implement a somewhat different take on the ACH methodology.

BASE, therefore, remains a dynamic and evolving process. In many respects, the BASE of 2013 is a richer and more detailed enterprise than the original version detailed in my earlier article, but it is also a far more demanding, high-pressure environment. But in its way that also plays into the pedagogical aims that lay behind creating BASE in the first place. This is because there was one other hands-on lesson I wanted students to take on board. And that is that the professional analyst undertakes his or her work in a demanding, fast moving environment in which any given assessment is only one of a stack of often very urgent appreciations in which he or she must participate. BASE has been described repeatedly by participants as the equivalent of a 40-hour-a-week full-time job, but one that must be undertaken in parallel with three other taught modules of a full-time student, or one other module and a nine-to-five full-time job for part-timers. And that is entirely intentional. Given the pace and pressures under which working analysts must do their jobs and the levels of uncertainty with which they must reckon in making their judgments, *it is often more surprising that intelligence analysis ever succeeds at all* rather than that it should, on occasion, fail and even fail spectacularly.

APPENDIX A: BASE TOPICS 2005–2012

2005   Assess the global strategic implications of the Shanghai Cooperation Organisation (SCO)

2006   Evaluate and forecast the effectiveness of the Association of Southeast Asian Nations as a partner in the war against terrorism

2007   Provide an assessment of the implications of Fidel Castro's death for Cuban political transition and stability, and for UK interests in the region

2008   Assess Russian capabilities and intentions with regard to the use of that country's energy assets as a means of strategic influence

2009   Assess UK medium- and long-term commitment to support of the Government Islamic Republic of Afghanistan

2010   Assess the risks and potential consequences of unilateral Israeli military action against Iran's nuclear and strategic missile programs within the next 24 months

2011   1. Threat assessment of Argentine military action against British interests in the South Atlantic in the next decade

       2. Prospects for and consequences of seizure of political power in the Islamic Republic of Afghanistan by the Afghan National Army

       3. Prospects for Chinese cyber-attack against the United Kingdom

2012   1. Risks and ramifications of militarization of the straits of Hormuz within the next 24 months

       2. Prospects for unilateral Japanese military action against North Korean nuclear and ballistic missile programs within the next 24 months

       3. Implications of a collapse of the euro for European collective security arrangements and for UK national security within the next 36 months

2013   1. Strategic ramifications of India's nuclear triad

       2. Prospects for confrontation and escalation in the Arctic region

       3. Stability and transition of power in Zimbabwe after the death of Robert Mugabe

APPENDIX B: ROUGH AND
READY MATRICES FOR SIS AND IRAQ

UNWEIGHTED

Hypotheses	*Iraq Has WMD*	*Iraq Does Not Have WMD*
Sources		
1	X	0
2	X	0
3	0	X
4	0	X
5	X	0
6	X	0
Net Judgment	4	2

SAMPLE WEIGHTED SUM (HIGH SCORE = HIGH RELIABILITY)

Hypotheses	*Iraq Has WMD*	*Iraq Does Not Have WMD*
Sources		
1	0 (reporting hearsay)	
2	0 (passing on reporting from subagent)	
3		3 (limited direct knowledge of WMDs)
4		3 (limited direct knowledge of WMDs)
5	2 (known dissident therefore questionable motivation)	
6	1 (new source on trial, no subsequent contact)	
Net Judgment	3	6

APPENDIX C: PARC ACH MATRIX FOR SIS AND IRAQ

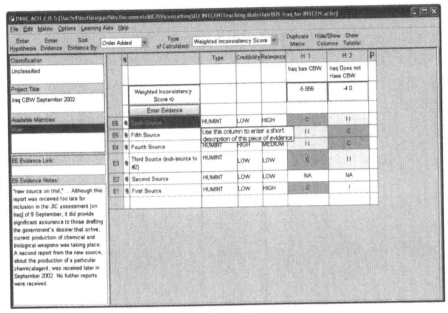

(N.B., Source numbers differ from the Excel version)

NOTES

1. In the United Kingdom, M-level programs (MA, MSc, and M Phil) typically run 12 months as compared to 2 years in the United States and Canada. It is worth pointing out, however, that there is no summer holiday, and apart from Christmas, Easter, and two midterm reading breaks, there are no holidays, and an MA is essentially 12 months of solid work.

2. For discussion of the transition between ORE, BNE, and the NIC, see Davies (2012, Vol. 1, especially pp. 125–126 and passim).

3. See, variously, Shulsky and Schmitt (2002, pp. 175–176); Warner (2002, pp. 15–22); Herman (1991, pp. 196–212); Betts (2007, p. 6).

4. On PHIA see Intelligence and Security Committee (2007, p. 23); within DIS PHIA's counterpart is the Professional Head of Defence Intelligence Analysis (PHDIA), and much of the development of a professional training practice in defense intelligence occurs through the Defence Intelligence and Security Centre at Chicksands.

5. It is worth noting that the "collection," "substantive," and miscellaneous DCI Committees were originally subcommittees of a precursor of today's National Intelligence Board called the United States Intelligence Board (USIB). They moved to the Office of the DCI in an attempt to reinforce the authority of the DCI during the intelligence furors of the mid-1970s. See Davies (2012, Vol. 1, pp. 12–122, 135–139 in summary, and passim).

6. For a blow-by-blow explanation of how a JIC Assessment is generated and details of JIC structure and process during the periods in question, see Davies (2012, Vol. 2, pp. 39–46 and pp. 186–192). For comparison with contemporaneous U.S. National Estimates practice, see Davies (2012, Vol. 1, pp. 214–215).

7. Downloadable as Windows and Java applications at: www2.parc.com/istl/projects/ach/ach.html.

8. See, for example, Borrion, Gaballa, Wapshott, Johnson, and Harvey (2011).

9. For an outline of the Admiralty Code, see DCDC (2011, pp. 3-20–3-21).

10. For a summary of the organizational development of DIS and the three decades this directorate structure remained largely unchanged, see Davies (2013).

REFERENCES

Betts, Richard. 2007. *Enemies of intelligence: Knowledge & power in American national security.* New York: Columbia University Press.

Borrion, Hervé, Gaballa, Mohamed, Wapshott, Charles, Johnson, Shane D., & Harvey, Nigel. 2011. An empirical study of the impact of reliability values on threat assessment. Presented at NATO Institute on Collaborative Human-Centric Systems for Prediction and Detection of Maritime Piracy, September 19.

Clauser, Jerome. 2008. *An introduction to intelligence research and analysis.* Jan Goldman (Ed.). Lanham, MD: Scarecrow Press.

Davies, Philip H. J. 2001. Spies as informants: Triangulation and elite interviewing in the study of intelligence and security agencies. *Politics, 21*(1), 73–80.

Davies, Philip H. J. 2005. Collection and assessment on Iraq: A critical review of Britain's spy machinery. *Studies in Intelligence, 49*(4), 41–54.

Davies, Philip H. J. 2006–2007. Assessment base: Simulating national intelligence analysis in a graduate teaching programme. *International Journal of Intelligence and Counterintelligence, 19*(4), 721–736.

Davies, Philip H. J. 2012. *Intelligence and government in Britain and the United States: A comparative approach.* Santa Barbara, CA: Praeger Security International.

Davies, Philip H. J. 2013. Defence intelligence in the UK after the Mountbatten Reforms: Organisational and inter-organisational dilemmas of Joint Military Intelligence. *Public Policy and Administration, 28*(2), 196–213.

Developments, Concepts and Doctrine Centre (DCDC). 2011. *JDP 2-00 Understanding and Intelligence Support to Joint Operations.* Shrivenham, UK: DCDC.

Herman, Michael. 1991. Intelligence and policy: A comment. *Intelligence and National Security, 6*(1), 196–212.

Intelligence and Security Committee. 2007. *Annual Report 2006–2007.* London: TSO.

Khalsa, Sundri. 2004. *Forecasting terrorism: Indicators and proven analytic techniques.* Lanham, MD: Scarecrow Press.

Lord Butler of Brockwell. 2004. *Review of intelligence on weapons of mass destruction.* London: TSO.

MacEachin, Douglas J. 1995. The Tradecraft of Analysis. In Roy Godson, Ernest R. May, and Gary Schmitt (Eds.), *US intelligence at the crossroads: Agendas for reform* (pp. 63–74). Washington, DC: Brassey.

Mercado, Stephen. 2004. A venerable source in a new era: Sailing the sea of OSINT in the information age. *Studies in Intelligence, 48*(3), 45–55.

Moore, David T. 2006. *Critical thinking and intelligence analysis: Joint military intelligence college occasional paper 14.* Washington, DC: JMIC Press.

Moore, David T., & Krizan, Lisa. 2002. Core competencies for intelligence analysis at the National Security Agency. In Russell Swenson (Ed.), *Bringing intelligence about: Practitioners reflect on best practices* (pp. 105–123). Washington, DC: JMIC Press.

Omand, Sir David, Bartlett, Jamie, & Miller, Carl. 2012. *#Intelligence.* London: Demos.

Richards, Francis Brooks. 1967. Francis Brooks Richards to Chairman of the Joint Intelligence Committee "Intelligence: Interdepartmental Committee Structure. J337/6 13 July 1967 in CAB 163/124 TNA.

Rovner, Josh. 2010. *Fixing the facts: National security and the politics of intelligence.* Ithaca, NY: Cornell University Press.

Shulsky, Abram N., & Schmitt, Gary J. 2002. *Silent warfare: Understanding the world of intelligence* (3rd ed.). Washington, DC: Brassey.

Trend, Sir Burke. 1967. Minute to Prime Minister Harold Wilson, 13 March 1967 in PREM 13/2688 in The National Archive (TNA).

Trend, Sir Burke. 1968. *Sir Burke Trend to Sir William Armstrong* A 03075, 2 February 1968 in CAB 168/124 TNA.

Warner, Michael. 2002. Understanding our craft: Wanted: A definition of intelligence. *Studies in Intelligence*, declassified ed., *46*(3), 15–22.

Watanabe, Frank. 1997. Fifteen Axioms for Intelligence Analysts. *Studies in Intelligence*, Semiannual Unclassified Edition No. 1, 45–48.

Webb, Eugene, Campbell, D. T., Schwartz, R. D., & Sechrest, L. (1966). *Unobtrusive measures: Nonreactive research in the social sciences.* Chicago: Rand McNally.

Young, John W. (Ed.). Minute to Prime Minister Harold Wilson, 13 March 1967. *Intelligence and National Security, 16*(2), 133–151.

14

Social Intelligence Survey: Mapping the Webs of Embedded Intelligence Functions

Wilhelm Agrell and Tobbe Petterson

Courses in intelligence analysis at Lund University were started by the Yugoslav émigré Stevan Dedijer in 1975 and are in their present form given annually since 2003. They are open both for academic students, who are required to have some previous experience in other academic disciplines, and for professionals from intelligence or related fields (defense, police, custom, private security sector). During the second semester, the students are working in mixed teams on a real-time case with the overarching aim to train them in information collection and assessments, as well as the ability to write and present finding within a given format. The more specific aim of the case is to train the students in encountering challenges where they will have to rely on their own inventiveness and where there is no clear-cut "teacher solution" at hand.

One of the cases developed and employed in the intelligence analysis course in Lund is the Social Intelligence Survey, where the students are given the task to identify, map, and describe the most vital surveillance and intelligence functions across the society associated with critical infrastructure. The students are instructed to, at least initially, disregard the traditional foreign and domestic intelligence institutions and instead start by analyzing the vital flows in the society and, once these have been mapped, investigate how they are being monitored. The purpose is to employ a broad social science perspective to study the features and dynamics of a primarily self-organizing web of mostly embedded intelligence systems. Social intelligence is a theoretical concept, but as such useful in academic and professional teaching on intelligence; it helps students think unconventionally on the nature and purpose of intelligence, as well as the potential of sources and methods employed outside the traditional intelligence domains.

Our experience is that the students find the task stimulating and thought provoking, forcing them to apply their (collective) knowledge in a new and unforeseen way. They need guidance and inspiration to grasp the task and get on track, but once there, they get absorbed by the case and produce some surprising and genuinely novel results. This case is designed for more extensive courses, with the aim of deepening and broadening the student's comprehension of intelligence beyond the traditional domains. It is probably less suited for shorter training courses where the participants have a homogenous professional and educational background.

This is a "live," open-ended case, dealing with a real-world investigation based on information available in the open domain. The findings are presented in a graphic flow chart, supplemented by a written report. Most of the work is done in subgroups, hence teamwork ability is essential. Supervisor input and guidance are crucial to get the groups going and to keep their work coordinated. Students on the whole find the case exciting but initially confusing. Both these reactions are intended and an important part of the purpose of the case, where the students, without knowing beforehand, experience the impact of the kind of unstructured and boundless tasks they might encounter as intelligence analysts.

THE "TIP OF THE INTELLIGENCE ICEBERG" AND THE TRANSFORMING SECURITY AGENDA

Intelligence is traditionally defined as a decision support within the domains of foreign policy and national security, with the main focus on monitoring and assessing threats. The *Encyclopaedia Britannica* refers to "evaluated information concerning the strength, activities, and probable courses of action of foreign countries or non-state actors that are usually, though not always, enemies or opponents." This definition reflects the twentieth-century paradigm of national security, based on the dominant realist perception of the international system shaped by the world wars and the Cold War, a paradigm that constituted the basis for the establishment of institutions for foreign and domestic intelligence purposes.

Social intelligence as a concept was introduced by Stevan Dedijer in the 1970s, based on the observation that all social actors are becoming increasingly dependent on their ability to collect, evaluate, and comprehend an increasing flow of information. In a transforming security environment, societies are becoming increasingly dependent on this ability, which is often dispersed among private and public institutions. Instead of focusing on the national level, Dedijer saw intelligence as a phenomenon transcending society, used not only by governments and their agencies, but also by banks and other financial institutions, business, nongovernmental organizations, and ideological movements or criminal networks. The conduct of intelligence was thus not limited to the governmental agencies, but far more dispersed and multifaced. In Dedijer's words, national security intelligence (foreign, internal, and counterintelligence) represents only "the tip of the intelligence iceberg in any society. It is, however, the tip which has been the most widely studied and which tends to attract public attention" (Dedijer, 1984; Jéquier & Dedijer, 1987, p. 23). Few attempts have been made to identify, quantify, and study the totality of intelligence activities in societies. Although formulated almost three decades ago, these observations are still valid. If there has been an intelligence revolution taking place in the meantime, social intelligence has passed remarkably unnoticed.

The tendency to broaden the definition of intelligence to include a wide range of horizon-scanning and information-collecting activities has been criticized for diluting the meaning of the term *intelligence* to a point where it becomes too vague. Social intelligence, however, is focused on the adaptation and diffusion of intelligence needs, customers, and providers through new domains in society. That intelligence, as a social phenomenon, should remain unchanged in the forms developed during the twentieth century must be regarded as the least likely of all unlikely predictions (Agrell, 2012). Although social intelligence can be criticized as being too broad a concept, covering very disparate forms and contexts of information processing and cognition, that very feature at the same time allows for a more open approach to intelligence as phenomenon and activity, outside the limitations imposed by the dominating organizational approach in intelligence practice and mainstream intelligence studies.

This becomes visible in the intelligence consequences of the transforming national and transnational security agenda after the end of the Cold War.[1] The focus on protection against terrorism has transcended intelligence communities after 2001, with radical changes in priorities, organizational structures, legal framework, and methods for information collection and dissemination.[2] Terrorism, however, is only one element in a transformed security agenda, with, on the one hand, a number of emerging transnational threats, and on the other, a growing awareness of vulnerabilities in the societies, especially in the domain of critical infrastructure.

The shift in security priorities toward the protection of key flows and critical infrastructure in society is clearly visible within the European Union in fields like energy, transport, and internal security (Boin, Ekengren, & Rhinard, 2007; Gheorghe, 2006). The European Union and its member states are dependent on these flows and the critical infrastructure upon which they are based. But, at the same time, the internal market and free movement has created or aggravated security problems. The EU's strategy for internal security thus displays the shift from the traditional interstate armed conflict paradigm to a new security agenda where external and internal threats are increasingly diffused and linked to risks and vulnerabilities in the European Union and its member states (Council of the European Union, 2010; Kaunert, Léonard, & Pawlak, 2012). The shift toward the protection of key flows and critical infrastructure is also visible in the U.S. Homeland Security and the focus on worldwide information security and the protection of global supply chains (*National Strategy for Global Supply Chain Security*, 2012).

Intelligence here is becoming an activity that transcends society and is not, in Dedijers words, isolated to the top of the "intelligence iceberg." Instead we can expect the emergence of intelligence *functions* that are not necessarily the tasks of intelligence *agencies*, but diffused or embedded within the operating structures. These diffused or embedded intelligence functions have received sparse attention in a literature still focused on the traditional concept of intelligence. The role of intelligence here is less on conventional threat assessments and more on what Mark Phythian (2012, p. 196) calls "policing uncertainty," that is, identifying latent risks that exist within uncertainty. This means that intelligence has to be performed over a wide span of fields, with the aim of monitoring flows and indicating anomalies with a potential to develop into threats.

THE CASE DESIGN: MONITORING OF THE FUNDAMENTAL FLOWS AND THEIR SURVEILLANCE SYSTEMS

Based on Stevan Dedijer's metaphor of the "intelligence iceberg," this case has the form of a survey of the major social intelligence systems in a society, where these systems are identified, mapped, measured, and analyzed. For practical teaching reasons, the survey is national, even though many, or rather most, of the structures studied are not. The survey could, however, also be designed on a regional or transnational level, as suggested by students. The Social Intelligence Survey Sweden was chosen to simplify information collection, given the high level of openness in Swedish public administration and the easily available statistics on a wide range of social indicators.

The starting point and guiding principle for the survey is the observation that societies are becoming increasingly dependent on the uninterrupted transfer of persons, goods, and various services. The crucial, and for any prolonged period catastrophic, impact of a stop in any of these systems was illustrated during the closing down of a large part of the northern and Western European airspace after the eruption of the Icelandic volcano Eyjafjallajökull in April 2010. Legal frameworks, public supervision, and private operators are all deeply engaged in the management, supervision, and development of these systems that facilitate these flows.

Five fundamental flows can be identified and constitute the basis for the survey:

- Persons
- Goods
- Energy
- Information
- Money

Persons consist of physical travel. The flow can be recurring or more permanent (migration), it can be either over longer distances or shorter commuter transports, and various transport systems can be employed. The flow thus has temporal, spatial, and technical dimensions. But the flow of persons is complex and also contains such elements as spread and control of epidemic diseases and the diffusion of a wide range of illegal activities.[3]

Goods are all kinds of commodities, legal as well as illegal. Goods represent the main content of sea and land transport, and the supply chain constitutes the traditional fundamental economic infrastructure, where trade routes and main nodes are defined as being of vital strategic importance. Like the flow of persons, goods have temporal, spatial, and technical dimensions. Important elements are just-in-time logistic systems, long-distance transports versus local supply, and the largely uncontrolled cross-border flow within the European Union.

Energy can to a considerable extent be regarded as a segment of the supply chain, especially on the global level. However, energy also includes specific infrastructure for production and distribution of electricity and natural gas. In the Swedish case, all categories of energy supply were dealt with as parts of the energy flow, but representing both product diversity and a temporal span from the real-time flows in the electrical grid to storable fossil and renewable fuels.

Information is both content and media. The flow is both analogue and digital, and consists of one-way, two-way, and multiway communications. The rise of the information society is linked to the development of means and infrastructure, but also to social patterns and attitudes. The information flow is to a large extent dependent on the energy flow and interlinked with the flow of goods and money.

Money can, as energy, in certain respects be regarded as a commodity, but also represents a nonmaterial flow and social construction (markets and transactions built on trust). The payment system constitutes a core element in the critical infrastructure and is the prerequisite for all of the other four flows.

Flows can be self-regulating and adaptive, but the facilitation and control of the flows early became concerns for the modern state and the state bureaucracy. Flows demand physical infrastructure, legal frameworks, reliability, and safety, all of which require supervision. Operators, whether public or private, have a need for monitoring for the purpose of collecting payment, fees, or taxes. Flows furthermore include unwanted or dysfunctional elements. This multitude of layered surveillance systems constitutes the main social intelligence web of a society.

Carrying Out the Survey

The purpose of the survey is presented to the students in general terms, and the social intelligence approach and concept of vital flows is dealt with in an introductory lecture. Given the character of the survey, the students are likely to experience some degree of confusion, which is unavoidable and intentional (see further below under supervisors' reflections). One group, ideally consisting of four or five participants, will deal with each flow. Depending on the composition and background of the students, they could either be assigned to a group or be able to join a group based on their own choice. (See Slides 1, 2, 3 in Appendix A.)

The case is divided into two parts. Phase 1, a pilot study, is a broad fact-finding mission where the groups search for information and, at the same time, learn about the structure and content of the flow. The groups will need assistance in information searching and, if qualified support is available, it will help them to get started. The purpose of the initial phase is more educational than substantial; the groups should get together and find ways of distributing tasks among the members. In phase 1, each group works independently, basically operationalizing the broad task in their own way. The reporting session at the end of phase 1 thus is likely to consist of not only five flows, but also five different interpretations of how to approach the flows. At this session, the groups should be stimulated to discuss various approaches, their pros and cons, and the means to select a common approach to the survey assignment. The more the students can figure this out themselves the better, but they will also need supervisor feedback and possibly guidance. The supervisors should underline at this stage that there is no "teacher solution," and hence no point in trying to figure one out (Slide 4).

Phase 2 is the actual survey. Here the students will proceed from information collection and shaping to a more focused analytic work, with the aim of constructing a graphic model of the flow and, based on this, a scheme of the attached surveillance systems. Using these empirical findings, the groups should *measure* the content of the flow and the extent of the surveillance system and *analyze* trends and consequences in terms of reliability, safety, and integrity. After the end of phase 1, the students are likely to have more questions than when they started with the survey. External lectures by researchers or experts from the public or private sector could be brought in during phase 2, helping the students to relate to real-world problems of system development, administration, and security. The external expertise should, however, not be brought in too early, but at a stage when students have reached a level of constructive confusion (Slides 5, 6, 7).

The goal of phase 2 is the commissioning and presentation of the Social Intelligence Survey. Some control stations, and a rehearsal and wrap-up session, are recommended. Toward the end of phase 2, the level of work will accelerate and include elements of coordination and editing between the groups to ensure that the survey—both in content and format—will constitute a uniform product. The employment of external reviewers as audience is recommended, both to stimulate the students and to facilitate the assessment of their performance (Slide 8).

Teaching Goals

The overall purpose of the cases is not the survey as such, but the work on the survey as training in creative intelligence work. In this case, the students will be confronted with a semistructured and boundless problem, and they will have to decide on definitions, models, and limitations in order to proceed. The intention is that the students, in the course of their work, should gradually discover and comprehend a social intelligence system.

The purpose could also be seen as introducing students with no professional experience in the intelligence field—and also as a "reminder" for those having it—that it takes a lot of hard work and creativity to get a result; but that getting a result does not always make the picture clearer. Neither in this case nor in "real life" as intelligence analysts is there a "teacher solution" (Clark, 2008).

Student Reflections—and Students Observed

> We would have needed more help to get started—but now in retrospect it seems right that we did not get it . . . but we did not understand the goal from the beginning.

From Student Evaluation Sheet 2012

Throughout the 2012 case, the different groups' progress was measured by observations as well as interviews. The observations were compiled in a table, showing how the group used different working concepts, such as assumptions, definitions, selections, models, and categorizing. At the first report, the pilot study, the groups had very different approaches to starting the work. One group, for example, had "only" been brainstorming, while another had used a more structured approach using a staff working plan as well as a definition of the desired end state. Later in the process—during the actual survey—the groups had converged; they clearly had learned from one another at the formal reporting sessions (between the reporting, the groups had very limited contact). This indicates that the case of Social Intelligence Survey, with its minimal formal guidance, forcing the groups to employ creative and innovative methods and thinking—as in "real life" for an intelligence analyst—is suited for different kinds of groups, irrespective of default working methodology.

Members of each group were interviewed. Three questions were asked during two different interviews, one halfway into the process, the second just before the final report. Question one was "How would you spontaneously, with a maximum of three words or short phrases, describe the case?" In total that opened up the possibility of 15 different answers, but only four were actually required at the first interview: complex, vague, broad, and "everything is related." At the second interview, the case was described as time consuming, complex, interesting, current, and "hard to see the wholeness." Vague was still used, but this time it described the case only until the guest lecturer (see below, under supervisors' reflections) had given his lecture; after this (and working with the case for a time, it can be assumed), things were getting more clear.

The second question was simple: "In a scale from one to ten, how would you describe your feeling of grasping the task?" Ten were "completely," one "not at all." Three of the groups had significantly higher numbers at the second interview, from six to eight in average, which could be expected as the learning process was going on, but, interestingly, two groups actually had lower numbers; from six to three, respectively.

Question three was "In a scale from one to ten, how would you describe the task's relevance to the purpose of the course?" The answers once again showed that two groups—the same as for question two—had lowers numbers, but this time from 10 to 8, respectively (the average for all groups was 8 at interview one and 8.6 at interview two).

The results of the observations and the interviews could be interpreted as:

- It takes a whole lot of effort to make the picture clearer, since it is a continuous learning process in a continuously changing environment—just as in the practice for intelligence professionals.
- At the end of the case, it still could be hard to see a *complete* picture—once again a mirror of the profession; the job will seldom be "done" in a way that a student may feel after the last examination of a course, or a project leader may feel at the end of a project.
- And, in fact, just as in "real life" in intelligence practice, the task may even be harder to grasp over time (and with an increased amount of collected information).

The formal student evaluation of 2012 supports this interpretation; the students want more guidance from the supervisors, more structure, more templates to fill in, and more time and space to report; but, at the same time, they understand the usefulness of not getting this.

Supervisors' Reflections

The student will, and should, be aware of the fact that the case is an educational exercise, not an investigation or an intelligence effort, thus the strict adherence to the use of open sources only. However, the work with authentic objects and the dependence on the OSINT (open source intelligence) performance of the respective subgroups introduce an element of realism into the case. Although most information will deal with incremental changes in technical and administrative systems, these processes can be faster and more sudden in some cases, the impact of the Icelandic ash cloud in 2010 being one example of singular events affecting flow supervision, risk management, and perceptions of warning and redundancy. Students should therefore be instructed to keep their surveys updated and be observant to new information or circumstances that could affect their results.

External stakeholders or experts would further underline realism. In the Lund cases, we had the opportunity of having Ulf Petersson, chief analyst at Saab AB, give a lecture and discussion with the students. This gave a sense of a link between the objects of the survey and a market in terms of security system outside the traditional defence domain. This role could also be fulfilled by representatives of governmental agencies or companies operating in one or several of the five flows. The existence of an external "customer" for the final survey makes the task more challenging for the students.

One problem occurred at the intermediate reporting session at the end of phase 1, when one of the groups had defined their task in a way completely different from the others. The supervisors did not intervene directly but underlined the importance of a joint product as the outcome of phase 2. The group subsequently adjusted to the approach of the other groups and managed to integrate their own initial approach within this framework.

The main task of the supervisors was to explain to and stimulate the students. The two-step approach was helpful in this respect, and the guest lecture from Petersson made all the difference at a stage when the students had to proceed from initial confusion to a more focused approach. Toward the end of the case period, the groups were more or less self-going, and by preliminary briefings in full class the groups became aware of links and gray zones between the groups, matters of coordination that were discussed with the supervisors, but which the students eventually were able to sort out among themselves. The process toward self-going groups can be interpreted as an indication that the case worked and that the overall purpose was achieved.

APPENDIX A: MATRIX FOR SUPERVISOR INSTRUCTIONS

Slide 1

Five Fundamental Flows:

- Persons
- Goods
- Energy
- Information
- Money

Slide 2

Purpose of surveillance:

- Monitor flow
- Debiting
- Safety
- Protection against unauthorized use
- Follow-up and system development

Slide 3

Goal of the case:

To jointly and in subgroups build up a skeleton for a Social Intelligence Survey, identifying, mapping, and measuring the surveillance systems within each flow, providing indicators comparable between the flows.

Five groups work separately, each with one flow.

Slide 4

Phase 1: Pilot study
Each group drafts and presents a plan of work and a preliminary stock-taking:

- Test the five categories of purpose of surveillance. Adaptation or additions?
- Which are the main surveillance systems?
- Which are the operators of these systems?
- To what extent can relevant information on the surveillance systems be acquired?

The result is presented at a joint briefing and in a written report (three or four pages).

Slide 5

Phase 2: Building the Survey:

- Each group is to commission a report on their respective flow and associated sur-veillance systems.
- Main focus is on overview and comprehension, not details.
- All five reports should have a similar structure to ensure comparability.
- Groups are to consult on interlinked and overlapping areas.

Slide 6

Main points in the final report and presentation:

- Summarize the flow in a graphic chart
- Make an overall assessment of the size and composition of the flow
- Describe the surveillance systems and their modes of operation
- Identify the main surveillance operators and their respective roles
- Identify to what extent surveillance is open or concealed
- Assess the capacity and limitations of the surveillance systems
- Discuss problems regarding efficiency, coordination, and integrity
- Indicate trends (well-established, ad hoc, gradual adjustments, or major changes)

Slide 7

Presentation: Oral briefing, 10 minutes per group
Written Report: 10 pages, including one page executive summary and graphic flow chart

Slide 8

Case wrap-up prior to final presentation:
Each group presents an outline of the report.
Focus on:

- Main findings
- Remaining knowledge gaps
- Overlaps

Goal:

- Check progress of work
- Adjust for comparability
- Plan for final editing and joint report

APPENDIX B: EXAMPLES OF SUMMARIES AND FLOW CHARTS FROM *SOCIAL INTELLIGENCE SURVEY*

Social Intelligence Survey Sweden: Monetary Flow (Summary)

Main Surveillance Operators

There are mainly two types of surveillance operators. The first group is involved in direct surveillance. Here you find the Swedish central bank (Riksbanken), which is the most important operator since it has the monopoly on creating both electronic and physical money and is also responsible that the entire payment system works. Other actors that also perform direct surveillance consist of payment intermediaries, such as banks. The second group is more involved in indirect surveillance, by monitoring other operators with the aim of compliance with laws and regulations, such as tax authorities and the Swedish Economic Crime Authority (Ekobrottsmyndigheten). E-money providers act as surveillance operators within their own system.

The Flows Scale

The amount of physical money is roughly 99 billion Swedish kronor, and every day the turnover in the electronic payment system RIX, which connects the central bank with the commercial banks, is around 661 billion Swedish kronor per day. The fluctuation in e-money providers and users combined with a lack of a governing body impairs an accurate estimation of the e-money flow scale.

The Main Systems for Surveillance

When it comes to physical money, there is no system that monitors the whole flow. Instead, the surveillance is conducted in special nodes in the flow. Most transactions involving the exchange of money are required by law to be recorded and, based on these records, it is then possible to monitor the flow. For e-money, all transactions are always recorded through different payment systems, so here the surveillance is much easier. One of the main reasons to monitor the flow of both physical and electronic money is to collect taxes.

Open/hidden Surveillance

Both for physical as well as for e-money, the operators are open with the fact that they perform monitoring activities. However, since not all of the flows can be monitored, operators do not state which of the actual flows they are monitoring.

The Surveillance Systems Capacity/flaws

There are mainly two flaws to the system, both of which relate to its capacity. The first is that the flow is so large that surveillance cannot cover every transaction and instead monitors by performing random samples. The second is that there is no operator charged with monitoring the whole flow, and the coordination between the different surveillance operators does not work perfectly.

Effectiveness, Coordination, and Integrity

There is always a trade-off between the gains from surveillance and the perception that citizens' personal integrity is being questioned. When it comes to physical money, individual payments are more or less totally anonymous, which makes illegal transactions easier to conduct. However, a higher degree of surveillance of physical money would mean a much more direct intervention in and thus a questioning of citizens' personal integrity, which many people would oppose. The opposite is true for electronic money; while all of these transactions are recorded, the public seems to accept this fact without complaint.

Development Trends

When it comes to physical money, there would be a lot of gains for society if the surveillance increased since it would make criminal activities more difficult. However, since this would be a huge intrusion into matters of personal integrity, the development trend is instead intended to increase the use of electronic money, where all transactions are recorded. For the electronic money, there is no clear development trend.

Flow Chart: Money

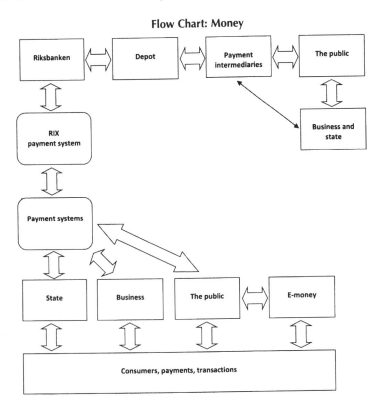

Example of Decption on Internet-Bank Transactions Illustrating Insufficient Surveillance

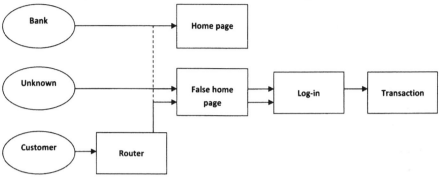

Social Intelligence Survey: Information Flow

The current systems for distribution of information in Sweden are extremely diversified. Most sectors have a multitude of private as well as semipublic operators. The least diversification is seen in the radio broadcasting sector, where the company Teracom—with its roots in the National Agency for Telecommunications (Televerket)—totally dominates the infrastructure of its sector. In the postal sector, Sweden has some 30 operators—however dominated by Posten AB—with its roots in the state agency Postverket.

Sweden still has a diversified newspaper business with over 300 published newspapers, and Swedes are still among the most newspaper-reading people in the world. The state commitment in the newspaper business is directed toward financially supporting various publishers and some planning for newspaper publishing in times of crises.

The most complex sector of the information flow system in Sweden is the electronic communication systems for telecommunications and the computer communication sector. There are a multitude of local, national, and international operators active in Sweden, operating cable as well as mobile communication networks. The dominant players regarding cable communications are companies with their roots in state agencies—Skanova with its roots from Televerket; Trafikverket ITC (telecommunication subsidiary of the Swedish Transport Administration) with its roots from the former state rail agencies; and Svenska Kraftnät (Swedish national grid) with its roots in Vattenfall (partly owned by the Swedish state) and its partially owned Triangelbolaget.

The responsibility for the monitoring of the different information distribution systems is managed by the respective operators. However, for electronic communications and radio systems, as well as for the postal system, the state executes a governance function through PTS—Post and Telestyrelsen (the Swedish Post and Telecom Authority)—the state agency that inherited the governance tasks of Postverket and Televerket. The governance is directed at the operators' surveillance activities as well as the function of the market for the respective services.

Information security has become a more important task for the society. Besides some involvement from PTS, it is the state agency MSB (Myndigheten för samhällsskydd och beredskap [Swedish Civil Contingencies Agency]) that heads these efforts. It is done through its subsidiaries SAMFI (Samverkansgruppen för informationssäkerhet—the collaboration group for information security) and through CERT.SE (Computer Security Incident Response Team)—that is part of the global information security collaborative network. For the protection of national security, the government has FRA (Försvarets radioanstalt [the National Defence Radio Establishment]) at its disposal. Although part of the Swedish Armed Forces, FRA also has nonmilitary missions regarding information security, as well as counterterrorism, where it collaborates with SÄPO (Säkerhetspolisen [Swedish Security Service]).

Swedish society and the Swedish government are to a very large extent dependent on private operators for its communication needs. However, as a complement and as an alternative with higher security levels, the state runs several autonomous communication systems. For emergency services, the digital and encrypted radio system RAKEL is available. The Swedish Armed Forces runs its own telecommunication system, FTN, and for highly sensitive communication within Sweden and to the EU authorities, MSB manages the SGSI (Swedish Government Secure Intranet) network.

NOTES

1. For the transforming security agenda, see Buzan (2007) and Wagnsson, Sperling, and Hallenberg (2009). For the theory of an emerging risk society, see Beck (1992, 2002).

2. One example of the structural adaption to a new threat environment is the establishment of counterterrorism fusion centers, such as the British Joint Terrorist Threat Assessment Centre (JTAC), created after the London bombings in 2003.

3. One example of the diffusion of illegal activities is the building of permanent roads and rail communications between Denmark and Sweden in 2000. A Swedish National Police intelligence report analyzed the assumed new pattern of criminal activities in southern Sweden that would be the result of the increased flow.

REFERENCES

Agrell, Wilhelm. 2012. The next 100 years? Reflections on the future of intelligence. *Intelligence and National Security, 27*(1), 118–132.
Beck, Ulrich. 1992. *Risk society*. London: Sage.
Beck, Ulrich. 2002. The terrorist threat: World Risk Society revisited." *Theory, Culture and Society, 19*(4), 39–55.
Boin, Arjen, Ekengren, Magnus, & Rhinard, Mark. 2007. *Protecting the European Union: Policies, sectors and institutional solutions*. Stockholm: Defence College.
Buzan, Barry. 2007. *People, states & fear: An agenda for international security studies in the post–Cold War era*. Colchester: ECPR Press.
Clark, Robert. 2008. Dividing up intelligence education. *Journal of Strategic Security, 1*(1), 1–6.
Council of the European Union. 2010. *Draft Internal Security Strategy for the European Union: "Towards a European Security Model."* March 8.
Dedijer, Stevan. 1984. The 1984 global system. Intelligent systems, development stability and international security. *Futures, 16*(1), 18–37.
Encyclopedia Britannica Online: intelligence (international relations), http://www.britannica.com/EBchecked/topic/289760/intelligence.

Gheorghe, Adrian V. 2006. *Critical infrastructure at risk: Securing the European electric power system*. Dordrecht: Springer.

Jéquier, Nicolas, & Dedijer, Stevan. 1987. Information, knowledge and intelligence: A general overview." In S. Dedijer & N. J'equier, *Intelligence for economic development. An inquiry into the role of the knowledge industry*. Oxford: Berg Publisher.

Kaunert, Christian, Léonard, Sarah, & Pawlak, Patryk (Eds.). 2012. *European homeland security. A European strategy in the making?* London: Routledge.

National Strategy for Global Supply Chain Security. Washington DC: White House, January 2012. Available at: www.whitehouse.gov/sites/default/files/national_strategy_for_global_supply_chain_security.pdf.

Phythian, Mark. 2012. Policing uncertainty: Intelligence, security and risk. *Intelligence and National Security, 27*(2), 196.

Wagnsson, Charlotte, Sperling, James A., & Hallenberg, Jan (Eds.). 2009. *European security governance: The European Union in a Westphalian world*. London: Routledge.

15

Multimedia Intelligence Products: Experiencing the Intelligence Production Process and Adding Layers of Information to Intelligence Reports

Rubén Arcos, Manuel Gértrudix, and José Ignacio Prieto

ABSTRACT

This simulation[1] is designed to be run for students of intelligence and intelligence analysis in postgraduate courses, once the students have already acquired knowledge on information gathering, analytic techniques, and intelligence writing bases and principles. The objective of the simulation is twofold. It aims to enhance the learning experience of the student by simulating the intelligence production and communication process. At the same time, the exercise seeks to improve the intelligence consumer experience by enriching intelligence reports' communication features. Divided into groups and playing the role of information gatherers, analysts, and managers, the students are asked by the instructor to address a real-time intelligence requirement and produce and present an intelligence report using online collaborative and multimedia communication tools and a report template located at a website. The simulation is divided into four phases, has a duration of several weeks, and combines in-class and distance learning: (1) getting organized, intelligence requirements, and role assignments (in-class, takes about 1 hour); (2) information gathering, analysis, and preproduction (distance, team members use online file sharing tools and software for analysis, the duration is at the instructor's choice); (3) multimedia reports production (in-class and takes about 4 or 5 hours where the students are instructed in the use of multimedia tools); (4) briefing and discussion (in-class, duration depends on the number of intelligence teams). Multimedia intelligence reports should be conducted at a maximum duration of 2.5 months, but this time can be reduced at the instructor's discretion to enable the students to experience the real pressure conditions of intelligence professionals.

KEYWORDS

Intelligence production; multimedia reports; intelligence analysis; intelligence cycle; team working; simulation

The field of intelligence studies has seen great development in the past three decades. There has been an exponential growth of intelligence literature on almost every aspect of the intelligence process. There is a proliferation of courses, seminars, conferences, and workshops focused on intelligence and intelligence analysis. However, and in spite of its importance, the reflection on the teaching/learning methods used in the field is not a common topic in this academic literature. It seems obvious that, if the aim of a seminar or a workshop is to provide training on intelligence analysis, the methods used cannot be the same ones as those intended for educating the general public on intelligence matters. The profile of students and their expectations and assumptions on the course are absolutely different and need different teaching approaches for providing value. Presentations and discussions, although necessary at a first stage, have a limited usefulness when the aim of the programs is to provide education and training on intelligence analysis. The growing interest in intelligence analysis demands a body of case studies, analytic exercises, as well as simulations/gaming that enhance the learning experience of the audiences of these courses.

Simulations constitute an important tool for academic scholars and intelligence schools' trainers to improve the learning experience of students. At the same time, these academic institutions constitute the ideal environment for testing new methodologies and practices that might be difficult to test or ill-timed in the daily work of intelligence agencies. Since a basic function of the intelligence enterprise is reducing uncertainty by delivering intelligence products to decision makers, communication is a cornerstone.

Taking all of this into account, a simulation exercise was designed for addressing the need of training the students of a practical-focused MA in intelligence analysis while testing the use of multimedia tools in enhancing the intelligence consumer's experience by enriching intelligence reports' communicative features. The simulation allows the students to experience the intelligence production process while role-playing and interacting as information gatherers, analysts, and managers addressing a real-time intelligence requirement. From the standpoint of the educator or trainer, it reinforces the concepts and tools taught to the students during the program.

TRAINING STUDENTS IN INTELLIGENCE ANALYSIS AND PRODUCTION OF REPORTS

In March 2009, Rey Juan Carlos University and Carlos III University of Madrid launched the first edition of the MA program focused on educating and training students in intelligence analysis. In September 2012, two additional Spanish universities joined the program: the Autonomous University of Barcelona and the University of Barcelona. As a result, the MA in intelligence analysis is an interuniversity postgraduate program offered and supported by four Spanish universities with two editions running in Madrid and Barcelona. Beyond the importance of the administrative support to the program, this agreement among the four universities established a benchmark in the field of intelligence studies for other Spanish academic institutions. On the other hand, the program does not award the PhD degree but is rather a professionally focused master's program. It implies that the teaching approach needs to be focused on the praxis of intelligence analysis. The modular structure of the program follows the intelligence cycle without forgetting the discipline of counterintelligence and influence operations. It also adds a module on economic and competitive/business intelligence that consists of 80 hours of in-class learning. The total length of in-class learning currently is 375 hours, with previous editions of the program being up to 500 hours.

Since its second edition, the program has increasingly introduced more hours of practical exercises and interactive learning for the students as a result of the feedback provided by the students and deficiencies observed actively in the classes. Practical exercises and simulations stimulate the student while allowing the instructors to introduce concepts and theories in relation to them. While it could be stated that there is nothing more practical than a good theory, reality shows that the students learn theoretical issues best when they are derived from the praxis. The importance of critical thinking, creativity, analytic techniques, formal logic, and communication for the intelligence analyst is best understood when it is shown in practice and the student has to face the challenge of producing a report or brief on some topic.

In 2011, the organizers of the program made the decision to introduce a new exercise for the students inside the module focused on reports production and communication techniques. While short in-class exercises had been useful, it seemed that a longer challenge could provide a more realistic experience for the students regarding the intelligence process. What if the students were required to prepare a report and brief it to a fictitious decision maker while the module is running? Wouldn't actual use of the techniques they had been studying help students to incorporate more effectively the practical concepts and techniques they had studied in the classroom? Also, would tomorrow's decision makers consume intelligence products in the same way as they do today?[2] What if students were required to produce not only a conventional textual report but also to use multimedia tools?[3] As a result, the simulation exercise was designed with two main objectives: to provide a realistic challenge with a training value for the students, and to experiment with the communicative potential of multimedia tools for conveying insights on topics of interest for decision makers.

The simulation is structured in four stages: (1) definition of teams and intelligence requirements; (2) open source intelligence gathering and analysis; (3) production of web-based reports and integration of multimedia interactive elements; (4) presentation and briefing to decision makers.

BASIC DATA

Instructional Objectives

To simulate the intelligence production and communication process;[4] to examine the use of multimedia communication for improving the experience of consuming intelligence reports; to provide a framework for putting participants' knowledge of methods and techniques for intelligence collection and analysis into practice; to show the difficulties inherent in intelligence work through an experience-based learning approach.

Simulation Objectives

To work in an open source intelligence team addressing an intelligence requirement; to produce an intelligence report using multimedia tools and web services; to brief main judgments and key findings before the class.

Debriefing Format

The instructors facilitate a discussion after the multimedia intelligence products have been briefed by all teams. The discussion is focused on (1) issues concerning the intelligence process; (2) evaluation of the insights on the intelligence requirements provided by the teams; (3) evaluation of the results achieved by integrating multimedia elements from the point of view of communication; (4) perspectives on the present and future of multimedia communication for intelligence production.

Target Audience

Students in MA programs or other specialized courses in intelligence analysis. Students in specialized courses on competitive intelligence.

Playing Time

5+ weeks

Debriefing Time

1 hour (an extra session for debriefing in hindsight is recommended)

Number of Players Required

20+. Groups of five or six members. A maximum of six groups is recommended.

Participation Materials Included

See Appendices A, B, C, and D.

Debriefing Materials Included

None.

Computer/Internet

Each participant and instructor should have a Windows- or Mac-based computer with a high-speed Internet access and the updated version of a web browser.

Other Materials/Equipment Required

A large classroom with Internet access for the sessions on applicable web services and tools and the session for integrating multimedia elements. For the briefing session, the use of a large classroom with a projector and audio system for showing the interaction with the multimedia products is recommended. A tablet for the instructor is also recommended.

FACILITATOR'S GUIDE

Materials

1. Online Collaborative Workspace. To facilitate the collaborative working among groups, instructors should create a working environment at Box.com (https://app .box.com/). A folder should be assigned to each group for sharing and editing files and posting comments on the contents (Figure 15.1). Instructors have access to these folders during the simulation for tracking and reviewing the process, communicating with the participants, and providing feedback.
2. Container. A Content Management System (CMS) has been selected from the existing different options for web development. A CMS is a system that contains a set of tools aimed at the production of multimedia contents in a simple and directed way. In spite of their technological complexity, content management systems' user interfaces for the production and management of content are very intuitive. This feature of CMS allows users to begin producing information very fast, without difficult procedures. The CMS facilitates the creation, maintenance, publishing, control of workflows and presentation, among others. Among the different freely available solutions, instructors can install Joomla! (www.joomla .org/), more precisely, Joomla! 2.5.11. Wordpress (wordpress.org/) is an excellent alternative. An easier substitute that does not require installing is Weebly (www .weebly.com/). Tutorials for instructors on how to install and configure the CMS can be downloaded at the publisher's website (https://rowman.com).
3. Appendix A: Guide for participants. Use the document as a template to be customized and uploaded to the collaborative workspace.
4. Appendix B: Applications and web services. To facilitate the autonomy of the teams and the selection of the tools to be used, a catalog of multimedia tools is

Figure 15.1.   Overview of the Collaborative Workspace at Box.com

available at the web portal of the Multimedia Intelligence Products Project. Access is only provided to registered participants (www.masteranalistadeinteligencia .com/pim). Appendix B presents the catalog of freely available tools, applications, and web services, organized according to typology of the resource, accessible for registered participants at the web portal of the multimedia reports project.

5. Appendix C: Evaluation alphanumeric system. Provides a standardized system for evaluating sources. It is intended to be used by participants in step 2 of the simulation.

6. Appendix D: Report template. Instructors can configure inside the CMS a template that serves as the standard format for the intelligence reports. Additionally, a set of plug-ins for presentation can be selected. Participants can use this set of tools for structuring information: tabs, slides, menus, tooltips, among others. The template follows the inverted pyramid structure and other usual principles for internal organization of intelligence reports.

Presimulation Briefing

Instructors inform participants that they are going to put their knowledge on information gathering, analytic techniques, and presentation of intelligence to decision makers into practice. Participants are informed that during the following weeks they will work as an intelligence unit charged with producing an intelligence report to be briefed on a particular date. The instructors tell participants that reports presented before the class must follow the principles of analytic writing taught during the course. Additionally, instructors inform participants that the report that they are going to produce is not a conventional textual report, but one that makes use of multimedia communication tools by integrating images, video, interactive maps, and timelines, as well as other multimedia resources that participants find suitable for providing intelligence to decision makers. Explain to participants that decision makers are increasingly exposed to information that is presented in very attractive and interactive formats, like, for example, infographics from media press. Communication technologies have changed the way that information is produced and presented, and it seems reasonable to think that the field of intelligence should not be any different.

Simulation Step 1: Getting Organized—Assigning Intelligence Requirements and Forming Teams

Divide the class into teams of five or six members and tell participants that they have to select a representative who will be responsible for presenting the report and briefing the decision maker. Tell participants they have to assign the roles of information collectors, analysts, and reviewers/managers to the different members inside their teams. However, caution participants that this division of labor should not be a hurdle for keeping all members involved in gathering information and sharing relevant documents by using the online workspace, as well as collaborating in the analysis and interpretation of information. This procedure is useful for giving more weight to some members in each of the phases, for preventing participants from being too tied to their responsibilities, and for ensuring their involvement in the project from the very first moment.

Provide access to the online workspace at www.box.com. It is recommended for instructors to do this on the day prior to the briefing session and to upload the guide for participants (see Appendix A) that explains the objectives of the simulation and the intelligence requirements assigned to each team. Table 15.1 of Appendix A shows the requirements assigned to participants. Once they log in to the workspace for the first time, participants can find the guide together with the relevant documentation that the instructors want to provide. Later, the instructor can use this workspace to provide the details for logging onto CMS to produce the multimedia intelligence product. This online collaborative tool is intended to be used as a repository of information and as a system for communication, information sharing, and discussion among members of each team during the different phases.

Simulation Step 2: Familiarization with the Portfolio of Applications and Multimedia Web Services (5 hours)

Instructors show participants a catalog of applications and web services that can be used for presenting their insights. The session is aimed at familiarizing participants with the possibilities offered by multimedia tools in the communication of intelligence. An effective session should cover the following topics: (1) initial reflections on multimedia tools and their applicability to intelligence reports; thoughts and issues regarding accessibility, use of someone else's materials, and applications and services in the Cloud; (2) procedures for entering the CMS and producing the multimedia report. Instructors show participants how to register the report inside the system, how to integrate different content (such as text, pictures, embedded content, etc.) by using the visual editor of the CMS, as well as the different menus available for structuring the information (tabs, slides, tooltips, etc.), how to save the changes and edit them later; (3) in-depth explanation of the catalog of multimedia applications and services. Instructors provide a detailed overview on the tools, addressing the following issues: potential contribution and value of the kind of media in the context of intelligence production; brief review of available tools; grounded selection of a specific kind of tool, according to its features and suitability for the production of the reports; brief clarification on how to use the tool and referencing to documentation and tutorials. The survey of the portfolio includes tools for integrating ePaper and repositories of documents, static images and slidecast, video, audio, animations, data visualization, maps, geopositioning and geolocation, timelines, and other useful applications such as reference managers, content curation, and systems for presentation.

Simulation Step 3: Information Collection, Analysis, and "Preproduction" (5+ weeks)

Work in teams using the online collaborative workspace. Participants assume their roles of collectors, analysts, or managers, and carry out their functions during the weeks available for this step. Participants focus on the intelligence requirements, conduct collection of information through open sources, tap the insights of experts, and begin the preproduction of the report through the platform for collaborative work. Likewise, in this step, teams conceptualize the product and do the searching and selection of multimedia elements to be integrated in the following step. The online platform is used both by the teams for sharing information, uploading documentation, and communicating among members as well as by the instructors for monitoring the process and handling queries.

Instruct participants to evaluate the information using international standards. Instructors can create a subfolder and share relevant documentation on how to rate the reliability of the sources and the credibility of the information. Appendix C includes the NATO standardized alphanumeric system for evaluation. Inform participants that they can customize the collaborative environment by adding pictures. Stress the importance of establishing a system for organizing subfolders and files inside the team's folder. Tell participants that this system also will be useful for providing transparency for the analytic process, since the collaborative environment can be embedded into the finished multimedia product, allowing the traceability of their assessments and the information underlying the analyses. Additionally, participants can use software or applications for analysis such as the "Analysis of Competing Hypotheses" (ACH) software (downloadable at: www2.parc.com/istl/projects/ach/ach.html). A collaborative version of the ACH tool can be found in the web-based package of tools TH!NK Suite™. (The suite includes: Te@mACH™, the Multiple Hypotheses Generator™, and the Indicators Validator™; see www.globalytica.com/thinksuite-html/.) Students are instructed in the use of "Structured Analytic Techniques" during the course (Heuer & Pherson 2011).

Participants are given access to the customized CMS for producing the multimedia report. Once the students have logged in to the system, they can find tutorials on how to use the tools, as well as a guide and a model of intelligence report that follows the inverted pyramid structure and includes recommendations and "don't forgets" for producing the report. Instructors can summarize content taught to students in specific sessions on analytic writing and communication. The instructors also caution participants to make the selection and integration of multimedia elements conditional upon their usefulness to the consumer and stress that there is no need to add elements indiscriminately or for aesthetic reasons. Students are told to conceptualize the final product and think about how multimedia elements can add value to the textual report. The use of interactive maps or timelines, for example, is justified as long as these elements provide clarification to intelligence consumers, and their use must not be seen as an end in itself. Students are told to finish their analysis and bring the completed textual report for the session focused on integrating the multimedia elements.

Simulation Step 4: Report Production and Integration of Multimedia Elements (5 hours)

Teams integrate text and other media and produce the finished multimedia intelligence report using the CMS. Instructors assist the teams in integrating the contents with multimedia elements and optimizing the layout. Instructors also make comments and suggestions on the structure and content of the reports. The teams' subfolders can be embedded in the multimedia product in this step. Once the session has been completed, the teams are ready to brief the intelligence product in a separate session. Instructors may find it useful to give students some additional time for reviewing their reports and making edits before the briefing session.

Simulation Step 5: Briefing (3 hours)

Teams present the report to instructors who play the role of decision makers. The estimated time of each presentation is 25 minutes. When the representatives of the groups have concluded their briefings, the instructors can require additional explanations on topics of interest. To improve the quality of briefings, it is recommended that instructors provide students with specific sessions on oral communication to provide knowledge and develop these skills prior to the briefing session.

The active phase of the simulation concludes when all teams have presented their reports and brief before the class.

DEBRIEFING

A debriefing session is conducted when all the intelligence teams have briefed and discussed their multimedia reports, and it is an essential part for meeting the learning objectives. Instructors may also choose to dedicate an additional session specifically for debriefing, if substantial changes have occurred in the course of the real events that were the objects of intelligence reports. This way, the conclusions reached by the participants can be compared in hindsight with the evolution of the different situations.

The facilitation of the debriefing should begin by summarizing the experience and then inviting participants to share their feelings. Instructors can start by asking each team in turns. An effective debriefing session can be run by focusing on the issues outlined in the following sections.

Intelligence Cycle

The design of the simulation assumes the cyclical model for representing the intelligence process. Discuss issues regarding this cyclical depiction of the intelligence process according to how participants experienced the process during the simulation. Discuss issues on planning, collection, analysis, and dissemination. Suggested questions for discussion are:

1. Did the intelligence process respond to a linear cyclical model?
2. Were the intelligence requirements well formulated? Did you experience the necessity to request clarification from policymakers?
3. Did you feel the pressure of meeting a deadline? How did this affect the final product?
4. Did you have the sense of working in a team? Did you feel comfortable with the roles assigned?
5. Did you experience problems with the collection process and the evaluation of the information sources? Did members disagree on the reliability of sources?
6. What analytic techniques did you use? Did you try to inculcate rigor into your analyses?
7. How important is subject matter expertise according to your experience?
8. Did you use any software tools for analysis? Did the tools provide significant value or make a difference?
9. Were there relevant discrepancies in the overall judgment among members of the group?
10. Was your analysis conducted according to standards?
11. Did you find problems when conceptualizing the report? Did you use any range for conveying uncertainty and level of confidence in your judgments (ODNI, 2012, p. 13)?
12. How did you prepare your briefing? How would you evaluate yourself?
13. How would you rate the usefulness of your product for a policy maker?

Insights Provided by the Teams

Instructors should facilitate a specific round of discussion focused on the intelligence requirements assigned to the teams. The questions for running this part of the briefing depend on the topics selected by the instructors. Substantial changes in the evolution of events or unpredicted developments can provide an excellent opportunity for discussion and for detecting problems and unveiling additional assumptions underlying the reports. In addition to specific questions, this part can be facilitated by asking the following questions:

1. How would you rate your knowledge on the topic assigned to your group before the simulation?
2. Do you think experience and expertise on a topic are important when doing intelligence analysis?
3. Do you feel satisfied with the work done? Would you add or make any changes to your report?

Finished Products and Communication

Facilitate an analysis phase of the debriefing focused on the results achieved by integrating multimedia elements from the point of view of the effectiveness of communication. Compare and make comments on the finished products. The results tend to be diverse in their quality and use of multimedia elements. Some groups are tempted to overuse multimedia elements, while, in the case of others teams, the use of these elements is scarce. Some questions to move the discussion forward are:

1. Did the possibility of adding visual or audible evidences to the text improve your communication options as analysts?
2. Did you find difficulties in using the multimedia tools?
3. How would you evaluate the integration of multimedia elements in the final report produced by your team?
4. Does your finished product bring interaction to the consumer?

Application of Multimedia Communication for Intelligence Production

Cover the issue of applicability of the multimedia technology for communicating analysis. Ask participants to think about the issue from the point of view of policymakers. Discuss advantages and problems posed by the use of multimedia communication. Questions to be asked are:

1. Do you think multimedia communication adds value to intelligence analysis? What advantages would you emphasize?
2. Do you find any problems for application by intelligence services?
3. Do you think policymakers will increasingly demand these kinds of reports?
4. Does multimedia communication require specific skills to be developed at intelligence agencies?
5. Do you think multimedia reports can improve the interaction and the relationship with the consumer?
6. Do you think the different layers of information bring transparency? How useful are they?

THE PRODUCTS

A total of 17 multimedia reports, covering a variety of topics (Figure 15.2), have been produced by the students of MA in intelligence analysis from 2011 to 2013 (three editions of the program). Note: All the reports can be found and consulted at www .masteranalistadeinteligencia.com/pim.

All of the products have been designed by adding layers of multimedia elements, in the form of charts, interactive maps, timelines, video, or images. The results from the communication perspective are diverse. Some of them integrate the different "layers of information" very well, while others fail in their efforts for different reasons. On the other hand, the solution provided by some groups produces a product that we may call "ready-to-tablet" format. The concepts of "layers" and "packaging" are useful for catching the nature of these intelligence products. The idea behind both terms is that, for communicating insights to the decision makers, the analyst can deliver them in a

Table 15.1. Multimedia Reports Produced from 2011 through 2013

2011	2012	2013
Illegal immigration to Spain: Networks, routes, factors, and potential evolution	North of Mali: Perspective on the consolidation of Azawad's secession and the crisis impact on regional stability	Ethnopolitical stabilization of Sri Lanka
Food safety and security: Impact in global economic development	Iran nuclear crisis: Likely evolution and impact of a potential war	Syria: Regional geopolitics of the current conflict
Indian economy: Evolution and perspectives in the light of demographics growth	The impact and significance of the Anti-Counterfeiting Trade Agreement (ACTA) for Business/Competitive Intelligence firms and digital content providers	Venezuela: Modalities of a potential transition post-Chávez
Naxalite insurgency: Destabilizing risks for India	Possibilities of a decline of Chavez's regime after the elections of October 2012	Colombia: Peace negotiations with the armed insurgency, and possibilities of success
Climatic change: Global influence in social, political, economic, and strategic fields	Economic growth of Turkey: Potentialities and limitations	China: Intelligence services and diasporic projection
Social media: Possibilities of influencing the democratic improvement and consolidation in the Andean world	Al Qaeda: Analysis of the growing irrelevance of its original nucleus, and the continuous validity of the jihadist effluence	

package of layers of information that provides and makes explicit the main judgment and the key findings (first layer); analysts' assumptions (second layer); visualizations that represent the topic/issue and its evolution over time (third layer); the evaluation of the sources (fourth layer); and the analytical process (fifth layer). All of this information is presented in an interactive package that allows the decision maker to:

1. Focus on the "What?" and the "So what?" in the traditional way.
2. Obtain a fast representation of what is happening while getting more knowledge on the origin, drivers, etc.
3. Know the assumptions underlying the findings and conclusions of the analytical teams that have been made explicit by them.
4. Track the analytic process, how the analysts have thought, and what techniques they have used for "connecting the dots."
5. Know the evaluation of the sources in terms of reliability and credibility.

Figure 15.2 shows a sample of a multimedia report with the textual report embedded.

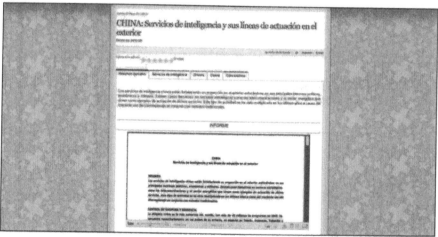

Figure 15.2. Sample of a Multimedia Report

Regarding the applicability of these "packages of intelligence" as intelligence products in the real world, there are some hurdles and problems that have to be considered:

1. Security issues related to the tools used for producing the reports. Since the tools used for the simulation are freely available, the feasibility of their application depends on the development of exclusive tools for the intelligence community or for specific firms.
2. Multimedia communication skills. Development of skills required for preparing the reports.
3. Timeliness. While the multimedia products can be feasible at a strategic level and in cases of limited time constraints, at the tactical level their use misses the mark.

4. Government use and business use. Its use in the field of business and competitive intelligence (BI/CI) presents fewer problems than in national security intelligence.
5. Contact with the decision maker. The relationship between the client and the producer is important and irreplaceable. No product can replace personal contact and face-to-face briefings and questions; that is, "the best of all possible worlds" in terms of interaction.

CONCLUSION

The simulation has been useful in providing a framework for the students to put intelligence collection, analysis techniques, and writing skills in action. By role-playing and being exposed to potential real requirements and uncertainties, the students experience the challenges intrinsic to intelligence analysis. It also provides the opportunity to test and innovate in the presentation of intelligence products to decision makers.

The use of multimedia elements also presents a challenge in terms of the skills required for conceptualizing and presenting finished intelligence to policymakers. At the same time, the fact that the product that the IC provides is just one of the many decision-making elements for the policymakers raises the question of making it at least as competitive as the other sources of informed decision making, including in terms of appearance. Today information and communication technologies are routine in developed societies, and it seems difficult to imagine that the product that the IC provides is not going to experience changes in the upcoming years.

APPENDIX A: PARTICIPANTS' GUIDE TO MULTIMEDIA INTELLIGENCE PRODUCTS PROJECT

Note: Customize this part by adding a few paragraphs that provide background on the project for participants. This content also can be published on the project's website as a presentation.

Objectives

The main objective of the project is to produce a multimedia intelligence report by the students of the X edition of the program. That is to say, to produce an intelligence report using multimedia tools and web services. As a participant, you have to put your knowledge of collection of information, analytic techniques, and writing of analytic products into practice. You will work in an open source intelligence team addressing an intelligence requirement. The intelligence topic assigned to your unit is: _____.

Multimedia products will be presented to decision makers in a scheduled briefing session. Please see the attached schedule.

Dynamics

Start by dividing the labor and assigning functions to the different members inside your team. Assume the role of collector, analyst, or reviewer/managers. Select a representative of your team to play the role of manager of the unit and be the person who briefs the report before the decision makers.

This division of labor should not be an obstacle for keeping all members involved in gathering information and sharing relevant documents by using the online workspace, as well as collaborating in the analysis and interpretation of information.

Use the collaborative workspace prepared for your unit at www.box.com. An invitation with the login details has been sent to your e-mail address. In the unlikely case that you have not received the invitation, please inform your instructor. Once you log in for the first time, you will find this guide together with other relevant documentation for the project.

Use this collaborative workspace for all communications and activities regarding the project: information sharing, discussion, repository of documents, platform for communicating with your team and instructors, etc.

Multimedia tools and web services to be used in the project will be the subject of a specific session in class. Please see the attached schedule.

Information on how to access the platform for integrating content and the multimedia elements will be provided through the online workspace. A session for integrating these elements and producing the finished intelligence report with the support of your instructor will be held on: see schedule.

When organizing the information in subfolders, keep in mind that the team's folder will be embedded in the finished product.

Instructors will monitor your developments and respond to your questions and queries. Use the collaborative platform for contacting your instructor.

Unit Number	Requirement	Participant Name	Main Role
			Collector
			Collector
			Analysts
			Analyst
			Manager (team representative)

Schedule

Date Session 1. Presentation
Date Session 2. Portfolio of multimedia applications and web services
Date Session 3. Report production and integration of multimedia elements
Date Session 4. Briefing

APPENDIX B: APPLICATIONS AND WEB SERVICES

ePaper

The capability to use electronic viewers (ePaper) for the publishing of office productivity documents allows the embedding of any document on a website. There are a number of tools available, ranging from those that combine capabilities for creating (substituting conventional office productivity suites) and sharing office productivity documents, such as Live Documents (www.live-documents.com) or Google Docs (www.docs.google.com), to virtual hard drives like Dropbox (www.dropbox.com), ThinkFree (www.thinkfree.com), and Box (https://app.box.com), as well as specialized tools for publishing presentations such as Slideshare (www.slideshare.net), and generic systems for documents sharing, mainly Scribd (www.scribd.com), Isuu (http://issuu .com), and Calaméo (http://en.calameo.com).

The report in its conventional textual format can be embedded by using any of these services.

Static Images

Many applications with diverse functionality are available for integrating static images such as photographs, illustrations, figures, among others.

First, there are applications that allow easy editing operations of users' images: adjust, rotate, correct, insert layers, and so forth. Among all existing applications for these aims, we recommend the following ones that allow the performance of processing and editing operations directly in the browser: Pixlr (http://pixlr.com) and Photoshop.com (www.photoshop.com).

Second, there are services aimed at producing screen captures for sequencing or providing illustrative elements for the report. Among these kinds of tools, the following are recommended: Curate (www.curate.us), which directly generates code (clipping) for integrating the capture instead of copying images files; or Capture and Annotate by Diigo, which is available as a plug-in for the web browser Firefox and Chrome.

Third, there are tools used as repositories for the publishing of images. These now have added extra features such as album creation, geopositioning, social functionalities, and so forth. We recommend the following: Flickr (www.flickr.com) and Photobucket (www.photobucket.com).

Slidecast

A slidecast is a presentation with built-in and synchronized audio. Slides are explained and commented upon in the presentation. The outcome is a file disseminated by streaming where slides are loaded in synchronous manner with the audio file. This audio file is normally prepared in MP3 format. Slideshare (www.slideshare.net) provides this functionality. Additionally, it can produce a slideshow that displays a sequence of images on the specific issue of the intelligence report, or it can present images of potential documents of interest.

A variant of slidecasting is slidevideocasting, which allows synchronizing a presentation with a video and can be used as a tool in webinar development. An available tool is Zentation (www.zentation.com).

Video

By integrating video sequences into the multimedia product, we can show processes, events, or behaviors or illustrate and document a specific fact. By doing this, facts can be contextualized, more information on the subject can be added, evidence underlying the fact can be provided, certain aspects can be analyzed, among others. Due to the size of this kind of content and the fact that some of the resources are available on the Internet, we have opted for using the usual Internet streaming services, including YouTube (www .youtube.com), Vimeo (https://vimeo.com), and DailyMotion (www.dailymotion.com).

For the creation of original video, there are three possible options: (1) own production and postproduction, with real image or animation; (2) clip remix produced from own static images and using services such as Animoto (http://animoto.com) or One True Media (www.onetruemedia.com); (3) clip video tutorial, generated from a screen capturer with applications such as Screenr (www.screenr.com).

Audio

For producing audio files, there are different options: (1) to use a voice manager that converts a text into an audio file through a voice synthesizer. This can be done with services such as: Sonowebs (www.sonowebs.com) or Loquendo (www.nuance .com); (2) to record voice directly through the recorder provided by services such as PodOmatic, using the web browser (www.podomatic.com/login); (3) to use a freely available desktop audio editor such as Audacity (http://audacity.sourceforge.net), and to publish the audio file later by using a podcasting service as PodOmatic or Podcast .es (www.podcast.es).

Data Visualization

There are a number of tools—collaborative or individual use—for information visualization that allow the visual representation of textual information and data. Examples include Many Eyes (www-958.ibm.com), which allows users to create different representations from the information and data that are provided. This tool offers 18 possible visualization types grouped according to their purpose: analyzing a text, comparing a set of values, detecting relationships among data points, seeing parts of a whole, tracking a phenomenon over a period of time, and discovering geographic evidence.

Other similar tools containing complementary or different usefulness are: Tableau Public (www.tableausoftware.com), Newsmap (www.newsmap.jp), datawrapper (http://datawrapper.de), Visual.ly (http://visual.ly), Touchgraph (www.touchgraph.com), Gephi (https://gephi.org), Google Chart Tools (https://developers.google.com/chart), and Jgraph (http://jgraph.com).

Geopositioning

The integration of systems of maps allows the geopositioning of information of different kinds, such as visual, audible, and textual. Google Maps (https://maps.google .com) allows, for example, the creation of maps with layers of information. Google Street View (www.google.com/maps/views/streetview) allows the making of panoramic views. Animaps (www.animaps.com) can produce animated maps showing the representation of routes and circuits. Stepmap (www.stepmap.com) is a tool for producing static maps with very effective visual representations in only a few steps. For producing interactive maps, we recommend the use of Geocommons (http://geocommons.com) or Crowdmap (https://crowdmap.com) as outstanding options.

Timelines

Web services for creating timelines are made up of a set of tools for creating visualizations in which we can integrate previously processed media. With any of the multiple existing applications, it is possible to produce complex timelines. Timelines' milestones can be grouped into periods, and visual, audible, textual, or audiovisual information can be added. Easy-to-use tools for producing timelines are: Timeline JS (http://timeline .verite.co), Timeline (http://thetimelineproj.sourceforge.net), XTimeline (http://xtime line.com), and Dipity (www.dipity.com).

APPENDIX C: EVALUATION ALPHANUMERIC SYSTEM

Reliability of the Source

A. Completely reliable.
Refers to a tried and trusted source that can be depended upon with confidence.

B. Usually reliable.
Refers to a source that has been successful in the past but for which there is still some element of doubt in a particular case.

C. Fairly reliable.
Refers to a source that has occasionally been used in the past and upon which some degree of confidence can be based.

D. Not usually reliable.
Refers to a source that has been used in the past but has proved more often than not unreliable.

E. Unreliable.
Refers to a source that has been used in the past and has proved unworthy of any confidence.

F. Reliability cannot be judged.
Refers to a source that has not been used in the past.

Credibility of information

1. Confirmed by other sources.

It can be stated with certainty that the reported information originates from another source than the already existing information on the same subject.

2. Probably true.

The independence of the source of any item or information cannot be guaranteed, but from the quantity and quality of previous reports its likelihood is nevertheless regarded as sufficiently established.

3. Possibly true.

Despite there being insufficient confirmation to establish any higher degree of likelihood, a freshly reported item of information does not conflict with the previously reported behavior pattern of the target.

4. Doubtful.

An item of information that tends to conflict with the previously reported or established behavior pattern of an intelligence target in a marked degree.

5. Improbable.

An item of information that positively contradicts previously reported information or conflicts with the established behavior pattern of an intelligence target in a marked degree.

6. Truth cannot be judged.

Any freshly reported item of information that provides no basis for comparison with any known behavior pattern of a target. This rating should be given only when accurate use of higher rating is impossible.

Source: NATO Standardization Agency 2003.

APPENDIX D: REPORT TEMPLATE

Note: Use this model report as a guide for configuring the template inside the CMS. Customize it according to the target audience and own preferences.

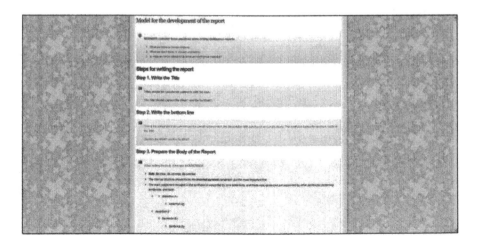

REMINDER: Consider these questions when writing intelligence reports:

1. What we know, or the *known knowns.*
2. What we don't know, or the *known unknowns.*
3. Is what we know relevant? Is what we don't know relevant?

Steps for Writing the Report

Step 1. Write the Title

Titles should be considered contracts with the user. The title should capture the "What?" and the "So what?"

Step 2. Write the Bottom Line

This is the paragraph that summarizes the overall assessment, the perspective with conclusion and implications. The synthesis keeps the promise made in the Title. Capture the "What?" and the "So what?"

Step 3. Prepare the Body of the Report

When writing the body of the report, REMEMBER:

- Rule: Be clear, Be concise, Be precise.
- The internal structure should follow the *inverted pyramid* paragraph—state the most important findings first.
- The main judgment included in the synthesis is supported by core assertions, and these core sentences are supported by other sentences containing evidence and facts. The outline of the report should have the following format:
  ○ Assertion A
    - Sentence A1
    - Sentence A2
  ○ Assertion B
    - Sentence B1
    - Sentence B2
- Use phrases such as we understand, we assess, we estimate, we consider, and we think, for conveying your analysis. For example: "Although we have little information on X, we estimate that Y." Use existing ranges of uncertainty and words for expressing confidence in your judgments.
- The body develops the argumentation supporting the *synthesis* (above) with *assertions* and *evidence*. It should include multimedia elements: images, video, audio, charts, timelines, maps, and so on.
- Depending on the length of the paper, consider the use of this formula:*

- *Background* on the situation (optional)
- *Explanation*
  - Argumentation based on facts that support the synthesis.
  - It can include headings that stress and attract attention on what follows next.
- *Deepening* (optional)
  - It can go into detail on the underlying reasons or consider alternative scenarios.
- *Outlook*
  - More detailed than in synthesis.
- *Implications*
  - More detailed that in synthesis.
- *Assumptions* (optional)
  - A paragraph can be included making explicit the main assumptions underlying the analysis.

*This structure is a model for internal organization. It does not imply that the different parts (background, explanation, implications) should be the titles.

Consult the *Analytic Thinking and Presentation for Intelligence Producers* (Office of Training and Education, n.d.) for further details on the structure of intelligence reports. Also see Pherson and Pherson (2012 and 2013).

NOTES

1. This chapter is partially based on the paper "Simulations in intelligence: Experience-based learning and testing in intelligence analysis and production" prepared by the author for presentation at the panel "Building Active Learning into Intelligence Studies" of ISA Annual Convention, San Francisco (Arcos, 2013). The authors thank our students of the MA in intelligence analysis for their contribution to the improvement of the simulation through their comments and queries. Also, we thank Sergio Álvarez for his invaluable contribution to the facilitation of the simulation, his expertise, and suggestions.

2. In fact, the use of multimedia and tablets for the PDB has been reported by the news press. See for example the article "Oval Office iPad: President's daily intelligence brief goes high-tech" by Greg Miller (www.washingtonpost.com/blogs/checkpoint-washington/post/oval-office-ipad -presidents-daily-intelligence-brief-goes-high-tech/2012/04/12/gIQAVaLEDT_blog.html).

3. With the previous reference to the Mercyhurst College's INSIGHT project in mind, I began to explore the idea of a collaborative project between the MA in intelligence analysis and the Spanish National Intelligence Centre that could be useful, both for providing education/training to our students, as well as for the service. This approach was discarded at an early stage. At the same time, there was the issue of the format. It had to be a web-based collaborative product but not necessarily a wiki in its final shape. After discussing the pros and cons of wikis, we decided to use the multimedia intelligence report instead. Since the beginning we counted on the priceless help and experience of Ignacio Prieto both in the design phase of the simulation and also with the definition of topics of interest that have been translated into intelligence requirements for the students during the 3 years that the simulation exercise has been run.

4. For an overview of the intelligence process, see Lowenthal (2006, pp. 54–67).

REFERENCES

Arcos, Rubén. 2013. Simulations in intelligence: Experience-based learning and testing in intelligence analysis and production." Paper presented at the ISA Annual Convention, San Francisco, California, April 3–6. Available at: www.isanet.org/Conferences/SanFrancisco2013/Program .aspx.

Heuer, Richards J., & Pherson, Randolph H. 2011. *Structured analytic techniques for intelligence analysis*. Washington, DC: CQ Press.

Lowenthal, Mark M. 2006. *Intelligence: From secrets to policy* (3rd ed.). Washington, DC: CQ Press.

Office of the Director of National Intelligence (ODNI). 2012. *Global water security*, ICA 2012-08, February 2. Available at: www.dni.gov/files/documents/Special%20Report_ICA%20Global%20 Water%20Security.pdf.

Office of Training and Education. n.d. *Analytic thinking and presentation for intelligence producers: Analysis training handbook*. Available at: www.scip.org/files/resources/analytic-thinking-cia.pdf.

NATO Standardization Agency. 2003. STANAG 2511 Intelligence Reports.

Pherson, Katherine Hibbs, & Pherson, Randolph H. 2013. *Critical thinking for strategic intelligence*. Thousand Oaks, CA: CQ Press.

Pherson, Randolph H., & Pherson, Katherine Hibbs. 2012. *Intelligence products and communications* (course materials). Madrid: Globalytica.

Index

Abt, Clark C., xiii–xiv
academic consultant, in cognitive strategies
  simulation, 94–95
access and agility, in collaboration, 109, 123
ACH. *See* Analysis of Competing Hypotheses
ACH exercise, xiii; aim of, 33; brainstorming
  hypotheses in, 31; diagnosticity of
  evidence in, 27–30, 32; evaluating, 33;
  evidence assessment in, 31–32; score
  sheet, *31*, 32
Admiralty Code, 213
Afghanistan, 145–46, 214
After-Action Paper, 216–17
Allen, George, 45
all-source analysis, 206, 216
alternative explanations, 165
analysis. *See* intelligence analysis
Analysis of Competing Hypotheses (ACH),
  24–27, *166*; in biological weapons
  simulation, 186, 196–98; complexity
  of, 28–29; matrix, 213; in migration
  simulation, 163, 165, *166*, 169, 172–73;
  in Multimedia Intelligence Products
  simulation, 246; PARC, 212–13, 217, 220;
  refuting power of, 28; scenarios for using,
  29; software, 163, 165, 210–11, 246

analytical professionalization, 212
analytic conclusions, 197
analytic process, 162–66, 171
analytic standards, 35, 38, 56
analytic tradecraft, xii, 4, 24–25, 36, 56,
  203, 205, 207. *See also* Brunel Analytical
  Simulation Exercise; intelligence analysis
argumentative capabilities, in cognitive
  strategies simulation, 86–89
arguments, 40–41, 77
Army Sniper School, U.S., 99–100
assessments: ACH exercise evidence, 31–32;
  BASE simulation, 203–11, 215; CAOC
  simulation, 152; competitive, 206;
  CyberSIM, 115; Iraqi WMDs simulation,
  10–13, 16
Athens office, 147
audio, 255
Autonomous University of Barcelona, 241

BASE. *See* Brunel Analytical Simulation
  Exercise
Bayes, Thomas, 194
Bayes' theorem, 185–86, 192–95
BCISS. *See* Brunel Centre for Intelligence and
  Security Studies

About the Editors

Dr. William J. Lahneman is an associate professor of homeland security at Embry-Riddle Aeronautical University in Daytona Beach, Florida. He holds a PhD in international relations from the Johns Hopkins University's School of Advanced International Studies and a BS from the U.S. Naval Academy. Lahneman has held academic positions as associate director for programs at the University of Maryland's Center for International and Security Studies (CISSM) and as associate chair of the Political Science Department at the U.S. Naval Academy. He is a former U.S. Navy surface warfare officer with specializations in strategic planning, international negotiations, and nuclear propulsion. His publications include "Examining the NGPI Dots" (*International Journal of Intelligence and Counterintelligence* [IJIC], Winter 2013–2014); *From Mediation to Nation-building: Third Parties and the Management of Communal Conflict* (Lexington, 2013); *Keeping U.S. Intelligence Effective: The Need for a Revolution in Intelligence Affairs* (Scarecrow, 2011); "The Need for a New Intelligence Paradigm" (IJIC, Summer 2010); "U.S. Intelligence Prior to 9/11 and Obstacles to Reform" (in Bruneau and Boraz, eds., *Reforming Intelligence: Obstacles to Democratic Reform and Effectiveness* [2007]); and *Military Intervention: Cases in Context for the 21st Century* (Rowman & Littlefield, 2004).

Dr. Rubén Arcos is professor of communication sciences at Rey Juan Carlos University (Madrid, Spain). He is deputy director at the Intelligence Services and Democratic Systems Chair, and coordinator of the MA program in Intelligence Analysis. Dr. Arcos is chapter chair of SCIP (Strategic and Competitive Intelligence Professionals) Spain. He is also country manager at 2creatEffects. Arcos is a certified instructor of Structured Analytic Techniques and the holder of a certification SCIP CIP™ Competitive

Intelligence Professional. He is deputy editor of the Spanish Intelligence Journal *Inteligencia y seguridad: Revista de Análisis y prospectiva* and co-director of the Intelligence Studies Series at Plaza y Valdés Publishers. His main research activity is focused on intelligence analysis, strategic communication and experiential learning. He has published articles in *Jane's Intelligence Review* and in the *International Journal of Intelligence & Counterintelligence*. Recent publishing includes a chapter on the Spanish system of intelligence included in the Routledge Companion to Intelligence Studies.

About the Authors

Dr. Wilhelm Agrell has a twin academic background in history, where he defended his PhD thesis in 1985 and became associate professor in 1987, and in peace and conflict research, where he became associate professor in 2003. Since 2006 he is professor in intelligence analysis at Lund University, the first on the subject in Sweden. He has written extensively on military R&D, security policy, regional conflicts, and the role and transformation of intelligence. He is a member of the Royal Swedish Academy of War Sciences and of the external advisory board to the Swedish Security Service.

Cristian Barna is associate professor at the "Mihai Viteazul" National Intelligence Academy (Bucharest, Romania), the head of the Political Science and International Relations Department, and former practitioner in the field of intelligence. His areas of expertise are intelligence and security studies, geopolitics, security organizations, organized crime, and terrorism. He is the author of several books, such as *Al-Qaida vs. The World: After 10 Years* (Top Form Publishing House, 2011), *Terrorism the Last Solution? The Rise and Fall of Al Qaida* (Top Form Publishing House, 2010), *"The Crusade" of Islam* (Top Form Publishing House, 2007), and of many articles such as "The Role of Intelligence in Combating Islamic Radicalization in Europe. Study case: Romania" (International Conference Academic Intelligence and Security Studies, 2011).

Dr. Vaughn F. Bishop, an executive associate at Globalytica, LLC, teaches critical thinking, leadership skills, and analytic tools and techniques to analysts in the intelligence community and the private sector. During his 30-year career in the intelligence community, he held a number of senior positions in the Central Intelligence Agency (CIA) and the Office of the Director of National Intelligence (ODNI). Among his assignments, he served as vice chairman of the National Intelligence Council; national intelligence officer for Africa and the first national intelligence manager for Africa; chief operating office for the Directorate of Intelligence (DI); and director of the Office of Asian Pacific, Latin American, and African Analysis in the DI. He also has served in a number of senior posts overseas. He is the recipient of the National Intelligence Distinguished Service Medal, the William Langer Award, and the George W. Bush Award for Counterterrorism. Prior to his government service, he served as an assistant professor of political science at Emory University in Atlanta, Georgia, teaching courses in comparative politics, African studies, and political science methodology. He received his BA, MA, and PhD from Northwestern University.

Dr. James Breckenridge is the executive director of the Institute of Intelligence Studies at Mercyhurst University. He is the former dean of the Walker School of Business and was appointed as the first chair of the Department of Intelligence Studies at Mercyhurst University. He designed the curricular requirements and gained accreditation for the new major in intelligence studies in 2002, the graduate program in applied intelligence in 2004, and the graduate certificate program in 2005. During his military career, his leadership responsibilities ranged from commanding the U.S. army's first unit to engage in combat since the Vietnam War (in Beirut, Lebanon 1983) to serving as a professor of military science. During his military career he taught Middle Eastern history and served as the course director for the world history program at the United States Military Academy at West Point. He is a founding board member of the International Association for Intelligence Education (IAFIE), a former president of the Fairview School Board, and a former member of the Transportation Committee of the Erie Chamber of Commerce.

Dr. Ella Magdalena Ciupercă is associate professor of sociology, social psychology, and research methods at "Mihai Viteazul" National Intelligence Academy (Bucharest, Romania). She is the author of five books, coauthor of three books, and author of many articles and studies published in specialized journals. She is also a member of the board of the Romanian *Journal of Intelligence Studies* and participates in different research projects on intelligence and security studies.

Professor Philip H. J. Davies is director of the Brunel University Centre for Intelligence and Security Studies (BCISS), having previously served as its founding deputy director between 2003 and 2008. He has published extensively on the organization and management of national intelligence institutions, the comparative study of intelligence, and the theory of national intelligence cultures. He is the author of *Intelligence and Government in Britain and the United States: a Comparative Approach* (2012), *MI6 and the Machinery of Spying* (2004), and *The British Secret Services* (1996); co-author of *Spinning the Spies: Intelligence, Open Government and the Hutton Inquiry* (2004, with Anthony Glees) and *The Open Side of Secrecy: Britain's Intelligence and Security Committee* (1996, with Anthony Glees and John N.L. Morrison). He recently co-edited *Intelligence Elsewhere: Spies and Espionage Outside the Anglosphere* (2013, with Kristian Gustafson) in which he also contributed a chapter on intelligence in Indian strategic thought. He was one of the authors of the current UK joint intelligence doctrine (2011) and joint doctrine on "understanding" (2010). In 2004 Professor Davies developed Brunel's heavily subscribed MA in Intelligence and Security Studies, including the Brunel Analytical Simulation Exercise and since 2013 he has led BCISS' delivery of analyst training for the European Union's Intelligence Centre (INTCEN).

Dr. Irena Dumitru is professor of communication sciences at "Mihai Viteazul" National Intelligence Academy (Bucharest, Romania), researcher at the National Institute for Intelligence Studies, and coordinator of the MA in communication and intelligence. In 2005 she received her PhD in sociology with a thesis on sociology of communication. She is the author of *Interpersonal Communication* (Tritonic, 2009), *Romania Abroad* (Defense University, 2006), and *Kamikaze Women* (Defense University, 2006). She contributed the chapters on "Communication in Preventing Terrorism" in *Terrorism and Counterterrorism: Security Education and Knowledge* (TopForm, 2007) and "Mass Media as an Instrument in Educational Counterterrorism Programs" in *A Non-violent Path to Conflict Resolution and Peacebuilding* (Fatih University Press). She is coeditor of *Counterterrorism and International Security* (TopForm, 2008), *The Dynamics of Intelligence: Challenges, Opportunities and Priorities* (Mihai Viteazul National Intelligence Academy, 2007), and a member of the board of the Romanian *Journal of Intelligence Studies.*

Dr. Manuel Gértrudix is currently professor of interactive multimedia and communication at the Rey Juan Carlos University, coordinator of the research group Ciberimaginario (Rey Juan Carlos University) and a member of the research group Socmedia (Complutense University of Madrid), and the group INNOVCOM (University of Malaga). He is the deputy director of the research journal in communication and emerging technologies, *Icono14.* He is a specialist in the area of multimedia and interactive communication. He holds a PhD in information sciences and has published extensively in monographs, journals, and collective books. His publications analyze the possibilities offered by new media and languages in the Internet applied to various fields such as communication, narrative, creativity, or learning. He has been technical director and head of the implementation of distance education provision in the Ministry of Education and Science of Spain, between 2001 and 2007, and coordinator of online degrees in the Faculty of Communication Sciences of the URJC between 2009 and 2010.

Chris Jagger is currently the managing director of a professional skills learning consultancy that specializes in delivering training that changes habits of mind. In recent years he has held several senior positions advising governments, the military, international organizations, private sector, and leaders of industry. The majority of these positions have involved inspiring innovative approaches and directing projects in both civilian and military "special operations" environments. Much of his time has been spent working overseas for the British government, NATO, and the United Nations in a wide range of challenging and culturally sensitive environments. These positions include: director of National Security Vetting, organized crime and border security adviser, intelligence and security adviser, head of military liaison (Kosovo), and director of the NATO Maritime Security Forum. He holds an MA in intelligence and security studies and has published numerous papers in his specialist field.

Dr. Hugo A. Keesing received his doctorate in behavior research in the early 1970s, based in part on his groundbreaking dissertation examining links between popular music and youth culture. He worked for the Defense Intelligence Agency from 1980 until 2006, where he served in a wide range of positions. As a faculty member at the Joint Defense Intelligence College, he taught courses on the psychology of intelligence analysis, group dynamics and the intelligence professional, leadership issues, and an intensive program called "Tomorrow's Intelligence Professionals," which assisted the acculturation of new DIA employees. He also served in leadership roles on intra- and interagency task forces that examined ways to improve intelligence education and training.

Luis Madureira graduated from NOVA School of Business and Economics with a top MSc in business economics, a major in marketing, and an accredited CIP-II Advanced Competitive Intelligence Professional, one of just 500 worldwide. He has gained extensive experience in consumer goods and consultancy industries in some of the world's most admired companies such as Diageo, Coca-Cola, PepsiCo, Red Bull, United Coffee, Heineken, and Ogilvy for the past 20 years, where he has held leadership roles in commerce, advisory, strategy, and intelligence at both developed and emerging countries. He founded CPCI (the Portuguese Community of Competitive Intelligence) and participates in the development of the CI discipline as an invited professor in University Masters presently being held in Europe. He created the Social Market Intelligence (SMINT) approach to CI, which was officially presented in the Strategic and Competitive Intelligence Professionals (SCIP) European Summit in 2012.

Dan Mazare is research assistant at KROSS, a Romanian think-tank. Dan has an academic background in computer and political science. His current research interests are centered on themes related to open source intelligence, with a particular focus on knowledge management and social network analysis.

Professor Sir David Omand, GCB, has been a visiting professor in the Department of War Studies at King's College in London since 2005, where he is responsible for delivering training to government intelligence analysts and lectures regularly to BA and MA level classes in intelligence studies. He is a Cambridge University graduate in economics, has an honorary doctorate from Birmingham University, and has just completed a degree in mathematics and theoretical physics with the Open University. He is a member of the editorial board of *Intelligence and National Security*. Prior to his academic career, he served many years in the British government. He was the first UK security and intelligence coordinator, responsible to the prime minister for the professional health of the intelligence community, national counterterrorism strategy, and "homeland security." He served for 7 years on the Joint Intelligence Committee. He was the permanent secretary of the Home Office from 1997 to 2000, and before that director of GCHQ (the UK SIGINT Agency). Previously, in the Ministry of Defence as deputy under-secretary of state for policy, he was particularly concerned with long-term strategy, with the British military contribution in restoring peace in the former Yugoslavia, and the recasting of British nuclear deterrence policy at the end of the Cold War.

He was principal private secretary to the defence secretary during the Falklands conflict, and served for 3 years in NATO Brussels as the UK defence counsellor.

Tobbe Petterson is a major in the Swedish Armed Forces and MSc in peace and conflict research. Since 2007 he has been managing an intelligence project that is a cooperation between the armed forces and Lund University. He has broad pedagogical experience from military academies, as well as a practical background as project manager at different military units.

Randolph H. Pherson, president of Pherson Associates, LLC and chief executive officer of Globalytica, LLC, teaches critical thinking and advanced analytic techniques to analysts throughout the intelligence community and the private sector. He co-authored *Structured Analytic Techniques for Intelligence Analysis* with Richards J. Heuer, Jr. and *Cases in Intelligence Analysis: Structured Analytic Techniques in Action* with Sarah Miller Beebe. He and his wife are the authors of *Critical Thinking for Strategic Intelligence* with Katherine Hibbs Pherson, and the *Analytic Writing Guide* with Louis M. Kaiser. He collaborated with Richards J. Heuer, Jr., in launching the "Analysis of Competing Hypotheses" software tool and has developed several other simple but elegant software tools for intelligence analysts. He completed a 28-year career in the intelligence community in 2000, last serving as national intelligence officer (NIO) for Latin America. Previously, at the CIA, he managed the production of intelligence analysis on topics ranging from global instability to Latin America, served on the inspector general's staff, and developed and implemented a strategic planning process for the CIA as chief, strategic planning and management staff under the deputy director for planning and coordination (ExDir). He is the recipient of both the Distinguished Intelligence Medal for his service as NIO for Latin America and the Distinguished Career Intelligence Medal. He received his BA from Dartmouth College and an MA in international relations from Yale University.

José Ignacio Prieto is a former colonel in the Spanish air force. He currently is a professor in the MA in the intelligence analysis program at Rey Juan Carlos University in Madrid. He previously has served as visiting professor at the U.S. Air Force Academy in Colorado Springs, at the University of Ankara, and at Andres Bello Catholic University in Caracas, Venezuela. He is an expert in political and cultural Islam. He holds an MA in physical education and sports.

Dr. Julian Richards obtained a PhD in political violence in Pakistan in Cambridge University in 1992. He then entered the UK Ministry of Defence, where he worked for a number of years on defense and security policy, returning to academic life as a research fellow with Brunel University's Centre for Intelligence and Security Studies in 2006. In 2008, he jointly founded the new Centre for Security and Intelligence Studies (BUCSIS) at the University of Buckingham, and joined the Global Affairs teaching staff 2 years later. He is also an associate of the Pakistan Security Research Unit (PSRU) at Bradford University, and an active member of the European Ideas Network (EIN), with whom he has published a number of articles and delivered addresses at various conferences and events. He has published two books with Oxford University Press: *The Art and Science of*

Intelligence Analysis (2010) and *A Guide to National Security: Threats, Responses and Strategies* (2012). In addition, he has published a number of articles and papers on intelligence issues, the security situation in the Afghanistan/Pakistan region, and international terrorism and counterterrorism policy in the United Kingdom and Europe.

Gabriel Sebe is professor at the University of Bucharest, faculty of political science, Romania. His research has primarily been concerned with the processes specific to the democratization of former nondemocratic regimes, such as the reform of the intelligence apparatus and the development of a free political market. He favors a transdisciplinary approach on research, basically due to his previous background and work as a mathematician.

Gheorghe-Teodoru Stefan is rector of the "Mihai Viteazul" National Intelligence Academy (Bucharest, Romania) and former practitioner in the field of intelligence (counterespionage and combating transnational threats). His areas of expertise are intelligence and security studies, management of the intelligence activity, and management of military higher education institutions. He is the author of several books, such as *Polarographic Techniques Used in the Analysis of Nuclear Materials: Environmental Security* (A.N.I. Publishing House, 2005), *Drug-trafficking: Landmarks, Scale and Perspectives* (A.N.I. Publishing House, 2005), *Globalization and Organized Crime—Global Landmarks from an European Perspective* (C.S.S.N., 2007), and *Globalization of Asymmetric Threats* (A.N.I. Publishing House, 2007).

Dr. Fernando Velasco is professor of moral philosophy and director of the chair intelligence services and democratic systems at Rey Juan Carlos University. He holds a PhD (University of Salamanca) and a BA in philosophy and BA in moral sciences (University of Comillas). He is codirector of Inteligencia y Seguridad: Revista de análisis y prospectiva and director of the master in intelligence analysis (Rey Juan Carlos University and Carlos III of Madrid University, Spain). He is author of books on ethics and coeditor of a number of books on intelligence. His main research interests are professional ethics, intelligence studies, and corporate social responsibility.

Dr. Kristan J. Wheaton (Kris) is an associate professor of intelligence studies at Mercyhurst University in Erie, Pennsylvania. He is a retired foreign area officer with the U.S. army who specializes in national security matters. He has served as a defense and legal attaché to various U.S. embassies and missions in Europe. He has also served in various intelligence or intelligence-related billets including the S-2 to the 559th Artillery Group in Vicenza, Italy; attaché to the Office of the Legal Counselor in The Hague; and chief of European analysis at the Directorate of Intelligence, EUCOM, in Stuttgart. He holds a juris doctor from the University of South Carolina, an MA (Russian and East European studies) from Florida State University, and a BBA (accounting) from the University of Notre Dame. Kris is also the author of *The Warning Solution: Intelligent Analysis in the Age of Information Overload* and coauthor of *Structured Analysis of Competing Hypotheses: Theory and Application*. His current research interests include the use of games in teaching intelligence analysis, and he is the author of "Teaching Strategic Intelligence Through Games." His research has been featured in the *Chronicle of Higher Education* and *USA Today*. He is the recipient of the CIA Seal Medallion and the State Department's Superior Honor Award and is a member of the South Carolina Bar.